ANCIENT EGYPT

ARTISTS AND EXPLORERS IN THE LAND OF THE PHARAOHS

Contents

GRAPHIC DESIGN
Patrizia Balocco Lovisetti
Clara Zanotti

1
Mirror image relief of Khaemhat, a
functionary of Amenhotep III reproduced by
Prisse d'Avennes, from the scribe's tomb in
the necropolis of Sheik Abd-el Qurnah.

2-3
Ramesses II, seated and dressed as a warrior,
awaits the start of the battle in the citadel of
Kadesh. A work by Ippolito Rosellini, the
drawing was inspired by the reliefs in the
Great Temple in Abu Simbel.

© 2003 White Star S.r.l.
Via Candido Sassone, 22/24
13100 Vercelli, Italy
www.whitestar.it

ISBN 88-8095-244-7

RISTAMPE:
1 2 3 4 5 6   07 06 05 04 03

Printed in Italy by Editoriale Johnson, Bergamo

© 2003 White Star S.r.l.
DESCRIPTION DE L'EGYPTE
Translation Richard Pierce
ISBN 88-8095-902-6

© 2003 White Star S.r.l.
ANCIENT EGYPT BY IPPOLITO ROSELLINI
Translation Richard Pierce
ISBN 88-8095-903-4

© 2001 White Star S.r.l.
EXPLORERS AND ARTISTS IN THE VALLEY OF THE KINGS
ISBN 88-8095-788-0

Preface

During the dramatic years at the turn of the nineteenth century, the world changed radically: revolutions, epic clashes between powerful armies, empires rising over the powers of the Old Regimes, and entire peoples that changed model of government, social behavior and ways of thinking. Fabled in the Middle Ages and explored by the occasional traveler and pilgrim in the seventeenth and eighteenth centuries, with Napoleon's expedition of 1789-1801 Egypt appeared majestically on the historical scene for the second time. What Herodotus had seen with his own eyes and heard tell by the priests of unknown liturgies, which he then recounted filtered through his own Greek understanding, was now brought once again before the eyes of Europe in a different light.

'Light' is indeed the most suitable word, because this was the era of Egyptology, one of the new sciences of the Enlightenment, in other words, the illumination of the world from the approach of the Age of Reason, another link in the chain of rationality exemplified by the Encyclopaedists and Positivism. Both France and Egypt suffered in the short term from the destruction of Napoleon's imperial dreams at the hands of the British, but it was not long before all the western world was consumed by a passion for this new and inexhaustible field of cultural investigation.

Like a reflection in the mirror of time, this extraordinary collection brings together three refined and exceptionally accurate works in the pages of which the masterpieces of ancient Egypt shine once more in artworks of unequalled beauty. These were produced by artists-cum-explorers, impassioned savants, linguists, naturalists, adventurers and 'proto-Egyptologists' who traveled far and wide in the land of the pharaohs, drawing the most exceptional monuments, gathering fragments of history, investigating in depth art, history, nature and the Egyptian people themselves in order to understand and illustrate something that was both incredibly ancient and yet absolutely new.

Their artistic talent combined with the power of scientific objectivity and nineteenth-century pragmatism give body to Egypt's seemingly endless marvels, in works of full color and forms that reflect the unmistakable lucidity of the wane of the Grand Siècle. The evocations of millennial history by names like Memphis, Giza, Saqqara, Giza, Medinet Habu and Mit Rahina are here bolstered further by the fame of figures like Jean-François Champollion, Prisse d'Avennes and Ippolito Rosellini from the Franco-Tuscan expedition of 1828-29, and David Roberts, John Gardner Wilkinson, Owen Jones and many other extraordinary individuals who, in less than two hundred years, brought the most impressive history ever told out of the darkness to the waiting world.

4-5
Women bearing offerings of fruit and
flowers; copied by Prisse D'Avennes from an
unknown Theban tomb.

DESCRIPTION DE L'EGYPTE

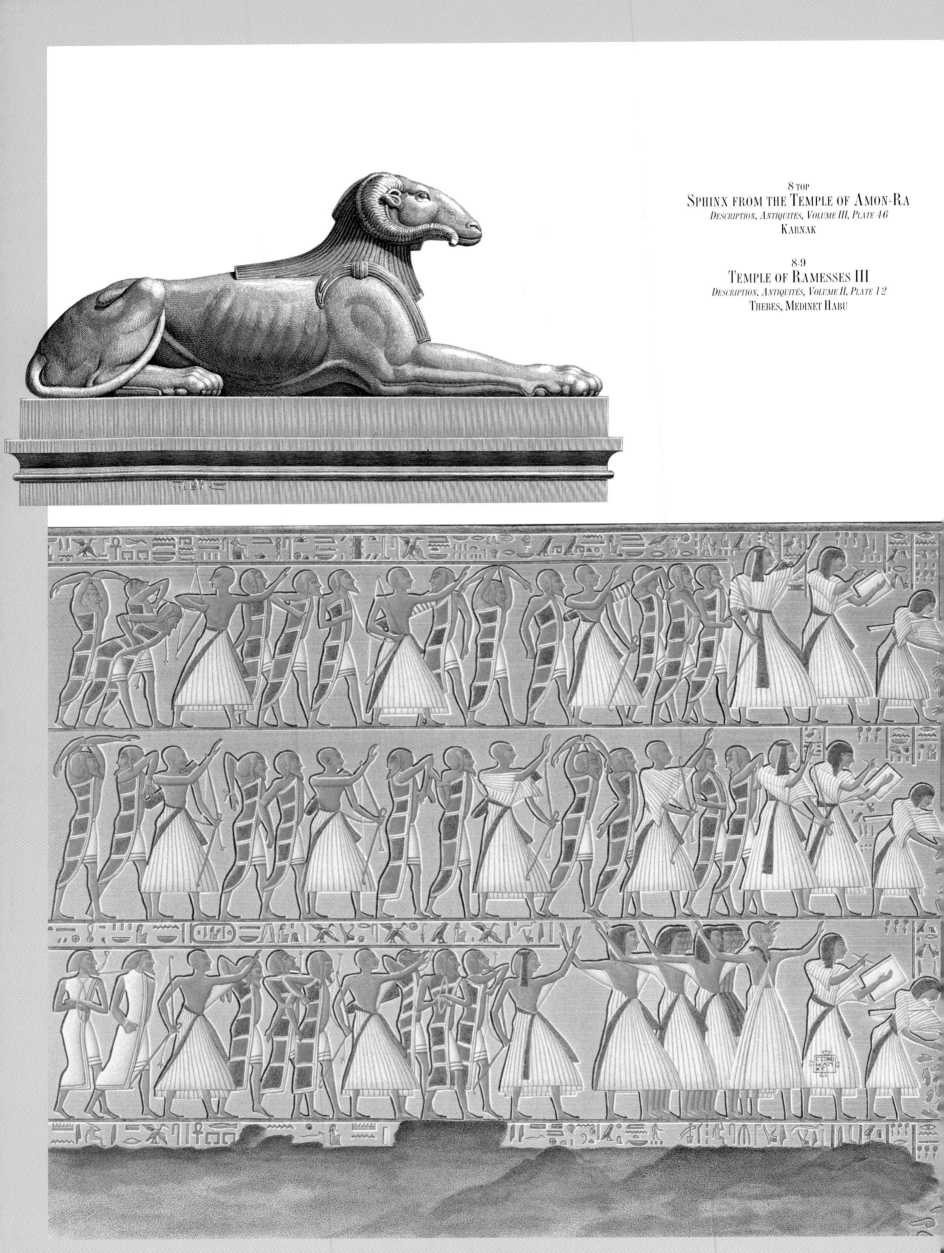

Contents

The 'Oriental Expedition':
THE REDISCOVERY OF EGYPT
(1798–1801)

"No sooner did the sun disappear over the horizon than the immense French fleet approached the canal. Upon seeing the surface of the sea covered with ships, the inhabitants of Alexandria were seized with fright and terror."

(Nakoul el-Turk, *Histoire de l'expédition des Français en Egypte*, trans. M. Desgranges Aîné Paris, 1839)

A French fleet, commanded by the twenty-nine year-old Napoleon Bonaparte (1769–1821) and consisting of over three hundred transport and war ships and about 50,000 men–the French troops and the ships' crews–was about to disembarque at the roadstead of Alexandria. This was the beginning of the Egyptian campaign. It was July 1, 1798.

This expedition was a romantic alternative to an impractical invasion of England, France's archenemy. Napoleon had decided to organize it with the political aim of challenging British hegemony of the Mediterranean and thus interrupting the routes to India of "perfidious Albion."

The Orient, with its pomp and mystery, had always fascinated the young commander-in-chief, so much so that he once stated, "Nothing great can be achieved except in the Orient." Because of its strategic position in the Mediterranean, the most favorable country in this regard was Egypt, which was virtually a gateway to the Orient. But what was Egypt like at the end of the eighteenth century?

The country had been invaded and conquered by the Arabs in AD 639, thus becoming part of the Islamic world and almost totally cutting its ties with Europe. After the dominion of the Mamluks, an old military

oligarchy of Turkish-Circassian origin (1250–1517), the Turkish sultan Selim I (the Grim) took control of Egypt, which became a province of the vast Ottoman Empire governed by a pasha chosen by the sultanate in Constantinople. The country's economic and social conditions worsened continuously because of the various military insurrections, epidemics, and famine. "In the seventeenth and eighteenth centuries," the French historian Edouard Driault summed up, "Egypt had indeed disappeared from history, cast into a corner of the Mediterranean, at the mercy of anarchy and misery, and therefore almost restored to the desert, to the void."

So when Napoleon arrived in Alexandria, he found a country with a population of less than three million,

still virtually governed by the Mamluks, in an extremely precarious condition because of the instability and difficulties in all spheres, both public and private.

Within a week of landing, Napoleon began his march to the interior, defeated Murad Bey's Mamluk army in the famous 'Battle of the Pyramids,' and on July 24, made his triumphal entrance into Cairo. Unfortunately, his dreams of glory and a possible conquest of India were thwarted a few days afterward by the loss of most of his fleet at the hands of the British admiral, Horatio Nelson at Abukir Bay, northeast of Alexandria. The Armée d'Orient thus found itself totally isolated with no means of receiving aid or supplies.

11
NAPOLEON DURING THE
BATTLE OF THE PYRAMIDS
PAINTING BY A. JEAN GROS

Napoleon is shown here leading his troops during the Battle of the Pyramids. An officer in the army by the name of Chalbrand reported that before the battle and in view of the famous monuments, the French leader proclaimed: "My soldiers, remember that forty centuries are looking down at you from the height of these Pyramids and will applaud your victory."

Although Bonaparte was well aware of the great danger involved, he did not lose heart, and embarqueed on a military campaign in Syria against the Ottoman Empire which, allied with Great Britain, had declared war against France. Despite some initial successes, the French campaign, which lasted three months, came to nothing. Furthermore, Napoleon's idea of maintaining a hold on Egypt proved to be only a dream. In fact, alarming news of political-military trouble in Europe forced Napoleon to abandon Egypt in August of that year and return to France, leaving General Kléber in charge of his troops. After Napoleon's departure the French army found itself in an extremely difficult situation:

hostility and revolts on the part of the local population, the assassination of Kléber in June 1800, and the defeats suffered by generals Belliard and Menou at the hands of the British in 1801 forced the French to abandon Egypt. Thus, from a military standpoint, the 'Oriental Expedition' was a failure and in some way anticipated the decline of Napoleon's plan for dominating Europe and the Mediterranean basin.

The first consequence of the failure of the military campaign in Egypt was the return of Egypt, the most important country in North Africa, to the British empire, which was traditionally hostile to France.

12
REVOLT IN CAIRO
LITHOGRAPH BY C. MOTTE

On October 21, 1798, the Egyptian capital was shaken by an insurrection against the occupying French forces. In this plate, Napoleon leads his soldiers against the rebels, whose uprising was quickly suffocated. However, on April 24, 1800, the episode was repeated and hastened the French surrender to the British.

12-13 TOP
NAPOLEON AND SHEIKH AL-BEKRY
LITHOGRAPH BY C. MOTTE

The lithograph is taken from *Vie politique et militaire de Napoléon* by A.V. Arnault. It shows Bonaparte, his retinue, and Sheikh al-Bekry, on August 20, 1798, commemorating the birth of Muhammad.

12-13 BOTTOM
LAND BATTLE AT ABUKIR BAY
WORK BY D.V. DENON

The land battle at Abukir Bay took place on July 25, 1799. About a year earlier, on August 1, 1798, during the Battle of the Nile fought in these waters a few days after the French victory at the Battle of the Pyramids, much of the French fleet was destroyed by the British, under the command of Horatio Nelson.

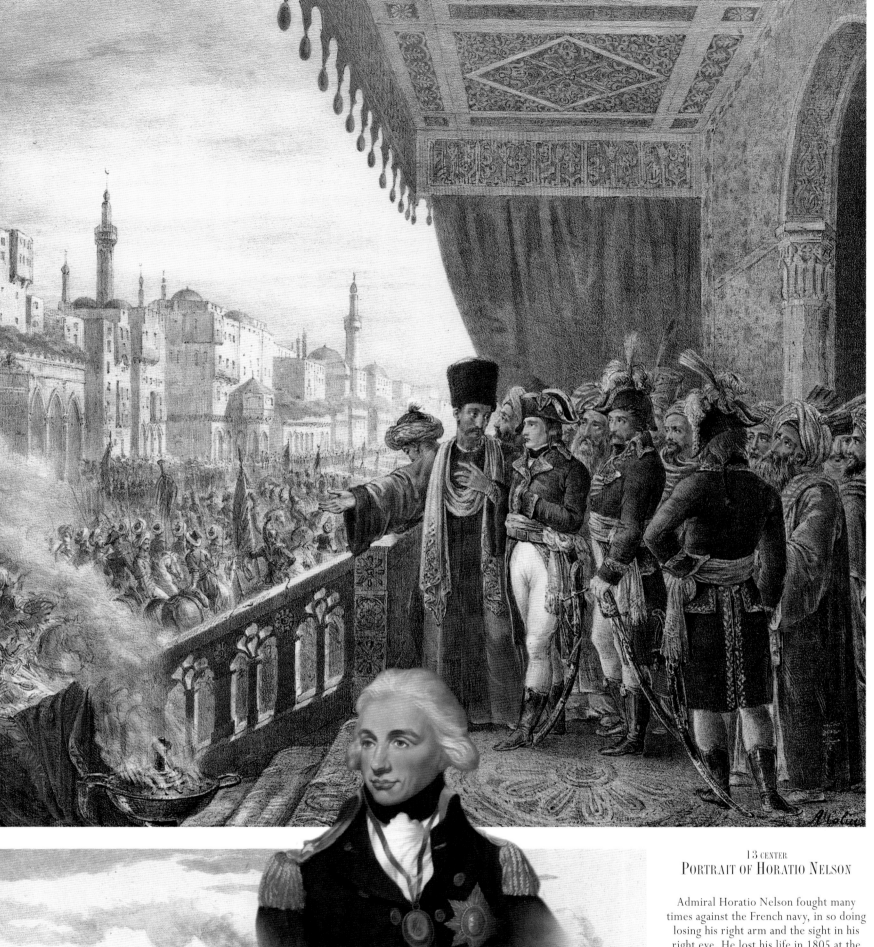

PORTRAIT OF HORATIO NELSON

Admiral Horatio Nelson fought many times against the French navy, in so doing losing his right arm and the sight in his right eye. He lost his life in 1805 at the end of the victorious Battle of Trafalgar against the French and Spanish forces.

BUT IT WAS NOT A USELESS UNDERTAKING...

THE INSTITUT D'EGYPTE

14
The *Commission des Sciences et des Arts* in Thebes

Several French scholars in the archaeological commission set up by Napoleon are shown taking measurements of antiquities and archaeological remains in ancient Thebes before they are transported to France. However, the British attack on the French forces interrupted the French campaign and the antiquities were never removed.

15
Map of ancient Egypt

Based above all on the representation left by the Jesuit Claude Sicard in 1722 and on the observations of the travelers Pococke and Norden, this map (taken from the work *Memoires sur l'Egypte ancienne et moderne* by J.B. Bourguignon d'Anville, 1766) is extremely accurate, in particular with relation to the course of the Nile and positions of the main cities.

The Egyptian campaign contingent did not consist only of infantrymen, artillerymen, cavalrymen, and sailors. It also boasted a group of 154 'savants'—engineers, architects, mathematicians, chemists, Orientalists, physicians, natural scientists, artists, and others who had embarqueed on a journey whose destination was kept secret from almost all the members and was revealed only during the sea voyage.

These scholars and experts all trusted the young Bonaparte: their revolutionary spirit, love of the ancient world, thirst for knowledge, and excitement over an unknown but surely prestigious enterprise for the young French Republic were instrumental in their accepting the risks and dangers involved in the mission.

For his part, Napoleon was gifted with keen intuition and an exceptional perception of history: he knew quite well that scientific conquests might prove to be more important and long-lasting than military victories. In fact, the future emperor once said, "We must hold scientists in great esteem and support science." For that matter, as the British historian J. Christopher Herold wrote, "Did not Alexander the Great take along philosophers and men of learning when he went to conquer Egypt, Persia, and India?"

So the French expedition included the *Commission des Sciences et des Arts* (the official name of the group of scholars), which was called upon to explore, make drawings, and write descriptions of all aspects of Egypt, which was for the most part unknown at that time.

Leaving aside the political motives, for Napoleon, the Oriental Expedition would represent a sort of 'moral supremacy' for France, whose 'regenerative mission' would leave a remarkable scientific and cultural heritage for all of Europe. Thus Napoleon, the 'civilizing hero' mindful of Alexander the Great, planned to bring to light a civilization that had disappeared two thousand years earlier, had been the mother and matrix of other Mediterranean civilizations and cultures, and had therefore played a vital and essential role in European history.

On August 22, 1798, a project that Napoleon had nurtured came into being: the foundation in Cairo of the Institut d'Egypte, modeled after the Institut de France. The main aim was to '*porter les lumières*' to Egypt, that is to say, disseminate progress and culture, support research, and publish the history of ancient and modern Egypt, including its customs and traditions. The original thirty-six members of this institute were chosen from among leading experts and scholars in various fields. Gaspard Monge was elected the first president. In July 1799, during the Napoleonic campaign, excavations effected at Fort Julien, near the village of al-Rashid (Rosetta) east of Alexandria, brought to light a find that proved to be of fundamental importance to the future science of Egyptology. This was the 'Rosetta stone,' discovered by the French officer Pierre Bouchard.

The stone is a black granite slab 114 cm long, 72 cm wide, and 28 cm thick, weighing 760 kilograms. It dates from 196 BC, when Egypt was ruled by the Ptolemaic dynasty. An incomplete text was carved on the stone in three scripts: the first, on top, was in hieroglyphs, the language of ancient pharaonic Egypt; the second was in demotic, used in Egypt from 700 BC; and the third was in Greek, the language of the heirs of Alexander the Great.

Bonaparte's scholars believed that the three inscriptions were versions of the same text, so by starting off from the ancient Greek, they felt they might be able to decipher hieroglyphic script, which had been incomprehensible for fourteen centuries. Thanks to his exceptional intuition and extensive linguistic knowledge, Jean-François Champollion succeeded in deciphering hieroglyphic text in September 1822. During its short-lived existence (three years), the Institut d'Egypte was forced to elect new members because some were killed in battle or died of illness, and others were sent back to France. In fact, of the 154 original 'savants,' 34 died for their country and for science.

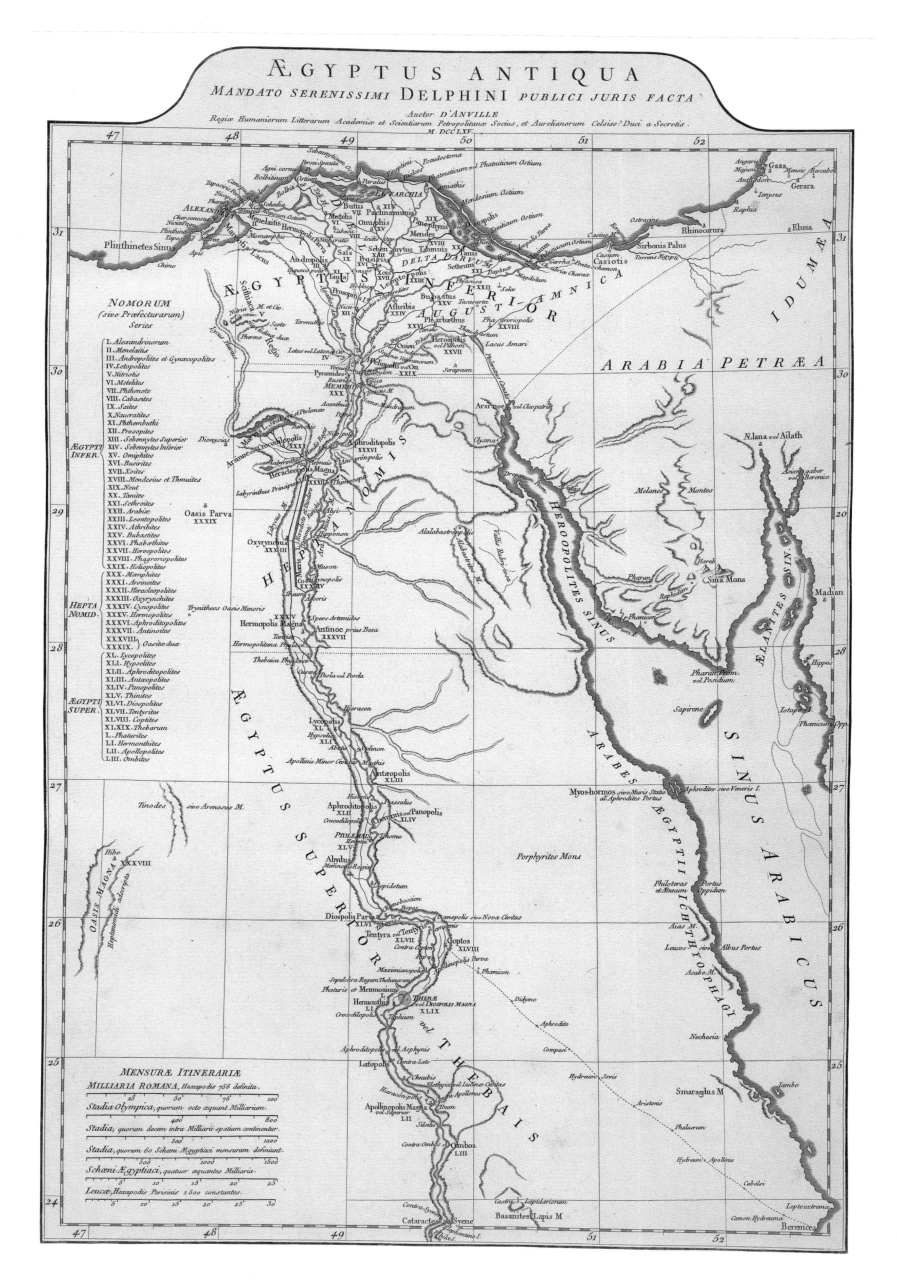

ÆGYPTUS ANTIQUA

MANDATO SERENISSIMI DELPHINI PUBLICI JURIS FACTA

Auctor D'ANVILLE

Regiæ Humaniorum Litterarum Academiæ et Scientiarum Petropolitanæ Socius, et Aurelianorum Celsiss? Duci a Secretis.

M. DCC LXV.

NOMORUM
(sive Præfecturarum)
Series

I. Alexandrinorum
II. Menelaitis
III. Andropolites et Gynæcopolites
IV. Letopolites
V. Nitriotis
VI. Metelitis
VII. Phthenote
VIII. Cabasites
IX. Saites
X. Naucratites
XI. Phthembuthi
XII. Prosopites
XIII. Sebennytes Superior
XIV. Sebennytes Inferior
XV. Omphites
XVI. Busirites
XVII. Xoites
XVIII. Mendesius et Thmuites
XIX. Nout
XX. Tanites
XXI. Sethroites
XXII. Arabiæ
XXIII. Leontopolites
XXIV. Athribites
XXV. Bubastites
XXVI. Phabethites
XXVII. Heroopolites
XXVIII. Phagroriopolites
XXIX. Heliopolites
XXX. Memphites
XXXI. Arsinoites
XXXII. Heracleopolites
XXXIII. Oxyrynchites
XXXIV. Cynopolites
XXXV. Hermopolites
XXXVI. Aphroditopolites
XXXVII. Antinoites
XXXVIII. }
XXXIX. } Oasitæ duæ
XL. Lycopolites
XLI. Hypselites
XLII. Aphroditopolites
XLIII. Antæopolites
XLIV. Panopolites
XLV. Thinites
XLVI. Diospolites
XLVII. Tentyrites
XLVIII. Coptites
XLIX. Thebarum
L. Phaturites
LI. Hermonthites
LII. Apollopolites
LIII. Ombites

AEGYPTI INFER.

HEPTA NOMID.

AEGYPTI SUPER.

MENSURÆ ITINERARIÆ

MILLIARIA ROMANA, Hexapodis 756 definita.

Stadia Olympica, quorum octo æquant Milliarium.

Stadia, quorum decem intra Milliarii spatium continentur.

Stadia, quorum 60 Schœni Ægyptiaci mensuram definiunt.

Schœni Ægyptiaci, quatuor æquantes Milliaria.

Leucæ, Hexapodis Parisinis 2500 constantes.

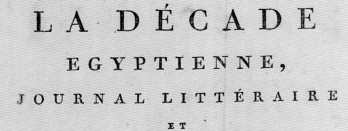

LA DÉCADE

EGYPTIENNE,

JOURNAL LITTÉRAIRE

ET

D'ÉCONOMIE POLITIQUE.

PREMIER VOLUME.

AU KAIRE,

DE L'IMPRIMERIE NATIONALE.

AN VII DE LA RÉPUBLIQUE FRANÇAISE.

16 TOP
**FRONTISPIECE OF THE
*Décade Egyptienne***

This is the frontispiece of the first volume of *La Décade Egyptienne*, the first literary and scientific periodical published in Egypt, in 1798. Only three very rare volumes and a few pages of a fourth remain of this important document (Franco Serino Collection).

16 BOTTOM
**INAUGURATION OF THE
*INSTITUT D'EGYPTE***
ÉTAT MODERNE, VOLUME I, PLATE 55
CAIRO

To mark the opening session, Bonaparte and a group of scholars joined Gaspard Monge in a room in the Institut d'Egypte, which was built in Cairo in August 1798.

In March 1801, in the wake of the military defeats and capitulation, the remaining group of scholars returned to France, each taking along his drawings, notes and collections, after having to overcome many an obstacle. On the other hand, the victorious English confiscated various archaeological finds, including the most prestigious of all, the world-famous Rosetta stone, which is now kept in the British Museum, London.

On occasion of the foundation of the Institut d'Egypte, Napoleon ordered that two periodicals be published—*La Décade égyptienne* and *Courrier de l'Egypte*. The first issue of the latter came out only seven days later, on 29 August 1798. It was the first periodical printed in Egypt; 116 issues were published up to June 1801. The semi-official organ of the French Army, it reported political and military news concerning Egypt as well as the principal current events in Europe and other useful information. Due to a printing error, in the first two issues the word 'Courrier' was spelled 'Courier'.

La Décade, on the other hand, was a scientific magazine that initially came out every ten days, and then monthly. Publication began on 1 October 1798 and continued until March 1801. For the most part it dealt with artistic and scientific matters and also featured a large number of memoirs and papers by the members of the Institut d'Egypte. The various issues were gathered together in three volumes, which are collector's items nowadays. There are also a few pages of a fourth volume that was never finished.

17 top
CARTOUCHE OF CLEOPATRA VII

This cartouche is taken from *Précis du système hiéroglyphique des anciens Egyptiens*, 1824. The original was inscribed on an obelisk that was at one time at Philae but is now in England. It was identified by being compared to the cartouche of Ptolemy that Champollion had already deciphered on the Rosetta Stone. The Egyptian form of writing was simultaneously figurative, symbolic, and phonetic.

17 bottom
ROSETTA STONE

Jean-François Champollion succeeded in deciphering the ancient Egyptian writing by comparing the hieroglyphic, demotic, and Greek inscriptions on the Rosetta Stone.

The 'Savants' and Egypt

During their three-year stay in Egypt the French scholars, who after returning to France were referred to as 'Egyptians,' had to overcome many adversities. For several of them—some of whom were quite young, while others were even university students who had never traveled—the impact of this country was nothing less than traumatic: everything was different and new compared to their beloved *douce France*.

But then, this was still Egypt, the cradle of an ancient civilization that had grown up along the banks of the Nile and distinguished itself for its brilliantly articulated thought, fantastic religious beliefs, and superb architecture. During the course of its history, Egypt had witnessed the rise of a sophisticated script and of belief in an afterlife, the organization of society into a pyramidal hierarchical structure, and the creation of monumental works that had defied time and awed people of all ages. These are only some of the reasons why Egyptian civilization has always been so fascinating to the Western imagination. Even two thousand years after ancient Egypt's decline, the French scholars—and many soldiers as well—were spellbound by the 'myth' of this country, considered the repository of ancient wisdom, much more ancient than Greek thought.

This is why the savants were eager to gain knowledge of everything they could: nature, all facets of Egyptian society, and in particular the monuments built during the three thousand years of the country's history and left as a cultural heritage for future generations.

Once they had overcome the initial difficulties, they adapted to the new reality and life and began their scientific exploration

18–19
THE SAVANTS
PORTRAITS BY ANDRÉ DUTERTRE

These are the savants that contributed to the production of the *Description*. From top to bottom: Joseph Fourier (1768–1830), mathematician and physician and secretary of the Institut d'Egypte; he was also author of the *Preface Historique* and of some chapters of the *Description*. The artist and draughtsman, Dominique Vivant Denon (1747–1825), became famous for his *Voyage dans la Basse et la Haute Egypte*, which was first published in 1802. François Cécile (1766–1840), engineer and draughtsman, produced thirty or so plates and the frontispiece of the first edition of the *Description*. Gaspard Monge (1746–1818), physician and mathematician, was appointed by Napoleon to form the scientific commission; he was nominated first president of the Institut d'Egypte. André Dutertre (1753–1842), draughtsman and engraver, illustrated many Egyptian monuments and produced numerous portraits. Claude-Louis Berthollet (1748–1822) next page, chemist and physician, made a notable contribution in the field of science. In Egypt he studied the natural formation of natron.

of Egypt as early as August 1798, when General Desaix set off in pursuit of the retreating Mamluks towards Upper Egypt, a vast region that was still relatively unknown at the time.

About twenty scholars were part of the military contingent that reached Aswan on February 2, 1799. These included the young Jean-Baptiste Jollois and Edouard de Villier, as well as the 'veteran' Dominique Vivant Denon (who will be discussed at more length later), ". . . who ran towards the monuments like soldiers run to the battlefield." Denon in particular journeyed through Egypt drawing continuously—while kneeling, on horseback, in the midst of battle. He drew everything he saw: landscapes, battles, ceremonies, mosques, various personages, and, above all, the stupendous ancient ruins.

In July 1799 he returned to Cairo. Napoleon was impressed by his drawings, which represented an extremely interesting aspect of the French campaign and a fairly complete picture of Egypt, both ancient and modern.

Although Denon had succeeded in doing all that work by himself, it was imperative to do even more. The following month, at the behest of Napoleon himself, two special commissions, each with a dozen scholars, left for Upper Egypt with the task of visiting and describing all the remaining monuments of the past. A month later, the members met at Philae, the southernmost point in the journey, and began to sail down the Nile in the direction of Cairo.

Whether following the troops or being escorted by them, the savants made topographical surveys, drew the ancient ruins, measured the monuments, and carefully copied the hieroglyphic texts. But they did not

always succeed in these tasks. For example, when there were sudden, unexpected attacks and their lives were in danger, they were obliged to suspend their work and, in order to be protected by the troops that closed their ranks, the scholars had to obey the famous order that inevitably made the soldiers laugh: "Donkeys and scholars in the middle!"

In such circumstances, even copying hieroglyphs, whose meaning was still undecipherable, was often a superficial procedure at best. And in their hypothetical reconstructions of some monuments, the artists made use of all their ability, going so far as to 'imagine' the decoration that no longer existed by re-creating scenes they had seen on other ancient ruins.

The fact is, they all did their utmost: for example, even when they ran out of pencils they replaced them with hastily melted lead bullets in order not to deprive future generations of this invaluable documentation. And it must not be forgotten how some savants, displaying great courage and abnegation, saved this documentation from falling into British hands.

19 TOP RIGHT
TOMB OF PAHERI
ANTIQUITÉS, VOLUME I, PLATE 67
AL-KA'B, LOCATED BETWEEN EDFU AND ESNA

In addition to the wall decorations, the deceased, an important Eighteenth Dynasty functionary, is also shown in the niche between his wife, to his right, and his mother. A French artist is shown drawing and a local Egyptian happily smokes his pipe.

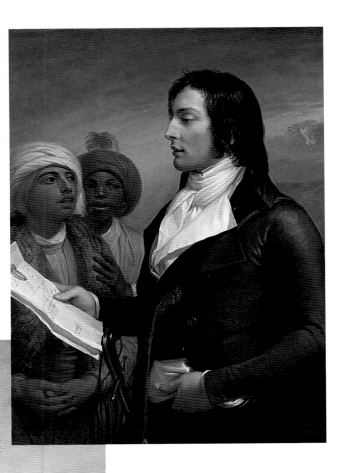

20 TOP
GENERAL DESAIX
PORTRAIT BY ANDREA APPIANI

General Desaix reached Aswan on February 1, 1799, thereby completing the occupation of all of Egypt. He is shown in a portrait reading Bonaparte's order of the day; the portrait was made in 1800 and is now in the Musée de Versailles.

20 CENTER
GENERAL KLÉBER
PORTRAIT BY ANTOINE ANSIAUX

Worthy successor to the commander-in-chief, Kléber (shown here in a portrait from the Musée de Versailles) was killed by a Muslim fanatic on June 14, 1800, the same day and at almost the same hour that Desaix fell at Marengo.

In fact, Article 16 of the French surrender, written at Alexandria on September 3, 1801, stipulates that, "The members of the Institut can take with them all the artistic tools brought from France; but the Arab manuscripts, statues, and other collections created for the French Republic shall be considered 'public property' and be placed at the disposal of the army generals." At this point the naturalists Geoffroy Saint-Hilaire and Raffeneau Delile, who represented the French Commission, threatened to burn all the collections if the French scholars were not allowed to take with them their 'intellectual property,'" that is, drawings, notes, and collections. General Hutchinson, the Englishman negotiating the French capitulation, concerned that unpleasant consequences might arise, allowed the savants to keep all their scientific information and collections, with one imperative exception: the British were to take possession of the archaeological finds, which included the Rosetta Stone.

Another important part of the Commission's work that should be mentioned was their drawings of monuments which, for various reasons, no longer exist today. In the descriptions of the illustrations selected for this volume, we have included monuments that were destroyed in the first half of the nineteenth century. Mohammed Ali, the founder of modern Egypt, implemented a wide-ranging program of reforms and renewal for his country, as he was eager to lead his country out of the 'dark ages' of the preceding centuries. But in doing so, he was often insensible to his nation's glorious past, allowing monuments to be demolished.

THE CONTRIBUTION OF THE FRENCH GENERALS

When speaking of the rediscovery of Egypt, the work of the French savants comes to mind first. However, it is only fair to add that some French generals also contributed to the scientific and cultural success of the Egyptian campaign. Among those who showed interest in ancient Egyptian history and monuments, mention should be made at least of Louis Charles Desaix (1768–1800) and Jean-Baptiste Kléber (1753–1800). The former has already been noted for his participation in the expedition to Upper Egypt, which allowed Denon to discover and make drawings of the ruins along the Nile Valley. This young general combined the qualities of a brilliant military strategist with the erudition of a scholar and noteworthy artistic taste. He is thought to have discovered the famous zodiac relief at Dendera.

General Kléber, who had many victories to his credit in Egypt and Syria, helped to mark a turning point in the history of the Egyptian expedition. A very cultured man who had studied architecture, he came up with the idea of creating a 'work in common.' In November 1799, he was enthusiastic about the drawings made by the two commissions that had returned from Upper Egypt and wrote, "One cannot but laud the amazing activity, the predominant harmony, and the precise division of labor among the members of the two commissions, and above all the liberal and patriotic idea of combining so much information into a single work . . . ." The aim of the work on Egypt was to ". . . spread culture and help to build a literary monument worthy of France."

This major work was of course to become the *Description de l'Egypte*, the most remarkable heritage of the Napoleonic expedition. The physicist Joseph Fourier was charged with coordinating the contributions, but he had to interrupt the preparation of the publication in 1801 when the French left Egypt, so it was continued and completed in Paris during the years that followed.

20 BOTTOM
THE HEAD OF THE SPHINX EMERGES FROM THE SAND
ANTIQUITÉS, VOLUME V, PLATE 11
GIZA

Khufu's pyramid and some secondary pyramids are seen in the background. From the time of the Napoleonic expedition, the monument has suffered a slow but progressive deterioration.

21
THE RUINS AT MEMPHIS
ANTIQUITÉS, VOLUME V, PLATE 3
MEMPHIS

About thirty kilometers south of Cairo lay Memphis, the capital of Egypt during the Old Kingdom. It was founded by Menes, the first pharaoh of the First Dynasty. This plate shows almost nothing of the few ruins still on the site, except for a colossal hand made of pink granite that was found there. In the foreground, in the midst of a vast palm grove, a French engineer and two assistants are removing and transporting this find, which is now kept in the British Museum, London. In the background are the three pyramids of Giza.

The Description de l'Egypte

"Egypt has been the object of various descriptions and of a great number of works, but until now it has not been possible to have exact and complete knowledge of this country.

What was needed was an extraordinary event, an extremely favorable circumstance such as the presence of a victorious army, in order to furnish the means needed to study Egypt with the attention it deserves. This country, visited by the most illustrious philosophers of antiquity, was the source from which the Greeks drew their principles of law, art, and science.

To describe and draw the ancient monuments with which one might well say Egypt is covered; to observe and find all the natural products, and prepare precise and detailed maps of the country; to collect ancient finds and study the soil, climate and physical geography; lastly, to gather together all the information concerning the history of the country's society, science and art—this is the aim of this undertaking, which required a great number of persons, all animated by the same ideas and ideals.

France had made every effort to conquer this country, and every artistic effort was made to describe it. A great number of draftsmen, painters, skilled typographers, mechanics and about four hundred engravers devoted themselves with admirable perseverance to the realization of this monument that merges the memories of ancient Egypt and the glory of modern France. This publication, dedicated to the description of so many gigantic monuments, is itself a colossal work in the field of literature, science and art" (Charles Louis Panckoucke, preface to *Description de l'Egypte*, 2nd ed., [Paris, 1821–29], n.n.).

After the French returned from Egypt, a consular decree of February 1802 announced the publication, at the government's expense, of the " . . . results in science and art obtained during the Expedition." This was the *Description de l'Egypte*. Written by a group of about fifty scholars whose contributions were coordinated by the physicist Joseph Fourier, the work involved about two thousand people and took about twenty years to complete. The gifted Nicolas-Jacques Conté invented a special, larger typographical machine, new printing methods were realized for the color plates, and special paper was utilized, particularly for the engravings.

By adopting the encyclopedic method, which called for the acquisition of a great deal of data (one should not forget the *Encyclopédie*, the famous work of the Enlightenment), the savants who prepared the texts compiled the most complete documentation ever realized, up to that time, of ancient and modern Egypt, as well as of the natural history of the country. As for the engravings, they were—and still are—the indispensable complement to the descriptions. Since the latter now seem to be partly out-of-date because of almost two centuries of Egyptological studies, it might be said that the illustrations form the most interesting part of this veritable literary monument, the *Description de l'Egypte*.

THE FIRST EDITION

Published in Paris between 1809 and 1828, the first edition of the *Description de l'Egypte ou Recueil des observations et des recherches qui on été faites en Egypte pendant l'expédition de l'armée française publié par les odres de sa Majesté l'Empereur Napoléon le Grand*, which was described as 'imperial,' consists of ten volumes of text and thirteen volumes of illustrations in folio plates (including two complementary volumes and an atlas). It is divided into *Antiquités* (five volumes), *Etat Moderne* (two volumes), and *Histoire Naturelle* (three volumes). It has 974 engravings (about seventy of which are in color) and more than three thousand drawings and illustrations. A thousand copies were printed.

"The day will come when the work of the Arts Commission," wrote the naturalist Geoffroy Saint-Hilaire, "will justify in the eyes of posterity the superficiality with which our nation rushed headlong, as it were, to the Orient. While deploring the fate of the many valorous soldiers who, after so many glorious feats, met their death in Egypt, future generations will console themselves with the existence of such a precious work."

The *Antiquités* section, which is presented in this volume, is the most fascinating part of the work because it deals with the archaeology of the ancient Egyptian, Ptolemaic, and Roman periods, and includes all the pre-Islamic sites and monuments visible at the time of the Egyptian campaign. The layout is systematic and not emphatic: the plates excel in their precision and the care with which they were drawn, while the captions, reduced to the minimum length, are considered indispensable. The order with which the plates are presented proceeds from south to north, from the island of Philae to the Mediterranean.

23
DESCRIPTION DE L'EGYPTE
FRONTISPIECE OF THE FIRST EDITION

Certain details in the work indicate that Napoleon Bonaparte was the sponsor of the *Description*, like this frontispiece designed by François Cécile, which celebrates both the monumental greatness of Egypt (all the country's principal monuments are shown in the central figure) and the military greatness of imperial France (symbolized in the frame where, for example, Napoleon is shown on a war chariot in the guise of Mars).

24
DESCRIPTION DE L'EGYPTE
FRONTISPIECE OF THE SECOND EDITION

The theme of monumental greatness combined with military conquest is taken up once more in the second edition which, after the fall of Napoleon, was cleansed of all imperial symbolism. In the center of the scene, there remain troops led by General Desaix to attest to the apotheosis of French colonial power. They are surrounded by some of the principal Egyptian monuments as observed by unidentified savants.

25
DESCRIPTION DE L'EGYPTE
FRONTISPIECE OF THE ATLANTE GÉOGRAPHIQUE.
SECOND EDITION

This frontispiece introduced the 'Geographical Atlas,' which is one of the volumes that complemented the second edition of the *Description*. This second edition was published in Paris between 1821 and 1829 and, though less popular than the first, it was well received throughout Europe and was a milestone in Egyptology.

However, the other two sections must not be neglected. The *Etat Moderne* features medieval and modern Egypt, Islamic architecture, and Egyptian customs, arts, crafts, and trades up to and including the eighteenth century, while the *Histoire Naturelle* contains descriptions and illustrations of animals and plants, classifications of minerals, and the results of research in various fields, including arms, music, and so on. Each plate has the name of the illustrator in the lower left-hand corner and the name of the engraver(s) in the lower right-hand corner and in the middle.

This plate, by François Cécile, symbolically synthesizes the military occupations and archaeological rediscovery of Egypt effected by the French. Under the archaizing cornice, the upper frieze represents, from left to right: the arrival of the French fleet at Alexandria, a procession of women, the symbols of art and science; in the middle, Napoleon in the guise of Mars on his chariot, is preceded by the imperial eagle and the fleeing Mamluk army. The Nile, personified in the figure at right, seems to be observing these events. Next to him is a crocodile, the symbol of Egypt.

In the two vertical registers there are military trophies and insignia commemorating the major battles and some of the localities the French explored. In the lower frieze, between two Egyptian-like symbols, is a procession of peaceful or subdued 'natives,' together with the initial of the emperor. The Nile is represented in the central section, which also shows the main monuments in Egypt: in the foreground, between an obelisk in Alexandria and 'Pompey's Pillar,' there are some archaeological finds, including the Rosetta Stone, the zodiac from Dendera, and a Theban ram-headed sphinx. Beyond the Great Sphinx at Giza, divided from one another by the Nile, are all the localities the French expedition reached, as far south as Philae.

In 1820 the publisher Charles-Louis Panckoucke printed the second edition of the *Description*, which was dedicated to Louis XVIII; it was less handsome but more practical in certain respects. It was published between 1821 and 1829—once again, in a print run of a thousand copies—and consisted of twenty-six volumes of text in octavo and eleven volumes of folio plates selected from among the original copper engravings. This publication, which stirred further interest in Egypt among the Europeans of the time, is still considered a fundamental part of Egyptology.

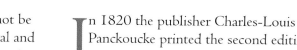

DESCRIPTION
DE L'ÉGYPTE
OU
RECUEIL
DES OBSERVATIONS ET DES RECHERCHE
QUI ONT ÉTÉ FAITES EN ÉGYPTE
PENDANT L'EXPÉDITION DE L'ARMÉE FRANÇAISE
SECONDE ÉDITION
DÉDIÉE AU ROI
PUBLIÉE PAR C. L. F. PANCKOUCKE
CHEVALIER DE LA LÉGION D'HONNEUR

ATLAS GÉOGRAPHIQUE

PARIS
IMPRIMERIE DE C. L. F. PANCKOUCKE
M D CCC XXVI.

Conceived by Panckoucke, who had not taken part in the expedition, the title page has a perspective view in color of the main ancient Egyptian monuments. After the fall of Napoleon, the title page with the apotheosis of the former emperor was obviously replaced. In the foreground are scattered ruins, including a column capital and the zodiac from Dendera, a head of Ramesses II, and a sarcophagus. In the middle, among obelisks and columns, are the ruins of Thebes and other monuments along the Nile. While French scholars undertake surveys at left, between the two columns, General Desaix is departing for Upper Egypt. In the distance is the island of Philae.

The Most Famous 'Savant'

After returning to France, almost all the scholars—even the generals and soldiers—in the Armée d'Orient published accounts or travel journals concerning their stay in Egypt. There was a flurry of memoirs that dealt not only with military events but also included descriptions of daily life and the marvelous ancient ruins.

To this day, the best-known work, besides *Description de l'Egypte*, is the *Voyage dans la Basse et la Haute Egypte* by Denon, briefly mentioned above, who became the most famous person in the entire Napoleonic expedition. It is impossible to mention all the events narrated by this author, much less all his descriptions of the sites he visited. But we will follow him in his '*Voyage*,' briefly touching upon some passages and impressions.

Dominique Vivant Denon (1747–1825) was an extremely cultured man, a former diplomat, artist, and traveler who managed to join the 'Oriental Expedition,' becoming a sort of special correspondent. He was the first of the French scholars to travel through Egypt. In November 1798, he left Cairo and joined General Desaix's troops, who were about to pursue the Mamluks and complete French military dominion of the entire country.

Despite the fact that he was over fifty, Denon proved to be more hardy than many of the soldiers. He survived the grueling marches in the desert, a bout of ophthalmia, and the torrid heat of Upper Egypt.

He was enthusiastic about Egyptian architecture and sculpture, which he was discovering little by little and which he drew continuously. He often worked alone and had to confront many difficulties. He traveled on foot, on horseback, or on camelback, drawing, as he said, " . . . for the most part on my knees, standing, or even on horseback: I was never able to finish one as I would have liked, because for a whole year not once did I find a straight table I could put a ruler on."

On more than one occasion Denon's life was in danger, but he was fortunate and, thanks to the protection and cooperation of the army officers and soldiers, always managed to achieve his ends. In December 1798, while traveling to Upper Egypt, Denon stopped for a short time at Hermopolis to see and draw the ruins of a temple (which no longer exists). In January of the following year, the French troops reached Dendera, where Denon was spellbound by the temple dedicated to the goddess Hathor. "I would have liked to draw all of it," he writes in his travel journal, "but I did not dare begin. Not being able to adapt myself to what I so admired, I realized I would only diminish the beauty of what I wanted to copy down. In no other place had I been surrounded by so many ruins able to stir my imagination." And he continued: "I thought I was—and in fact, I really was—in the sanctuary of art and science. Upon seeing such an edifice, how many epochs my imagination conjured up! How many centuries it took a creative nation to achieve such results, at such a perfect and sublime level of artistic production!"

A few days later, Desaix's army, which was moving along the west bank of the Nile, spotted on the opposite shore the extensive ruins of a city: the legendary, ancient Thebes. Then something unforgettable occurred. As soon as they reached the ruins, the French soldiers stopped and spontaneously began to applaud. "I did my first drawing," writes Denon, "as if I feared that Thebes would escape me. In order to draw another scene I found—thanks to the thoughtfulness and enthusiasm of the soldiers—knees that served as a table and bodies which shaded me from the blinding sun so that I could draw."

With unflagging energy and a great thirst for knowledge, Denon continued his search for monuments. With the army, he arrived at other localities, including Edfu, Aswan, and Philae, their final destination. In February, during his return trip, he was able to stop at Kom Ombo and return to Luxor and Karnak Temple with its obelisks ("the most perfect and elegant achievement of Egyptian architecture").

In July 1799, Denon went back to Cairo with over two hundred drawings that depicted everything: battles, monuments, towns, landscapes, ceremonies, animals, and various objects, and portraits of notables, artisans, and peasants. During a meeting at the Institut d'Egypte he read a report of his journey that excited the members. Napoleon himself examined his drawings and was so impressed that he immediately decided to promote two more expeditions to Upper Egypt. The following month, Denon left Egypt with Napoleon, Monge, and Berthollet and a few weeks later was back in Paris. After he had put his notes and drawings in order, in 1802 he published his *Voyage dans la Basse et la Haute Egypte*, in two folio volumes with 142 engravings—and was thus the first of the savants to do so.

A chronicler bridging the ages of Enlightenment and Romanticism, Denon revealed the monuments of ancient Egypt and Islam to European culture, thus helping to suppress the memory of the military failure of Napoleon's expedition.

His *Voyage* is characterized by very accurate drawings and comments that are often quite lively (and sometimes better than the illustrations). Although it is not arranged systematically, it was the most complete iconographic collection on Egypt published at the time. It enjoyed a great success and made Denon famous, so much so that in the course of the nineteenth century about forty editions of the work came out, including reprints and translations.

As one can clearly see, *Voyage dans la Basse et la Haute Egypte* was of fundamental importance to the rediscovery of Egypt. Furthermore, it was the prelude to the more wide-ranging and complete *Description* and marked the definitive triumph of the mania for ancient Egypt, a sort of aesthetic-cultural passe-partout that lasted for decades. Lastly, it made a basic contribution to the rise of a new discipline, Egyptology. But that is another story.

28 AND 29
DETAILS FROM THE *VOYAGE DANS LA BASSE ET LA HAUTE EGYPTE*

Denon's *Voyage* has many detailed illustrations. On this page, from top to bottom and from left to right, we see two capitals of columns, the zodiac relief from Dendera, and the upper part of a Hathoric column. On the page on the right, Denon has illustrated 'Pompey's Pillar' (left) and one of 'Cleopatra's Needles' (right), both of which were found in Alexandria. They are framed by representations taken from Theban tombs and, below, by a reproduction of the measurements taken of the Sphinx in Giza.

30-31
HYPOSTYLE ROOM IN THE TEMPLE OF ISIS
ANTIQUITÉS, VOLUME I, PLATE 18
PHILAE

The superb polychromy that decorated the interior of the hypostyle room was still visible at the start of the nineteenth century and is shown here in careful detail. Now, however, it has almost all been lost.

Denon del.   I. Pass sculp.

A View of the Sphinx at the Pyramids at Gizeh; a Patera, charged with the Portraits
of Osiris and Isis, and Sculptures of Egyptian Musicians. Pompey's or Dioclesian's
Pillar; and Cleopatra's Needle.

London Published as the Act directs July 18.th 1804 by J. Wilkes.

Antiquités

Volume 1

Contents

32–33
GENERAL VIEW FROM THE NORTHWEST
Antiquités, Volume I, Plate 2
PHILAE

"Upon entering this plain, one suddenly catches sight of the island of Philae. Large monuments, the trees surrounding them, the waters of the river, the luxuriant vegetation on its banks, all make for a picture that appears extraordinary and is enchanting because one has just come out of an arid valley."
(Description de l'Egypte, *Volume I, p. 10*)

This was the first impression Napoleon's savants had when they arrived at Philae, the final destination of their expedition. This was in February 1799. The entire archaeological site, which was surrounded by tall granite rocks, seems to be mirrored in the tranquil waters of the Nile.

35 TOP
GENERAL VIEW FROM THE NORTHEAST
Antiquités. Volume I. Plate 3
PHILAE

Located two kilometers south of Aswan and the First Cataract, Philae was a small island known since ancient times as the 'pearl of the Nile' because it lay in an incomparably beautiful natural setting.

Besides its location, the site became famous due to the great importance attached to the cult of Isis, especially during the Greco-Roman period. This engraving shows, on the right, the

Ptolemaic temple of Isis; at left is 'Trajan's Kiosk.' In the background, at right, are the granite rocks of the island of Biga, which was sacred to Osiris, the husband of the great universal mother.

36-37 and 36 bottom
SECTIONS AND VIEWS
Antiquités, Volume I, Plate 6
PHILAE

The plate shows the first pylon in the
Temple of Isis, with low reliefs of
Ptolemy XII, the father of the well-known
Cleopatra VII, in the symbolic act of
striking his adversaries with a club. The
representations of the Ptolemaic rulers
and gods such as Hathor, Isis, and Horus
have been copied quite faithfully.

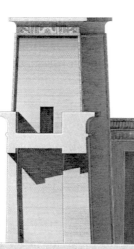

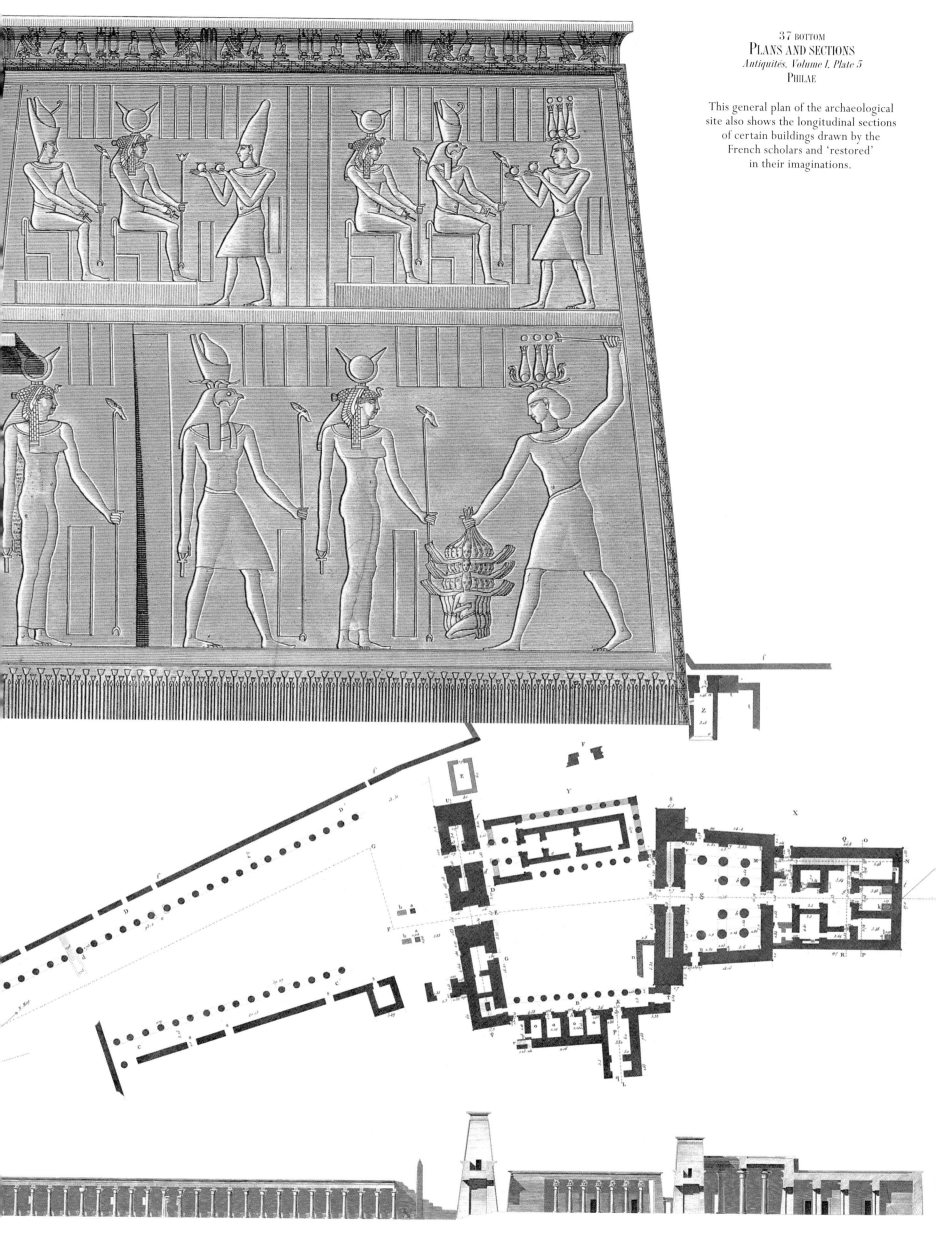

This general plan of the archaeological
site also shows the longitudinal sections
of certain buildings drawn by the
French scholars and 'restored'
in their imaginations.

38 TOP
LOW RELIEFS FROM VARIOUS BUILDINGS
Antiquités. Volume I. Plate 6
PHILAE

The low reliefs carved in the hypostyle room in the Temple of Isis depict Ptolemy VIII make offerings to Khnum, the god of the first cataract, and to Satet, his consort (top left), and to divinities believed to be Shu (the air) and Tefnut (moisture), who were children of Atum (top right). All are wearing symbolic crowns.

LOW RELIEFS FROM VARIOUS BUILDINGS
Antiquités. Volume I, Plate 13
PHILAE

The low reliefs represent gods and rulers and are taken from the colonnade to the east, and from the temple to the west or *mammisi*. This term, from the Coptic and meaning 'birthplace,' was used by Champollion to indicate smaller, less important buildings during the Ptolemaic period that were connected with the large sanctuaries, in which the mystery of the maternity of Isis was celebrated, and of the birth of her son Horus with whom the pharaoh was identified.

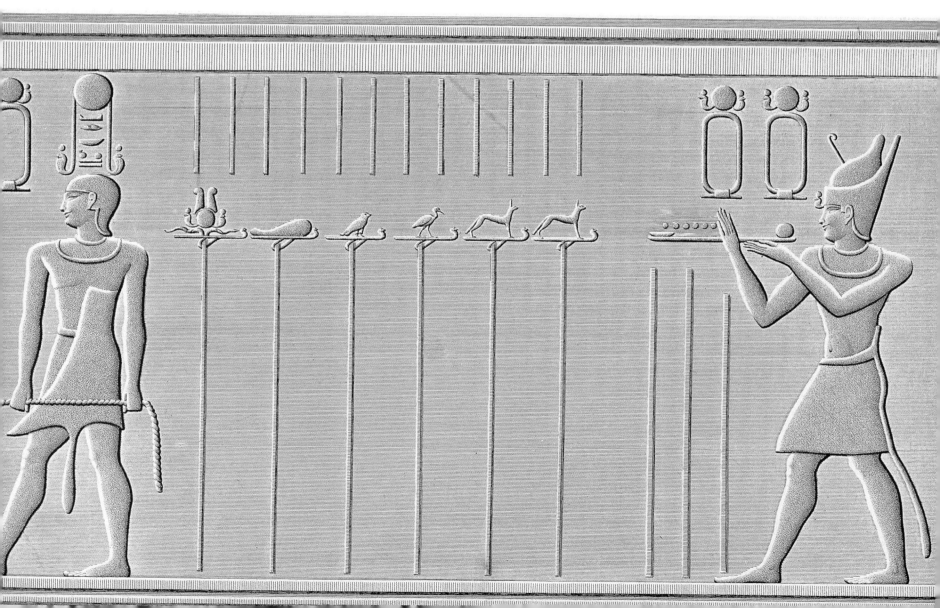

40–41
VIEW OF THE WEST TEMPLE
Antiquités. Volume I. Plate 24
PHILAE

In the foreground of this engraving is
a small temple known as a "mammini,"
a name invented by Champollion.
In Coptic the word means "place of
birth." During the Ptolemaic period,
the "mammini" were minor edifices
connected to large sanctuaries where
the mystery of the maternity of Isis
was celebrated. The two pylons of the
temple dedicated to this goddess-mother
are partly visible.

40 bottom
VIEW OF THE SECOND PYLON
Antiquités. Volume I, Plate 17
PHILÆ

Preceded by an internal court, the decorations and low reliefs of the second pylon are quite evident. The draftsmanship of the French artists reveals a surprising degree of precision and detail.

41 top
PANORAMIC VIEW OF THE EAST BUILDING
Antiquités. Volume I, Plate 28
PHILÆ

This is the building known as 'Trajan's Kiosk,' one of the last manifestations of ancient Egyptian art. The elegant, harmonious monument was erected in honor of the Roman emperor around AD 96, when the country had been a province of the Roman Empire for some time. The unfinished building features fourteen columns with elegant composite capitals.

41 bottom
VIEW OF THE EAST BUILDING AND NUMEROUS MONUMENTS
Antiquités. Volume I, Plate 25
PHILÆ

From right to left we see a view of the East Temple and 'Trajan's Kiosk.' The presence of visitors in western dress is characteristic of the engravings of the period and is an elegant expedient to give the viewer a sense of the dimensions of the buildings.

42-43 TOP AND 43 BOTTOM
VIEW
Antiquités. Volume I, Plate 32
ASWAN

The ancient Syene of the Greeks and Romans represented, with the island of Elephantine, the gateway to Nubia. At the time of the Napoleonic expedition, Aswan, today known as the main tourist destination in Upper Egypt, and which lies 950 kilometers south of Cairo, was only a village and a marketplace that attracted goods from the center of the continent. During the pharaonic period, Aswan was known for its granite quarries.

42 BOTTOM
TEMPLE OF AMENHOTEP III
Antiquités. Volume I, Plate 34
ELEPHANTINE

The island of Elephantine stretches in front of Aswan for one and a half kilometers. In ancient times, Elephantine, the gateway to the heart of Africa, was a flourishing trade center. It was the site of several monuments, but almost nothing remains of them today.

This small temple in the southern part of the island was built at the behest of Amenhotep III during the Eighteenth Dynasty and dedicated to Khnum, the god of the First Cataract. It was destroyed in 1822. The ruins in front of the temple consist of the remains of a stairway and the unfinished statue is probably a portrait of Osiris. Another small temple dedicated to Thutmose III in the northern part of Elephantine was also destroyed in 1822.

43 TOP AND CENTER
LOW RELIEFS FROM THE TEMPLE OF AMENHOTEP III
Antiquités. Volume I. Plate 37
ELEPHANTINE

In addition to the temple, much of the internal decoration was also destroyed in the nineteenth century when the modern city of Aswan was built. The scene shows Amenhotep III (his cartouches appear twice in the inscription) and his wife Tiy making offerings to the boat of Amun-Ra. The goddess with the head of an antelope, Satet, presents the pharaoh to Khnum, the god with the ram's head who was also her consort.

LOW RELIEF OF THE *MAMMISI*
Antiquités. Volume I, Plate 45
KOM OMBO

Not far from the Great Temple, there used to exist a smaller temple that commemorated the birth of Horus (see previous caption). Its walls were decorated with symbolic scenes of rulers and gods, including this one of the god Bes (top right), who was a sort of bearded dwarf. Despite his deformed appearance and scornful sneer, he protected the home, women in childbirth, and men from evil influences.

44 TOP
VIEW OF THE TWO TEMPLES
Antiquités. Volume I, Plate 46
KOM OMBO

An imaginary reconstruction by the French artists of the temple at Kom Ombo and its *mammisi* (left). At right is the wall and large gate of Ptolemy XII. The Nile in the foreground had eroded the banks over the centuries, thus causing great damage to the monuments.

44 CENTER
VIEW OF THE ROCK SHRINES
Antiquités. Volume I, Plate 47
GEBEL AL-SILSILA

This archaeological site on both sides of the Nile, sixty-five kilometers north of Aswan, was famous because of its sandstone quarries, as this stone was used to build the temples in Upper Egypt. The Arabic name of the locality means 'mountain of the chain'; according to legend, it derived from the fact that a chain was laid across the river from this rock to collect tolls from the boats passing by. The two rock-hewn shrines, whose entrances can be seen in this illustration, belonged to Merneptah and Ramesses II, two Nineteenth Dynasty rulers.

44-45
VIEW OF THE GREAT TEMPLE
Antiquités. Volume I, Plate 40
KOM OMBO

This is what the impressive ruins of the temple at Kom Ombo (about forty kilometers north of Aswan) looked like during the time of the Napoleonic scientific mission. The monument dates from the Ptolemaic-Roman age and consisted of two sanctuaries dedicated to the falcon-headed god, Horus 'the Ancient,' and Sobek, the crocodile-headed god. The illustration shows locals preparing dinner (right), a French scholar approaching the temple, and a soldier on patrol (left).

46–47
GENERAL VIEW
Antiquités. Volume I. Plate 48
EDFU

Situated little more than a hundred kilometers south of Luxor on the west bank of the Nile, the city of Edfu, famous for the beautiful temple dedicated to the god Horus, was called Apollonopolis Magna by the ancient Greeks after the first Ptolemaic rulers (ca. 300 BC) instituted religious syncretism that

identified the god Apollo with the local god Horus.

At Edfu, the son of Isis and Osiris was worshipped as the sun god, represented as both a falcon and a human being with a falcon's head. Construction of the temple began in 237 BC under Ptolemy III Euergetes and was completed almost two centuries later, during the Roman era. This is how the monument appeared to the French mission: half buried under sand, as it had been for several centuries. Rubble and modest dwellings lie both in front of the temple and on the roof of the hypostyle. At left is a well shaded by a sycamore tree.

"I set off at a gallop to pass the first soldiers and arrive before the last rays of the sun left off illuminating the town. This time I barely had time to go around and through this edifice on horseback: its grandeur, magnificence, and state of preservation surpassed everything I had seen until then in Egypt and other places. The impression it made on me was as great as its size." (D. Vivant Denon, *Voyage dans la Basse et la Haute Egypte*, vol. I, text; Cairo, 1989, p. 124). With the Nile in the background, the plate shows the sheer majesty of the temple, which is 140 meters long and has a pylon thirty-six meters high. Next to a tent are some members of the French mission and local inhabitants who are preparing lunch. Architecturally complete and richly decorated, this is the best preserved temple in Egypt.

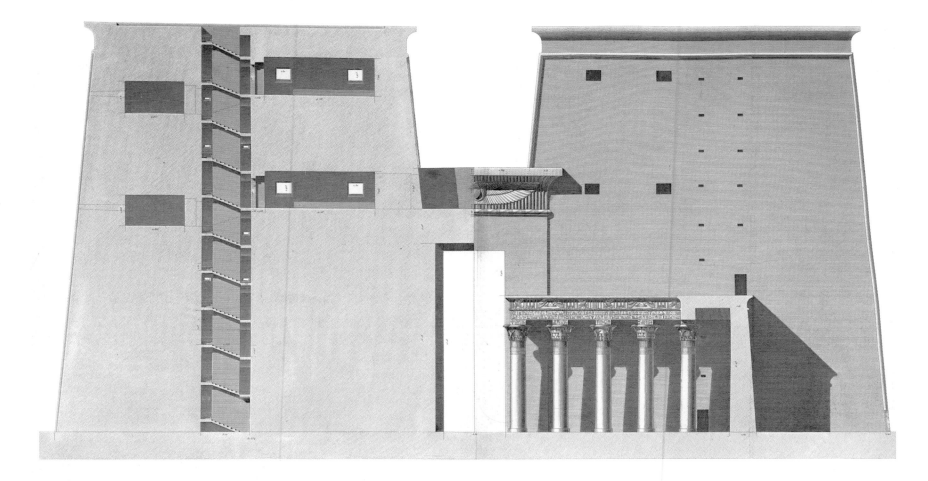

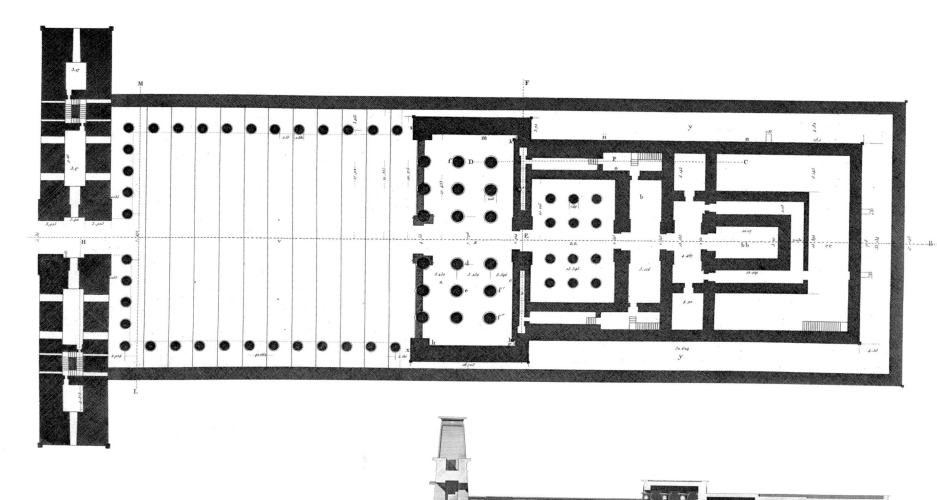

50 top
SECTION AND VIEW OF THE TEMPLE
Antiquités. Volume I. Plate 52
EDFU

The drawing by the French savants shows the two truncated pyramidal towers that formed the pylon, and the series of steps inside that led to the summit of the temple.

50–51
VIEW OF THE PYLON
Antiquités. Volume I. Plate 51
EDFU

This is the monumental entrance as imagined by the French artists without the sand and rubble under which it had been buried for centuries. A recurrent motif is the sovereign sacrificing prisoners of war in the presence of one or more gods.

51 top
PLAN AND SECTION OF THE TEMPLE OF HORUS
Antiquités. Volume I. Plate 50
EDFU

The architectural dictates of the New Kingdom remained in force even during the Ptolemaic era. 'The abode of the gods' was characterized by a pylon (monumental entrance) as seen here from left to right. Then there followed a vast open court surrounded on three sides by a portico with thirty-two columns, a pronaos, and a vestibule with twelve columns surmounted by splendid capitals. The vestibule was the preserve of the priests and perhaps dignitaries. There was also a hypostyle hall with twelve columns. The architectural structure of the temple was completed by other smaller rooms, including the cella (the most sacred section of the temple) which contained a statue of the god. The cella could only be entered by the pharaoh and the high priest for the carrying out of daily rituals.

Lepère Arch. del.

Louvet Sc.

52-53
VIEW OF THE FAÇADE OF THE PRONAOS
Antiquités. Volume I. Plate 53
EDFU

The illustration shows the façade of the pronaos with a row of columns decorated with elegant floral capitals. As a section of the decoration has been destroyed, the French artists completed the scenes using their imagination inspired by similar monuments.

52 BOTTOM
INTERIOR VIEW OF THE HYPOSTYLE HALL
Antiquités. Volume I. Plate 55
EDFU

The view of the temple, covered with sand and rubble, shows once again the splendid composite capitals. Together with the columns, their decoration is based on plant life and is typical of the Ptolemaic era. The scene is animated by the two natives in the typical dress of the time. The enormous quantity of sand suffocated the temple until 1860 when the French Egyptologist Auguste Mariette (1821–81) began to remove it, thereby making access possible to all of the complex.

53 CENTER AND RIGHT
DECORATIONS AND SCULPTURES
Antiquités. Volume I. Plate 58
EDFU

The many reliefs distributed on several registers in the hypostyle hall show offerings' and astronomical scenes. Note the ornamental motifs in these details.

This lovely illustration represents the rear
of the temple pylon, which consists of
two truncated pyramidal towers and the
entrance. The decoration, on two
registers, has scenes of the pharaoh
making offerings to various divinities.
The vast court is surrounded by a
peristyle with thirty-two columns, each
with a different capital.

55 BOTTOM
PANORAMIC VIEW OF THE SMALL TEMPLE
Antiquités. Volume I. Plate 65
EDFU

Opposite the large temple there is another much smaller one in a rather poor state of preservation–the *mammisi*. The floral capitals of the columns are crowned with sculptures of the god Bes, a disfigured domestic god considered the guardian of expectant mothers and newborn infants.
Since the beautiful scenes carved on the outside had been destroyed, the French mission artist executed an imaginary reconstruction of the temple with all the decoration typical of similar monuments.

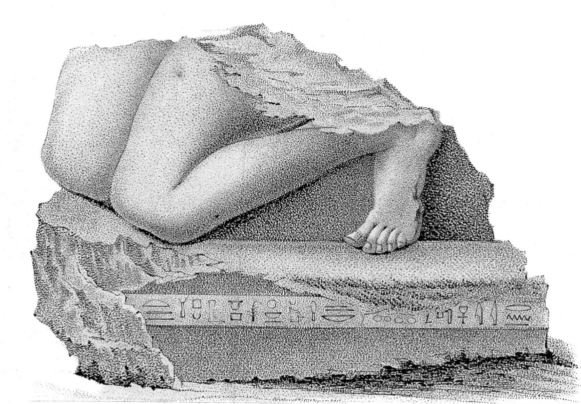

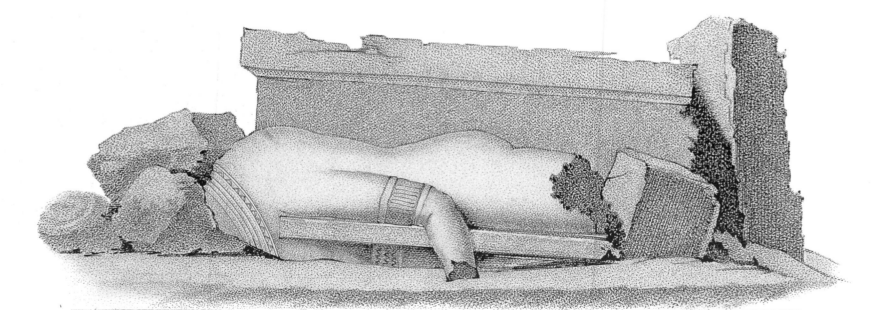

56 AND 57
LOW RELIEFS AND FRAGMENTS
Antiquités. Volume I, Plate 69
AL-KA'B

The modern-day town of al-Ka'b, which the ancient Greeks called Eileithyiaspolis, lies between Esna and Edfu on the east bank of the Nile and is one of the most ancient localities in Egypt. An important religious capital whose history dates from around 6000 BC, it was the ancient

Nekheb, which was consecrated to the vulture goddess, Nekhbet, one of the guardian deities of Upper Egypt. Identified by the Greeks with their Selene-Eileithya, it still has a series of interesting rock tombs, including that of Paheri, an influential figure who lived during the reign of Thutmose III (circa 1500 BC). The reliefs show funerary offerings and work in the fields. The fragments of statue were found among the ruins of the city.

<table>
<tr><td>

58 top
INTERIOR DECORATIONS
Antiquités. Volume 1. Plate 81
E S N A

The low reliefs, from the Greco-Roman
era, are from the interior of the temple
dedicated to Khnum in Esna and show
a pharaoh carried in procession on
a sort of litter.

</td><td>

58 bottom
VIEW OF THE TEMPLE OF KHNUM
Antiquités. Volume 1. Plate 73
E S N A

Esna, a locality in Upper Egypt, was called
Latopolis by the ancient Greeks because a
sacred fish, the Nile perch (*Lates niloticus*),
was worshipped there. The remains of a
large temple, dedicated to the ram-headed
god Khnum and dating from the Greco-
Roman period, can still be seen below the
road level of the present-day agricultural
town, about sixty kilometers south of
Luxor. This plate shows a hypostyle hall
with faithfully-copied low reliefs. The
lower part of the structure was not drawn,
as it was hidden by sand.

</td><td>

58–59
VIEW OF THE HYPOSTYLE HALL
Antiquités. Volume 1. Plate 83
E S N A

This is a hypothetical reconstruction of
the hypostyle hall, the only part of the
temple that has remained intact. Shown
with all the sand removed, the vault and
twenty-four columns are decorated with
signs of the zodiac, astrological scenes,
and important mythological texts. Priests
carrying statues of the deities complete
the fictitious scene. Along with the
names of Domitian, Trajan, and Hadrian,
the temple also has the most recent
cartouche of a Roman emperor,
Decius (AD 249–251).

</td></tr>
</table>

Antiquités

Volume 2

Contents

60 TOP
HEAD OF RAMESSES II
ANTIQUITÉS, VOLUME II, PLATE 32
RAMESSEUM

The engraving represents the granite head of a colossus dedicated to the famous pharaoh of the Nineteenth Dynasty. Ramesses II wears the regal linen *nemes* headdress and the false beard. On his forehead there is the uraeus serpent; this sacred cobra was a symbol of royalty.

60-61
GENERAL VIEW FROM THE NORTHEAST
ANTIQUITÉS, VOLUME II, PLATE 26
RAMESSEUM

The plate shows the funerary temple that Ramesses II had built for himself around 1250 BC. Here we see a part of the second courtyard with four, large headless statues of Ramesses II as Osiris set on pillars, and then the hypostyle hall, which had forty-eight papyrus columns. At left, on the ground, are the remains of the colossal statue of Ramesses himself.

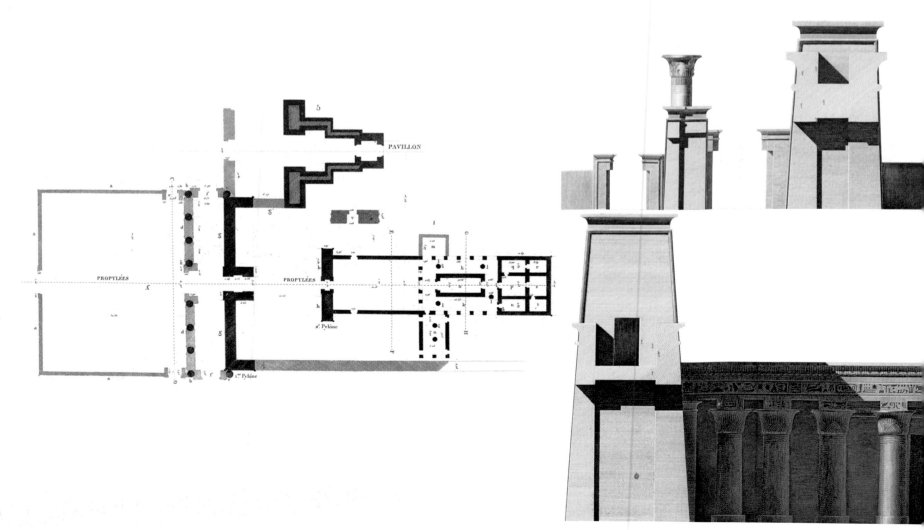

62-63 TOP
PARTIAL VIEW OF MEDINET HABU
ANTIQUITÉS, VOLUME II, PLATE 3
WESTERN THEBES

62-63 BOTTOM
PLAN AND LONGITUDINAL SECTIONS
ANTIQUITÉS, VOLUME II, PLATE 4
THEBES, MEDINET HABU

West of modern Luxor and south of the Theban necropolis lie the ruins of the funerary temple at Medinet Habu, a vast complex of buildings constructed by Ramesses III shortly after 1200 BC, at the end of the New Kingdom. The various buildings were surrounded by a thick stone wall and by a fort that was military in design, in imitation of Asiatic forts. The engraving shows part of the archaeological site. In the background we see the Ramesseum.

Drawn up by the Commission, these are the plans and longitudinal sections of various buildings that made up the vast monumental complex. The enormous temple comprises two courtyards, each of which is preceded by a pylon. Then come the hypostyle hall and other, smaller rooms, but, of these, only ruins remain. At the time of the expedition, identification was impossible due to the mountains of rubble in the complex. In a spirit of emulation and self-glorification, the last of the great pharaohs had the walls of this large monument covered with various military scenes and rhetorical texts, including the defence of the Asian and Nubian borders of the empire by Ramesses himself.

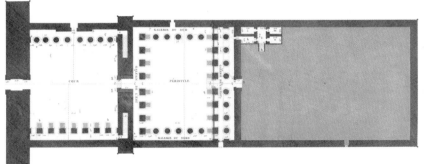

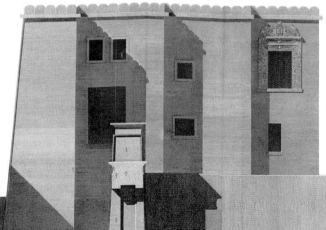

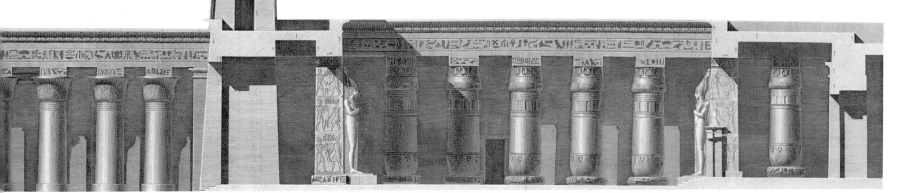

64–65 TOP
OSIRIAN PILLAR AND COLUMN
Antiquités, Volume II, Plate 7
THEBES, MEDINET HABU

Next to the drawing of a column in the form of a papyrus is a frontal and profile view of a statue crowning a pillar. It shows the pharaoh identified as Osiris and therefore wearing the characteristic clothing of the god of the underworld.

64–65 BOTTOM
NAVAL BATTLE
Antiquités, Volume II, Plate 10
THEBES, MEDINET HABU

The original low relief is actually twenty-eight meters long. It illustrates the attempted invasion of Egypt by the 'Sea Peoples' from the Mediterranean and Asia Minor who were active between the thirteenth and eleventh centuries BC. Around 1180 BC, the Sea Peoples were repelled by Ramesses in a battle that was perhaps decisive for the independence of the country. The engraving shows the pharaoh in battle, while his forces fight on land and at sea.

The scene is carved on a pylon in the temple of Ramesses III. It shows the pharaoh with a spear ready to strike as he hunts by chariot. A lion lies dead on the ground and another flees terrified. The scene is completed by a procession and drawings of architectural fragments.

66

THE 'COLOSSI OF MEMNON'
DETAILS OF THE NORTH STATUE
ANTIQUITÉS. VOLUME II. PLATE 22
THEBES

This is the frontal and profile representation of the colossus on the right in Plate 20. The sandstone statue of Amenhotep III seated in majesty, about eighteen meters high, has many carvings in Greek and Latin on the legs. The two figures on the right side of the throne are personifications of the Nile, which bring together the symbolic plants of Upper and Lower Egypt–the lotus and the papyrus–to represent the union of the two countries.

66-67

THE 'COLOSSI OF MEMNON'
ANTIQUITÉS. VOLUME II. PLATE 20
THEBES

The characteristic feature of the west bank of the Nile, chosen by the rulers of the New Kingdom as the site of their necropolis, is the two gigantic statues commonly known as the 'Colossi of Memnon.' This was the name given to them by the ancient Greeks, since they believed the statues portrayed the Ethiopian hero/king Memnon–son of the goddess of dawn Eos–who was killed by Achilles at Troy and celebrated in Homer's *Illiad*. In fact, these statues are the only remains of the funerary temple of Amenhotep III, which was built around 1400 BC. During the Roman period, the 'Colossi' were a major attraction: an earthquake in 27 BC made a crack in the statue seen at right in this plate. After this, due to a singular natural phenomenon–the stone dilating at dawn–the statue emitted strange vibrations, a sort of lamentation that the Greek visitors interpreted as the 'voice' of Memnon, who greeted his mother when she appeared every morning.
Among the most famous visitors attracted by this seemingly magical musical sound (who carved many inscriptions on the colossi) were Strabo, Hadrian, and Settimius Severus. Around AD 200, the last-mentioned emperor had the statue restored, with the result that the vibrations no longer occurred, as if Memnon had been offended and decided to remain silent for ever.

68 TOP
GENERAL VIEW FROM THE NORTHWEST
ANTIQUITÉS, VOLUME II, PLATE 23
THEBES, RAMESSEUM

Not far from the Colossi of Memnon
stands the Ramesseum, the mortuary
temple of Ramesses II. From the early
nineteenth century on, this poorly
preserved monument was known as the
'Memnonium' and was also described
with this name in the *Description de
l'Egypte* (see vol. II, page 237f.).
Another much older appellation is the
'Tomb of Ozymandias,' given by the
Sicilian-Greek historian Diodurus Siculus,
who had visited the site around 60 BC and
wrote the first description of the entire
mortuary complex and the fragments
of a colossal statue scattered around.
Why did he use the name Ozymandias?
This was the Greek transliteration of
Ramesses II's first name, User-Maat-Re
('mighty is the justice of Re').
This plate shows an overall view
of the ruins and part of the plain
of Thebes; in the background are
the Colossi of Memnon.

68–69
VIEW OF THE COURT WITH THE REMAINS OF A COLOSSAL STATUE
ANTIQUITÉS, VOLUME II, PLATE 25
THEBES, RAMESSEUM

This plate illustrates the first courtyard,
which is surrounded by papyrus-shaped
columns and Osirian pillars representing
the pharaoh, who is identified with
Osiris, the god of the underworld. On
the ground at right is the mutilated torso
of a colossal statue of Ramesses II, the
mighty 'Ozymandias.' According to the
famous British archaeologist William
Petrie, the colossus was nineteen meters
tall and weighed about a thousand tons.
It may well have been the largest
monolith ever raised.

69 TOP
GENERAL VIEW FROM THE SOUTHWEST
ANTIQUITÉS, VOLUME II, PLATE 24
THEBES, RAMESSEUM

On the basis of the description furnished
by Diodorus, the French architects Jollois
and Devilliers deduced that they had
found the 'Tomb of Ozymandias' in these
ruins. During their trip to Egypt in
1828–29, Champollion and Rosellini
confirmed this identification but,
believing that the monument was
a funerary temple rather than a tomb,
they gave the entire complex the
name Ramesseion.

This lovely low relief in the hypostyle hall illustrates another offensive in Syria by Ramesses II. After invading the territory of the Hittites around 1271 BC, the pharaoh took this city situated to the north of Kadesh. In the right hand scene, the fort, built on a rocky embankment, is being attacked by Egyptian troops. At bottom, the attackers are shown continuing the assault while they protect themselves with shields. At top left, the pharaoh discusses military tactics with his advisors. In the third scene, we see a Hittite chariot carrying three soldiers.

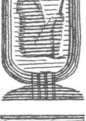

70
ARCHITECTURAL DRAWINGS
ANTIQUITÉS, VOLUME II, PLATE 30
THEBES, RAMESSEUM

The engraving depicts several architectural elements from the second court and the hypostyle hall on the Theban site. An Osirian pillar is shown in profile and from the front, as well as two capitals in the form of an open and closed papyrus.

70-71
LONGITUDINAL SECTION
ANTIQUITÉS, VOLUME II, PLATE 28
THEBES, RAMESSEUM

Here we are given the monumental complex as imagined by the Commission. At bottom: the first pylon (seen only in part) led to a courtyard in which there stood the seated colossus of the pharaoh. Then followed a second pylon, which had almost completely disappeared, and another courtyard with Osirian pillars. This led into a large hypostyle hall of which twenty or so of the original forty-eight columns remain.

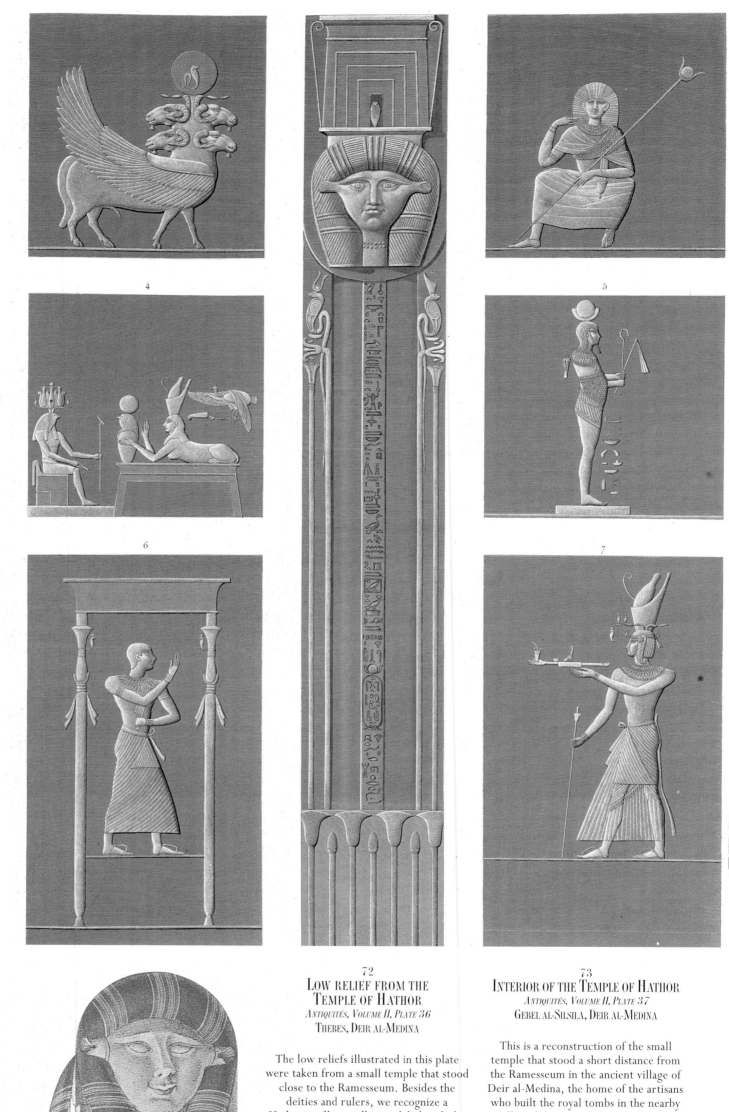

72
Low relief from the Temple of Hathor
Antiquités, Volume II, Plate 36
Thebes, Deir al-Medina

The low reliefs illustrated in this plate were taken from a small temple that stood close to the Ramesseum. Besides the deities and rulers, we recognize a Hathoric pillar-a pillar modeled with the image of the goddess with the human face and calf's ears.

73
Interior of the Temple of Hathor
Antiquités, Volume II, Plate 37
Gebel al-Silsila, Deir al-Medina

This is a reconstruction of the small temple that stood a short distance from the Ramesseum in the ancient village of Deir al-Medina, the home of the artisans who built the royal tombs in the nearby Valley of the Kings. The temple dates from the Ptolemaic period and was dedicated to the goddess Hathor, the goddess of joy, dance, and music. Some of the wall paintings were copied faithfully by the Napoleonic campaign artists.

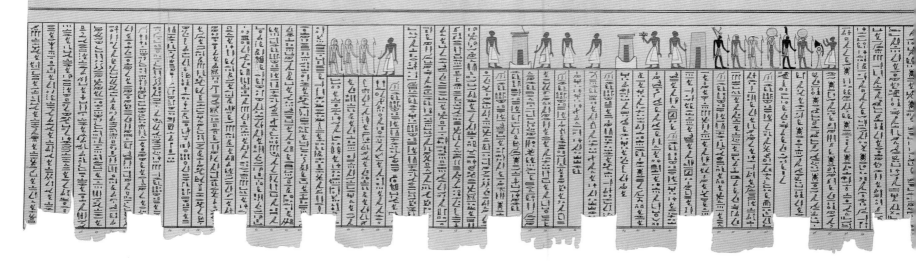

74 TOP
THE 'BOOK OF THE DEAD'
BELONGING TO PADIAMON
NEBNESUTTAWY
ANTIQUITÉS, VOLUME II, PLATE 72

The modern term 'Book of the Dead,' which was coined in 1842 by the great Prussian Egyptologist Richard Lepsius (1801–84), but which the Egyptians referred to as 'formulas for returning to daylight,' is a collection of magical and ritual prayers and charms used in a funerary context. They were written on papyrus, sarcophagi, and tomb walls. Papyrus was an important element in the

burial accoutrements, and was prepared during life in proportion to the authority of the client. The Book of the Dead was written in hieroglyphs or hieratic script and was later placed in the sarcophagus, usually on the deceased's chest. Beginning with the New Kingdom (ca. 1550–1080 BC), the Book of the Dead was composed of 192 chapters and was embellished by illustrations. It had the function of protecting the deceased from various dangers and of ensuring his survival and rebirth in the afterworld (*Duat* to the ancient Egyptians). These pages show the largest of the papyruses found in Thebes by the Commission. Currently held in the

Bibliothéque Nationale in Paris, it dates from the Ptolemaic era (304–30 BC). Written completely in hieroglyphs, it is a little over nine meters long and twenty-two centimeters wide. As the papyrus was written from right to left, the first plate represents the end. The total number of columns is 515. The many red characters between the hieroglyphs very probably indicate the start of a new phrase or chapter in the manuscript. Plate 72 describes the ancient belief of the Egyptians in a life after death, which is summarized in chapter 125 of the Book of the Dead; this is the best known chapter and refers to the

episode of the 'weighing of the heart.' It was believed that to enter Duat the heart of the deceased–in other words, his consciousness–was subjected to a moral code and weighed on a scale. In the scene illustrated, we see, on the right, Padiamon standing and reciting prayers, accompanied by Maat, the goddess of justice and the personification of the balance of the cosmos. The heart of the deceased lies in the dish on the right; in the other, the god Horus places an ostrich feather, which is the grapheme and symbol of Maat. The god Anubis checks that the two dishes are perfectly balanced. In this case, the heart is shown to be free from sin, therefore it is as light as 'Maat's feather.' This is the only way Padiamon can be deemed just and worthy of entering the 'Field of Rushes' where he will be able to cultivate fertile soil. If the heart is heavy with sin and weighs down its dish, it will be presented to Ammet 'the Devourer,' who is present at the judgment in front of Osiris. The monstrous animal is formed by the parts of a crocodile, lion, and hippopotamus. It symbolizes the annihilation of an aspect of the soul (*ba*) of the deceased and therefore the impossibility of rebirth. The scene is completed (top) by forty-two judges in charge of other sins that the deceased may have committed, and the ibis-headed god Thoth, who was the 'chancellor' of Osiris' court and took notes of the final sentence.

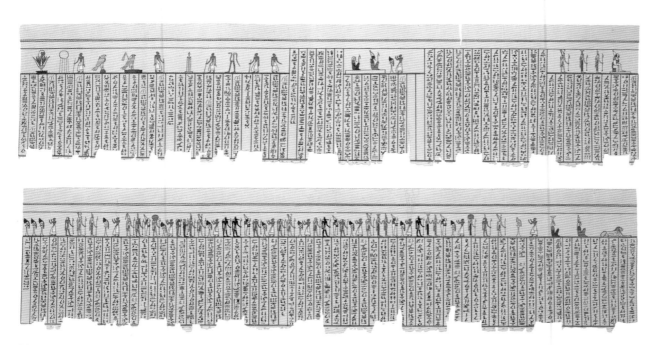

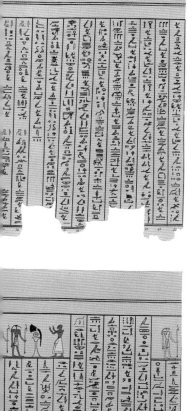

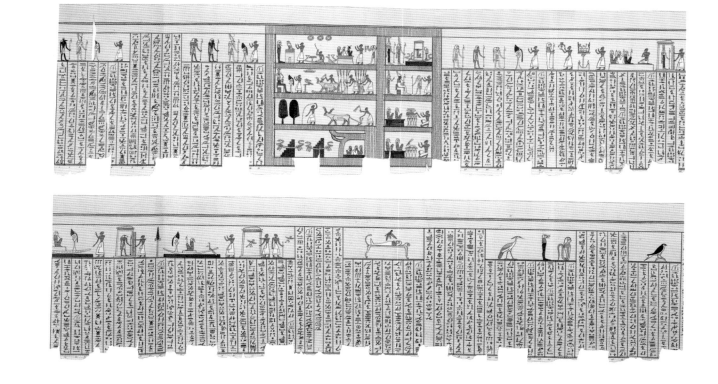

74 BOTTOM
THE 'BOOK OF THE DEAD' BELONGING TO PADIAMON
NEBNESUTTAWY
ANTIQUITÉS, VOLUME II, TAVOLE 73

Plate 73 shows the deceased reciting prayers or making offerings before various deities such as Osiris, Isis (his consort), Nephthys, and Horus (top right, chapter 18 of the Book of the Dead). In the upper section of the papyrus, two columns (between nos. 42 and 43) are free of text, perhaps for the scribe's requirements.

75 TOP
THE 'BOOK OF THE DEAD' BELONGING TO PADIAMON
NEBNESUTTAWY
ANTIQUITÉS, VOLUME II, PLATE 74

Plate 74 shows illustrations and formulas that allowed the deceased to be turned into a heron or swallow. Padiamon is then portrayed–after opening the doors of the three chapels (or naos) in which we see images of the gods–seeming to beseech the gods that he will be allowed to do in the afterlife all that he has done on earth, basically, continue his existence.
In accordance with chapter 110 of the ritual, the upper panel shows the deceased reaching the 'Jaru Fields' and is represented sowing and reaping the grain. The zigzag lines represent irrigation channels.

75 BOTTOM
THE 'BOOK OF THE DEAD' BELONGING TO PADIAMON
NEBNESUTTAWY
ANTIQUITÉS, VOLUME II, PLATE 75

Column 136 (the first in the bottom right) and on in Plate 75 refer to the initial part of the path that leads to the afterlife. After worshipping the god Ra-Horakhty (the sun god united with Horus of the Horizon), Padiamon begins his long journey towards the 'Fields of Rushes' or 'Jaru Fields' (this section is developed in chapters 16 and 17 of the Book of the Dead). The journey is made by boat in the company of certain gods, including Ra-Horakhty, Osiris, and Khepri (upper scene).

76
WALL PAINTINGS FROM VARIOUS TOMBS
ANTIQUITÉS, VOLUME II, PLATE 83
THEBES, VALLEY OF THE KINGS

The scene at the top is taken from the tomb of Ramesses VI and refers to the 'Book of Doors.' According to the magical and religious beliefs of the ancient Egyptians, this text gives a fantastic description of the journey of the sun through the twelve doors which, watched over by genies and serpents, represented the twelve regions of the underworld. At top we see the god Osiris seated on a throne and holding the symbol of life, the scepter, in his hand. Then there are nine characters (the souls of nine dead persons) arriving to be judged. A scale, carried by a mummy-like genius, is ready to weigh these individuals' deeds on Earth. The scene in the center shows a serpent that seems to divide the two inclined banks (of a lake or a river) on which twelve figures can be seen, and who represent the 'hours that are in the Duat.' The two drawings at bottom depict Osiris 'in the bandages' and Ptah, the god of Memphis, wrapped like a mummy.

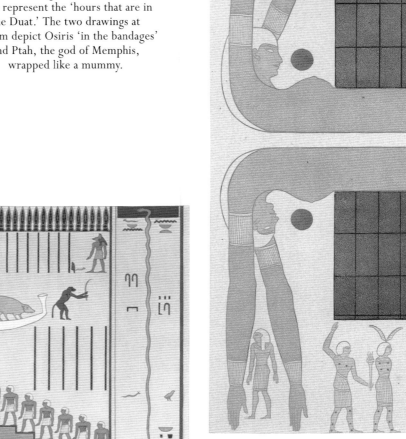

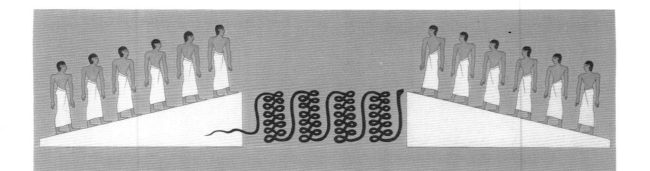

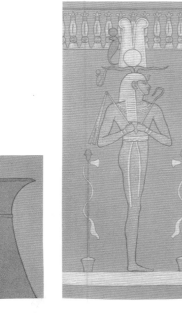

76–77
ASTROLOGICAL CEILING
ANTIQUITÉS, VOLUME II, PLATE 82
THEBES, VALLEY OF THE KINGS

This scene is of the ritual known as the 'Book of Day and Night.' It appears on the ceiling of the tomb of Ramesses VI and occupies an area measuring 8 x 4 meters. According to an ancient Egyptian cosmogonic system of beliefs, the sky was in fact a goddess, Nut, whose body, bent like a bow, covered the world below. The wife of Geb (god of the earth) and the mother of Ra (the sun), every evening Nut swallowed the sun disk to give birth to it once again the following morning. The plate shows Nut embracing the night sky (at top) and the day sky (at bottom). The fantastic figures and monsters represent the various constellations in the night sky.

77 BOTTOM
THEBES
VALLEY OF THE KINGS
TOMB OF RAMESSES III, DECORATION
ANTIQUITÉS, VOLUME II, PLATE 87

The plate shows wall paintings of a series of vases and fish, and a symbolic bull. At left there is a low relief of the goddess Maat on a basket supported by lilies, who spreads her wings as a sign of protection.

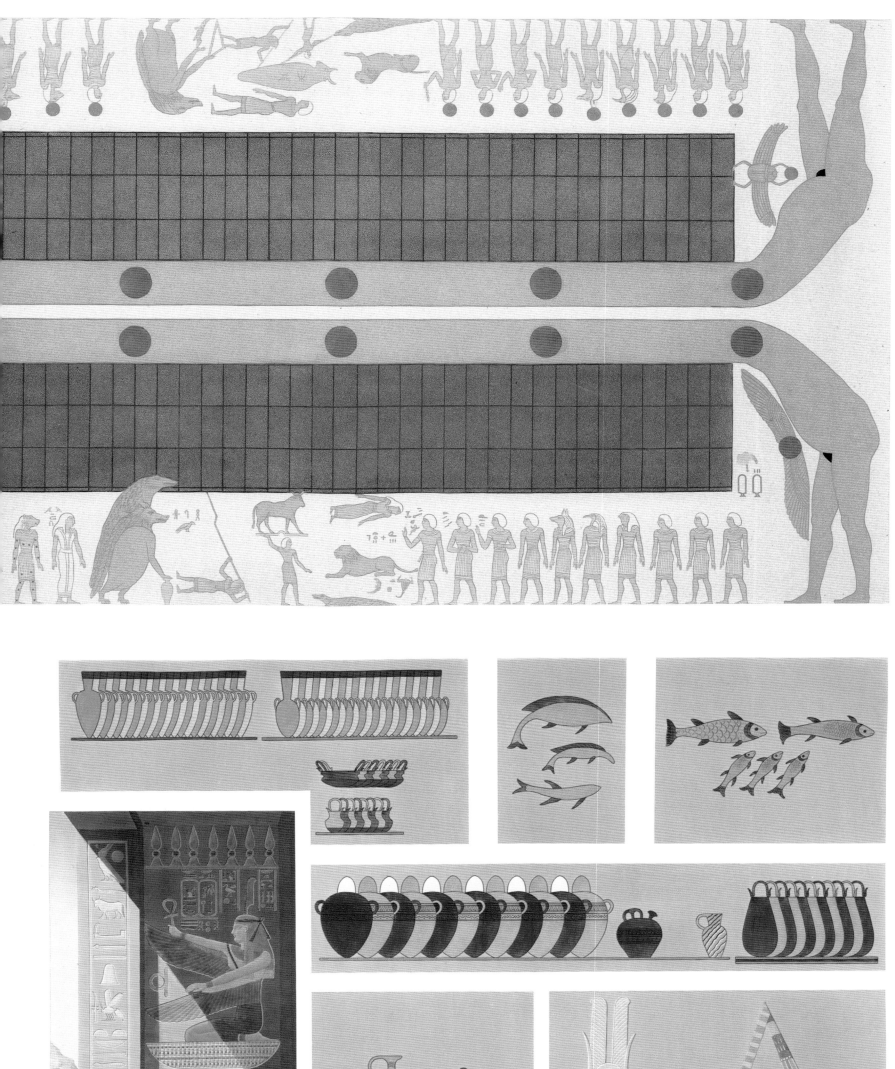

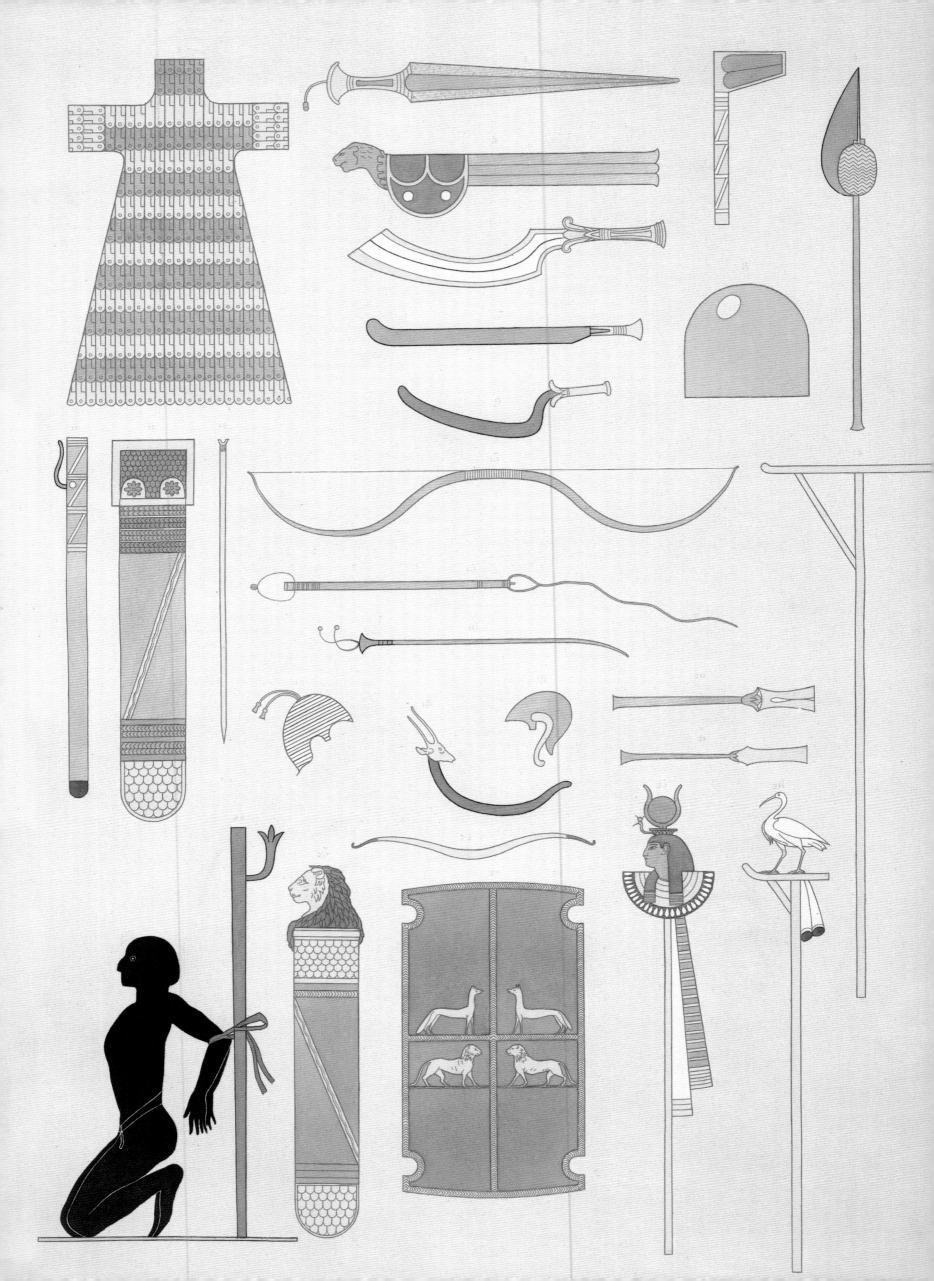

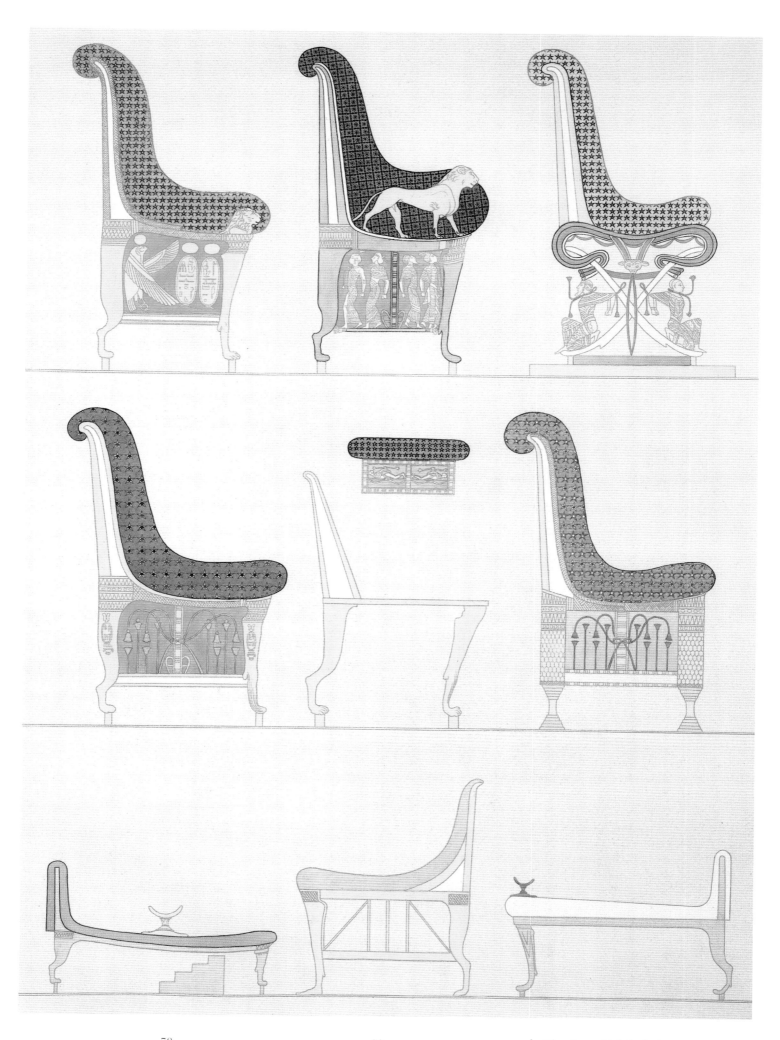

78
WEAPONS AND INSIGNIA
ANTIQUITÉS, VOLUME II, PLATE 88
THEBES, VALLEY OF THE KINGS
TOMB OF RAMESSES III

The engraving illustrates a number of defensive and offensive weapons used by the Egyptians. From top to left: a coat of mail, a dagger, two curved swords, a saber, and a pike. Then there are quivers, whips, military helmets, a shield, and two insignia.

79
ROYAL THRONES AND SEATS
ANTIQUITÉS, VOLUME II, PLATE 89
THEBES, VALLEY OF THE KINGS,
TOMB OF RAMESSES III

Here we see examples of royal thrones and seats painted on the tomb walls as part of the dead pharaoh's funerary goods. The elegant high-backed seats were finely decorated, had lion's paw feet, and were padded with polychrome cushions. The symbolic ornamentation on the side panels was created using gold, semi-precious stones, and ivory. On either side of a royal seat in the lower section of the illustration, we see two beds with headrests.

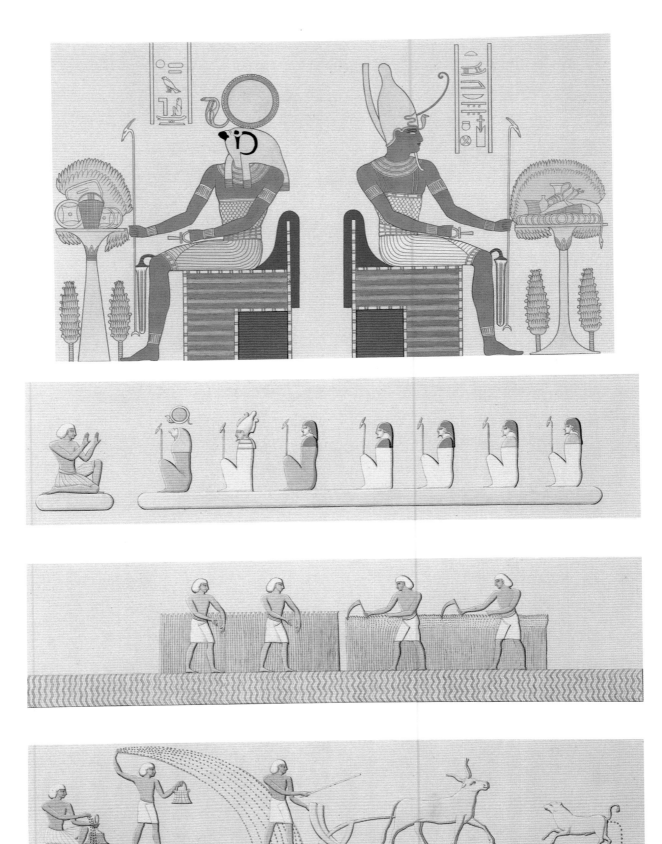

80
TOMB OF RAMESSES III
ANTIQUITÉS, VOLUME II, PLATE 90
THEBES, VALLEY OF THE KINGS

The wall paintings show Ra-Horakhty and Atum, two sun gods worshipped at Heliopolis, which was at one time an important religious center in Lower Egypt. Before them stand tables of offerings. The illustration is completed with imaginary scenes in the 'Field of Rushes' that represent the harvesting of lotus plants and *durra* (a sort of wheat), sowing, and plowing.

81
TOMB OF RAMESSES III
HARPISTS
ANTIQUITÉS, VOLUME II, PLATE 91
THEBES, VALLEY OF THE KINGS

The two famous scenes in this plate are on the walls of a small hall in the huge tomb of Ramesses III. They are now in a rather poor state of preservation, but at the time of the Napoleonic campaign their beauty and splendor were still intact.

Two blind harpists are playing their instruments, which have eleven or more strings. The sound boxes bear the image of the pharaoh wearing the crown of Lower Egypt (at top) and with the double crown of Upper and Lower Egypt (at bottom). The two divinities are Anhur (above) and Shu, the sons of Ra. In addition, there are a pair of vases and two other stringed instruments, probably similar to the harps. Ramesses III's tomb was discovered in 1768 by the Scot, James Bruce and the Italian, Luigi Balugani during their adventurous and dramatic journey to modern-day Ethiopia in search of the source of the Nile.

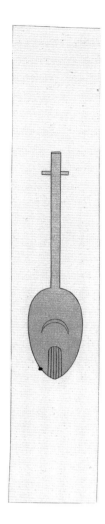

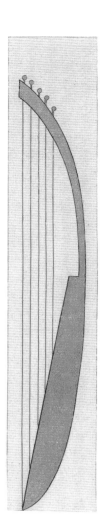
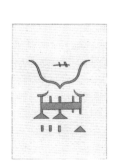

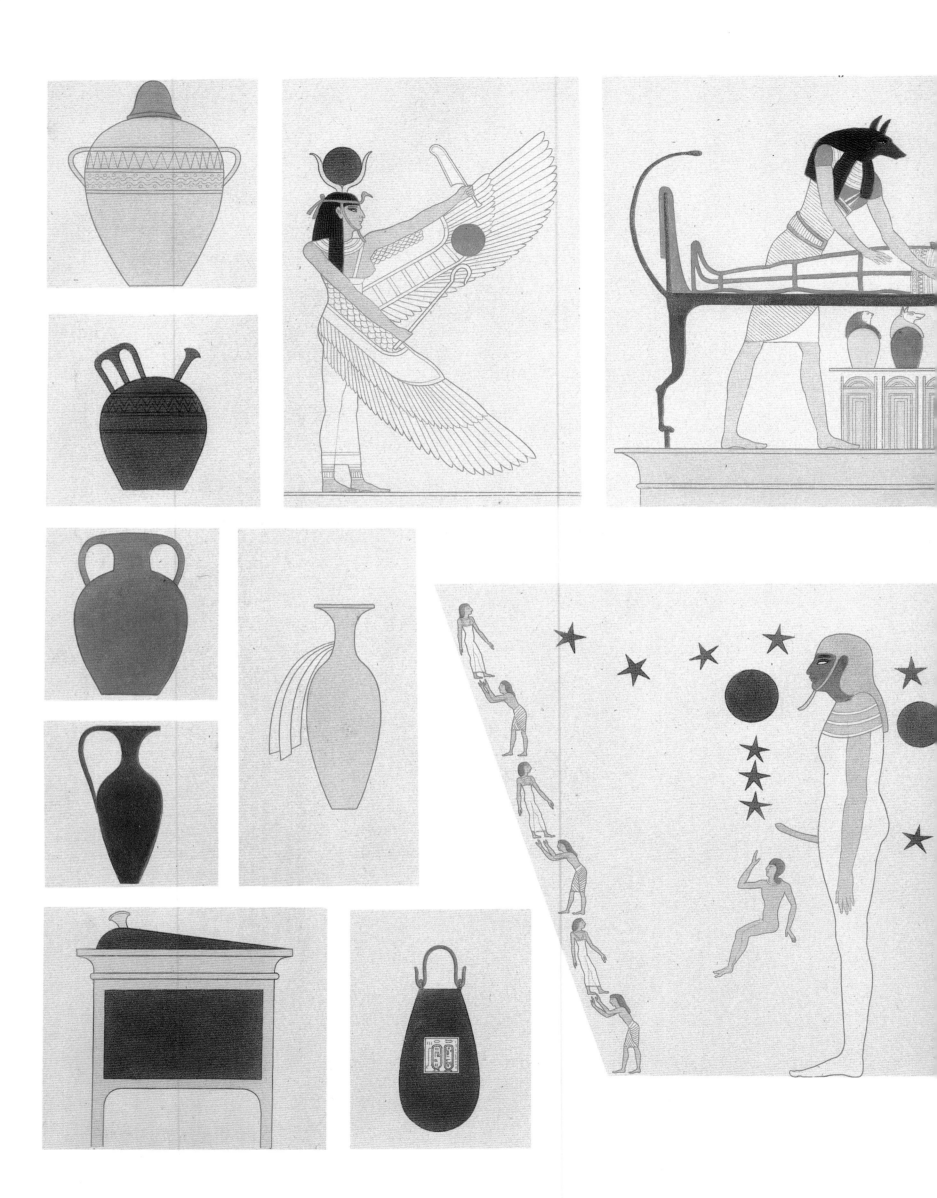

82 and 83

THEBAN TOMBS
ANTIQUITÉS, VOLUME II, PLATE 92
THEBES, VALLEY OF THE KINGS

In addition to vases in various styles and colors, the upper section of the plate shows a winged goddess with the characteristics of Maat, Isis, and Hathor. Next to her is Anubis, the god of embalming, as he performs rites on the deceased. At bottom center, the scene describes the magical ritual of the 'Creation of the sun disk' and shows an ithyphallic god, 'he who hides the hours,' surrounded by twelve female figures who represent the hours of the night.

Antiquités

Volume 3

Contents

84–85
**FIRST PART OF THE LONGITUDINAL
SECTION OF THE HYPOSTYLE HALL**
ANTIQUITÉS, VOLUME III, PLATE 22
KARNAK, TEMPLE OF AMUN-RA

This partial reconstruction of the second
pylon and hypostyle hall in Karnak temple
reproduces part of the decorations on the
walls and columns in detail. When the
French expedition reached Karnak and
the plate was produced, the mass of
rubble that covered the room built by
Thutmose III, prevented part of the room
from being seen, forcing the artist to
exercise his imagination.

Karnak

Village de Louqsor
élevé sur des décombres

Terreins cultivés

PALAIS

LE NIL

86 TOP
TOPOGRAPHICAL PLAN
ANTIQUITÉS, VOLUME III, PLATE 1
LUXOR

This is the rectangular plan of the famous archaeological site that lies about 750 kilometers south of Cairo. Owing to an error, the Commission had placed the bank of the Nile about thirty meters from the ancient wharf. However, the wharf was often reached by the waters of the river and at times even lapped against the base of various buildings. At top we see the mountains of rubble that stretched as far as Karnak. The ancient Egyptian name of the city was Waset, 'the powerful,' and it is not known why the Greeks referred to it as Thebes. Homer described the city in the *Iliad* as "the thousand-gated Thebes" (IX, 383–385) to indicate the number of majestic pylons. The name Luxor is a derivation of the Arabic *al-qusur*, 'the palaces,' which was given to the site in the seventh century by the Arabs who marveled at the extraordinary temples.

86–87
GENERAL VIEW
ANTIQUITÉS, VOLUME III, PLATE 2
LUXOR

This view of the ruins was taken from an island in front of the ancient site. Behind the pylon and the two obelisks (only the tip is seen of one), there is the mosque of Abu al-Haggag. Then follows the entire monumental complex built by the two great rulers of Thebes, Amenhotep and Ramesses II (14–12th centuries BC) and dedicated to Amun-Ra. French troops on land and boats fire blanks while locals seem frightened. In the right foreground there is an enormous crocodile which, at that time, still ruled the Nile; today, it is almost extinct in Egypt.

Entrance to the Temple of Amun-Ra
Antiquités, Volume III, Plate 3
Luxor

This engraving shows the pylon in the great temple, preceded by the last pair of obelisks that still existed in Egypt in the early nineteenth century. Behind the two pink granite monoliths, twenty-five and thirty-three meters tall respectively, one can see the two partly buried statues of Ramesses II. The reliefs on the pylon narrate episodes from the famous Battle of Kadesh, which the renowned Nineteenth Dynasty pharaoh fought against the Syrians around 1275 BC. Modest dwellings with dovecotes, heaps of sand and rubble inside and outside the sanctuary remained there for several decades. The obelisk at right, donated to France by Mohamed Ali, was transported to Paris and raised in Place de la Concorde on October 25, 1836. In the foreground we see a French soldier, a scholar making a drawing, and a blind man being led by a young girl.

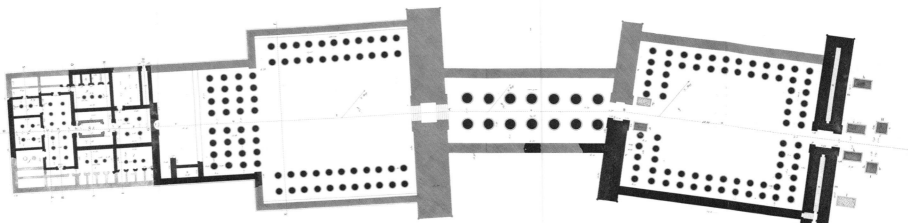

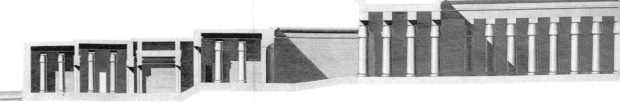

90-91 TOP
VIEW OF THE TEMPLE FROM THE SOUTH
ANTIQUITÉS, VOLUME III, PLATE 1
LUXOR

The engraving shows the Temple of Amun-Ra seen from the south. The temple is composed of the hypostyle hall with thirty-two papyrus columns, the processional colonnade with fourteen columns, and the large court of Amenhotep III. In the background there are the mosque of Abu al-Haggag, the pylon, and the two obelisks. This superb temple complex was also half-buried in sand.

90 CENTER AND 90-91 BOTTOM
PLAN AND LONGITUDINAL SECTION OF THE TEMPLE
ANTIQUITÉS, VOLUME III, PLATE 5
LUXOR

Amenhotep III's colonnade is reached after passing through the pylon and first courtyard. Then one comes to the vast central court, also built by Amenhotep, the hypostyle hall, and other less important areas such as the sanctuary with the cella that held the simulacrum of the god Amun-Ra.
In front of the pylon at right, and behind the two half-buried obelisks, was where the six great statues of Ramesses II stood. Only two of these are still here, one of the pharaoh seated and the other standing. An avenue of sphinxes more than two kilometers long connected this temple to Karnak.

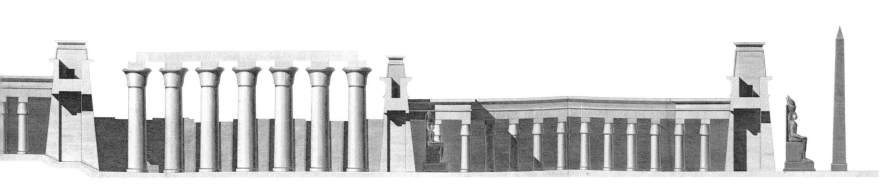

This plate shows the three faces of the
tallest monolith, which is recognizable at
left in the picture of the monumental
entrance. When the drawing was made,
almost five meters of the base of the
obelisk were covered by sand. While
observing what remained above the sand,
which still stands in front of the entrance
to the temple, the scholar Leslie Greener
(1900–74) remarked, "The monumental
pylon will always look like an elephant
with just one tusk!"

VIEW OF THE MONUMENTAL ENTRANCE
Antiquités, Volume III, Plate 6
LUXOR

This hypothetical representation shows
the pylon of the Temple of Amun-Ra
without the rubble that covered much of
the statues and obelisks. "The low reliefs
on the pylon were not copied exactly:
their state of conservation was somewhat
poor and the height at which they stood
made the work very difficult" (*Antiquités*,
Volume 10, p. 259).

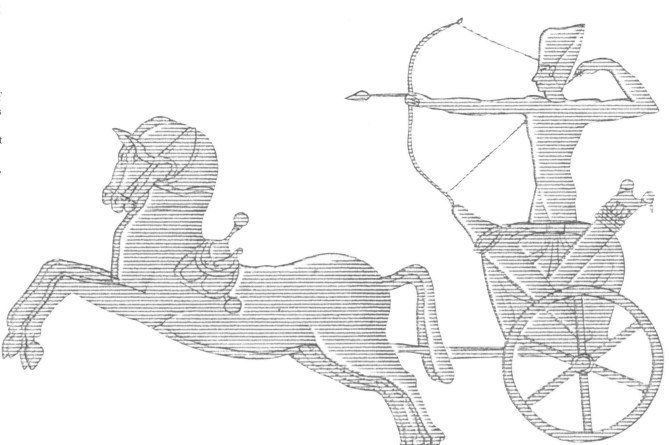

The first three representations in the
plate are an imaginary reproduction of the
east statue, which stands to the left as the
observer looks at the façade of the
temple. It is shown frontally (not on this
page), in profile, and from behind. In this
last view, we note the level of the sand,
which reached right up to the shoulders
of the colossus. The final drawing shows
the west statue in profile.

96–97 bottom
VIEW OF THE RUINS FROM THE NORTHWEST
Antiquités, Volume III, Plate 17
KARNAK, TEMPLE OF AMUN-RA

96–97 top
TOPOGRAPHICAL PLAN
Antiquités, Volume III, Plate 16
KARNAK

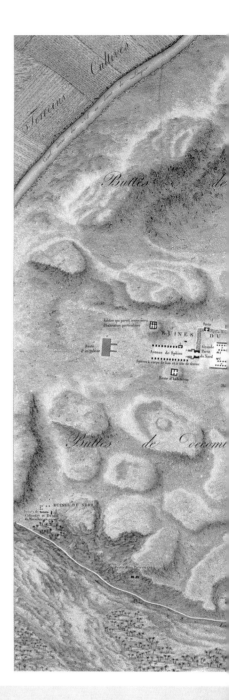

The archaeological site of ancient Thebes, on the east bank of the Nile, was always an obligatory attraction for those visiting Upper Egypt. During the New Kingdom, the city, which had been the leading cult and political center in Egypt, witnessed the construction of a grandiose temple dedicated to the god Amun-Ra, then considered the most important divinity in the Egyptian pantheon. This plate has a general view of the ruins as they appeared to the French savants. From right to left we have the first pylon, which for the most part collapsed, the courtyard with a large papyrus column, the heap of granite blocks from the second pylon, and the ruins of the immense hypostyle hall with an obelisk at one end.

Lying about three kilometers northeast of Luxor, this is how the Commission saw the temple area of Karnak, one of the largest archaeological sites in the world.
Three majestic complexes, each surrounded by a vast wall, are aligned on a north-south axis. The temples are dedicated respectively to the Theban gods Montu, Amun, and Mut (from left to right). An avenue of ram-headed sphinxes (the ram was sacred to Amun) connected the latter two, while a much longer avenue of human-headed sphinxes (with the image of the pharaoh) led to Luxor.

This granite statue currently stands in front of the second pylon of the temple and portrays the famous Nineteenth Dynasty pharaoh. The engraving shows how the statue appeared at the time of the expedition–without its head or arms. At left, a Napoleonic savant (wearing clothes more suited to the European climate than the Egyptian one) appears to be contemplating the statue with delight.

Because of its great size (over 2.5 kilometers long), the temple at Karnak is unique in the ancient world. This other view shows, from left, the rear of the hypostyle hall, and the colonnade of Amenhotep III. It was built by Seti I and his son Ramesses II around 1300 BC with no fewer than 134 papyrus columns from fifteen to twenty-three meters high in sixteen rows–a hymn of stones sung in praise of the god. Two obelisks can be seen clearly; in the background is the one built by Thutmose I around 1500 BC, while the other, built at the behest of Queen Hatshepsut in the same period, is in the foreground. At left is the top part of another monolith, which was also erected by the queen. At present, this find lies near the sacred lake.

Here we have the heap of rubble that was found in the first court of the sanctuary. The partially collapsed second pylon is clearly visible, and behind it, we catch a glimpse of the central aisle of the hypostyle hall. In the foreground is a large papyrus bundle column, the only remaining part of a kiosk dating back to the Ethiopian pharaoh Taharqa (seventh century BC). At right is the pylon of the temple of Ramesses III.

100–101 TOP
SECOND PART OF THE LONGITUDINAL SECTION OF THE HYPOSTYLE HALL
ANTIQUITÉS, VOLUME III, PLATE 23
KARNAK, TEMPLE OF AMUN-RA

A partially hypothetical reconstruction of the second pylon and the hypostyle hall. Part of the decoration on the walls and columns was copied, but the rest was imagined, as the mass of rubble that covered the room built by Thutmose III was enormous.

100 CENTER AND 101 BOTTOM
INTERIOR OF THE HYPOSTYLE HALL
ANTIQUITÉS, VOLUME III, PLATE 32
KARNAK, TEMPLE OF AMON-RA

The reliefs that decorated the internal walls of the hypostyle hall in the Temple of Amun-Ra were copied with extreme care paid to the details by the French draftsmen. The scene at left shows a pharaoh offering prisoners to the Theban triad (Amun, Mut, and Khonsu). The drawings of the reliefs in the hypostyle hall, published on the next page, show a pharaoh and a priest making offerings to an ithyphallic god.

100 BOTTOM
CULT SCENE
ANTIQUITÉS, VOLUME III, PLATE 32
KARNAK, TEMPLE OF AMUN-RA

A low relief in the hypostyle hall shows the transportation of the sacred barque of Amun-Ra by priests. It is decorated with the head of a ram at either end; the animal was sacred to the Theban god.

101 CENTER
CULT SCENE
ANTIQUITÉS, VOLUME III, PLATE 33
KARNAK, TEMPLE OF AMUN-RA

While the pharaoh burns incense as an offering to the sacred barque of Amun-Ra, the barque is drawn by a boat that transports a number of gods.

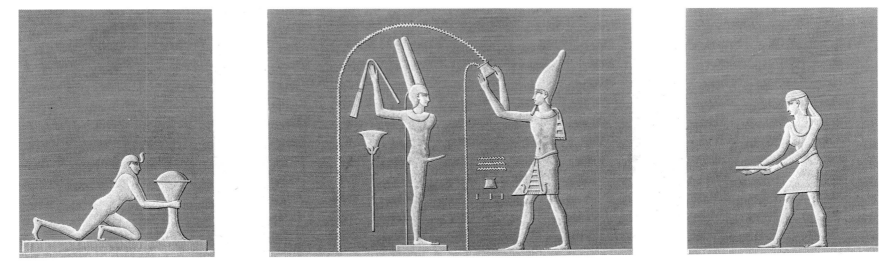

102–103 TOP
CULT SCENE
ANTIQUITÉS, VOLUME III, PLATE 34
KARNAK, TEMPLE OF AMUN-RA

The two decorations bear the name of Amun-Ra and some of his epithets, and the cartouches (at bottom) of the names of Thutmose III.

102–103 CENTER AND BOTTOM
CULT SCENE
ANTIQUITÉS, VOLUME III, PLATE 34
KARNAK, TEMPLE OF AMUN-RA

These low reliefs are from a wall in the cella. At the time of the French expedition, they still showed their original colors. On the upper register (from left) the sequence shows: the purification of the pharaoh, his coronation by Thoth and Horus, the presentation of the pharaoh to Thoth by Atum and Montu, and, lastly, Philip Arrideus (323–316 BC), the half-brother of Alexander the Great, kneeling before Amun-Ra. The lower register shows two barques of Amun-Ra being transported in procession by priests. A drape hides the image of the god Amun (Imn means 'the hidden one').

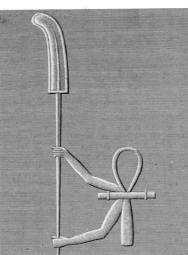

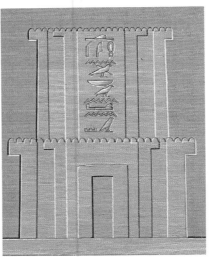

104 TOP LEFT AND BOTTOM
MILITARY SCENES
ANTIQUITÉS, VOLUME III, PLATE 40
KARNAK, TEMPLE OF AMUN-RA

In this war scene taken from a relief on the outside of the temple, the pharaoh Seti I (with his face half-erased) has got down from his chariot and is receiving the honors resulting from a victorious campaign.

104–105
MILITARY SCENE
ANTIQUITÉS, VOLUME III, PLATE 40
KARNAK, TEMPLE OF AMUN-RA

This war scene from a relief on the outer wall of the temple shows Seti I, with his face half erased, having got down from his chariot and receiving the honors due to him after an evidently victorious campaign.

105 CENTER
MILITARY SCENE
ANTIQUITÉS, VOLUME III, PLATE 39
KARNAK, TEMPLE OF AMUN-RA

The apotheosis of Ramesses II's father continues, here in a classic image. This time the pharaoh, no longer on his chariot, stamps on one adversary with his foot as he shoots another with an arrow.

105 BOTTOM
MILITARY DEEDS OF SETI I
ANTIQUITÉS, VOLUME III, PLATE 38
KARNAK, TEMPLE OF AMUN-RA

This low relief is taken from the hypostyle hall. It shows Seti I on his war chariot defeating the enemy. The scene commemorates the pharaoh's campaign in Palestine and Syria around 1320 BC.

104 CENTER
MILITARY SCENE
ANTIQUITÉS, VOLUME III, PLATE 40
KARNAK, TEMPLE OF AMUN-RA

The central figure, Seti I, is shown loosing an arrow among a mass of dead, then pursuing other retreating enemies. Some of these seem to be crying out for mercy with their arms flung upwards toward the king.

This is an imaginary reconstruction of the forecourt of the great temple. While the various components of the archaeological site date from different epochs (Eighteenth to Twentieth Dynasties), the papyrus columns, which formed a kiosk commissioned by the Nubian pharaoh Taharqa, date to the Twenty-fifth Dynasty and were all destroyed except for one (see plate 19 above). Preceded by high flagstaffs and standards fluttering in the wind, the pylon has representations of gods and scenes that commemorate Ramesses II at the battle of Kadesh. It should be noted that there were only ten columns rather than the twelve shown in the illustration.

GENERAL VIEW OF THE HYPOSTYLE HALL
Antiquités, Volume III, Plate 42
KARNAK, TEMPLE OF AMUN-RA

An imaginary reconstruction of the hypostyle hall, with its 134 columns. The plate shows the central colonnade composed of twelve columns, each twenty-one meters high, with capitals in the form of open papyrus plants.

108–109
GENERAL VIEW OF THE RUINS FROM THE NORTHEAST
ANTIQUITÉS, VOLUME III, PLATE 43
KARNAK, TEMPLE OF AMUN-RA

Another general view of the vast and impressive ruins of Karnak. Pylons, columns, and obelisks are seen among the architectural elements lying here and there on the ground, and masses of standing granite, overall looking like wounded giants on a battlefield. While visiting Karnak as leader of the Franco-Tuscan expedition with Rosellini, Jean-François Champollion wrote to his brother, "In Europe we are like Lilliputians; no ancient or modern population has conceived the art of architecture on such a sublime, vast, and grandiose scale as the ancient Egyptians." (From a letter of November 4, 1828).

SPHINXES
ANTIQUITÉS, VOLUME III, PLATE 56
KARNAK, TEMPLE OF AMUN-RA

An avenue of ram-headed sphinxes joined the Temple of Amun-Ra to that of Mut. The engraving shows the head of a half-buried ram. Other similar images, seen in Plate 56 (but not published here), show the rest of the creature's body, which was probably a reconstruction of how the statue would have appeared.

View of the Temples to the South
Antiquités, Volume III, Plate 49
Karnak, Temple of Amun-Ra

The expansion of the monumental complex southward led to the construction of more temples, including those dedicated to the goddess Mut and her son Khonsu who, with Amun, made up the triad of gods worshipped at Thebes. The illustration shows the Temple of Khonsu that was built by Ramesses II. It is preceded by a magnificent portal from the Ptolemaic era and by the avenue of human-headed sphinxes. Then follow the hypostyle hall of the great temple and the two obelisks of Thutmose I (in the background) and Hatshepsut. French soldiers and local inhabitants (including veiled women carrying water) have been added to give the scene some life.

View of the South Portal
Antiquités, Volume III, Plate 51
Karnak, Temple of Amun-Ra

This is the portal built during the reign of Ptolemy III, around 230 BC, in front of the Temple of Khonsu and facing the Temple of Luxor. Shown as a sort of triumphal arch, the Commission has portrayed it with a pharaoh returning from a victorious military campaign, preceded by soldiers and servants, and watched by priests and local inhabitants. The decorations and low reliefs were copied with great accuracy, but this was not the case with the hieroglyphs which were still completely incomprehensible.

112–113
FAÇADE OF THE TEMPLE
ANTIQUITÉS, VOLUME IV, PLATE 7
DENDERA

The plate depicts the façade of the large hypostyle hall, half-covered by piles of sand. The first six of the twenty-four columns have Hathoric capitals, that is, with the image of the goddess with cow's ears. The façade also has cartouches of the Roman emperors Tiberius, Caligula, and Claudius (AD 14–54). On the roof are the usual ruins and dwellings of the locals.

Half hidden by sand, this is the sandstone portal on which the cartouches of the Roman emperors Domitian (AD 81–96) and Trajan (AD 98–117) were carved. Also of the Roman era was the *dromos* that led to the temple and which had mostly disappeared.

VIEW OF THE RUINS FROM THE WEST
ANTIQUITÉS. VOLUME IV. PLATE 3
DENDERA

The temple site of Dendera (the ancient
city of Tentyris), sixty kilometers north
of Luxor, was a major cult center in
ancient Egypt. It extended (and to some
degree still extends) over a vast area
surrounded by a massive wall twelve
meters high. Construction began under
Nectanebo I (Thirtieth Dynasty),
continued under the last Ptolemy rulers
in the first century BC, and was finished
during the Roman age. The complex was
dedicated to the goddess Hathor, the
goddess of joy, love, and music, and
stands in splendid isolation on the left
bank of the Nile. Among the enormous
heaps of ruins that lay there during the
time of the French campaign, we can see,
from left, the remains of the north gate
and the great temple of Hathor.

RECONSTRUCTION OF THE NORTH PORTAL
ANTIQUITÉS. VOLUME IV. PLATE 6
DENDERA

This plate is a hypothetical reconstruction
of the north gate of the Dendera complex
as conceived by the French engineers
Chabrol and Jomard. As had been done
for the south portal of Karnak (see
Volume III, Plate 51), the entranceway
was envisioned as a sort of triumphal arch
covered with low reliefs portraying
divinities and pharaohs. The ceremony
depicted in one relief is connected to the
annual flooding of the Nile and included
manifestations of joy on the part of the
entire population.

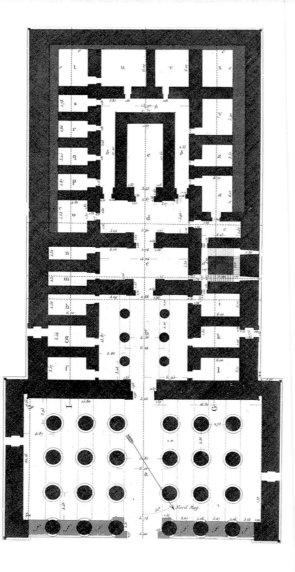

116-117
VIEW OF THE WEST SIDE OF THE TEMPLE
Antiquités, Volume IV, Plate 10
DENDERA

This engraving is of the outer wall seen from the west side. Completely decorated with reliefs, it shows scenes typical of Egyptian iconography, such as the adoration and offerings by the pharaohs to the various deities of Dendera.

PLAN OF THE TEMPLE
Antiquités, Volume IV, Plate 8
DENDERA

Like the temple in Edfu, the temple dedicated to Hathor in Dendera is a classic example of Ptolemaic architecture. It was built in sandstone, but lacks a pylon and courtyard. The plan shows the hypostyle hall with twenty-four columns, a vestibule, and other less important areas, including the cella that held the simulacrum of the goddess.

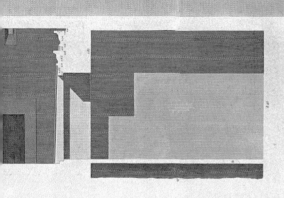

117 RIGHT
DETAIL OF A COLUMN
ANTIQUITÉS, VOLUME IV, PLATE 12
DENDERA

This drawing depicts one of the twenty-four columns in the hypostyle hall, reconstructed and colored (only in the first edition of *Description de l'Egypte*) partly thanks to the traces of color still visible in the early nineteenth century. The capitals of these columns are similar in shape to a sistrum, the musical instrument of the goddess Hathor. On the top there is also a *naos*, a sort of small shrine that housed the image of the goddess's son Ihy. The central scene shows the goddess and her young son holding a sistrum, and the emperor Claudius. The hieroglyphs were drawn at random.

VIEW OF THE REAR OF THE TEMPLE
ANTIQUITÉS, VOLUME IV, PLATE 16
DENDERA

The plate depicts the rear wall of the temple. In the center we recognize the goddess Hathor; below a lion-headed gargoyle, the large scene portrays (from right) the famous queen Cleopatra VII, identified with Hathor, with her son Caesarion burning incense to various deities worshipped at Dendera, including Hathor and Horus. This mirror image (the scene is also carved on the left side with other deities) is the only one remaining of the last queen of Egypt (51–30 BC), and of Caesarion (whose ruling name was Ptolemy XV [44–30 BC]), the last representative of the Ptolemaic dynasty.

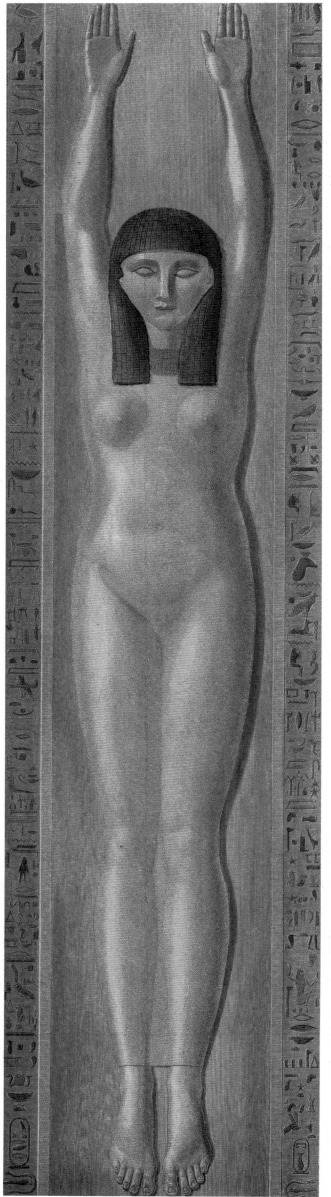

120 AND 121
ZODIAC
ANTIQUITÉS, VOLUME IV, PLATE 21
DENDERA

This Zodiac was carved on the roof of an upper chamber in the temple of Hathor. It is a representation of the sky, with the different constellations. At right and left, the goddess Nut is portrayed in a style that recalls the classic epoch. In 1821 the piece was removed and taken to Paris in a rather adventurous manner by the French engineer Jean-Baptiste Le Lorrain, who then sold it to Louis XVIII. The Zodiac was at first considered quite ancient but in fact dates back to the Greco-Roman period. It is now kept in the Louvre and a copy has been installed in its original location.

122 TOP
INTERIOR OF THE HYPOSTYLE HALL
ANTIQUITÉS, VOLUME IV, PLATE 30
DENDERA

This reconstruction is of the hypostyle hall, which is made up of twenty-four columns, each measuring fifteen meters high, and arranged in four rows. An imaginary procession is taking place in the hall, and the dim light does not obscure the Hathoric capitals with the impassive portrait of the goddess.

122–123
RECONSTRUCTION OF THE FAÇADE
ANTIQUITÉS, VOLUME IV, PLATE 29
DENDERA

Napoleon's savants were obliged to imagine the façade of the Temple of Hathor. Note that it lacks the pylon and forecourt that usually formed the entrance to a temple complex. The low reliefs reproduced were mostly exact copies of the originals.

Antiquités

Volume 5

124-125
GENERAL VIEW OF THE PYRAMIDS
AND THE SPHINX AT SUNSET
ANTIQUITÉS, VOLUME V, PLATE 8
GIZA

When the Greeks called the Giza Pyramids one of the 'Seven Wonders of the Ancient World,' the monuments had already been standing there for over twenty centuries. Today, very little or nothing remains of the other six wonders, but the Pyramids, now almost five thousand years old, are still the most evocative images of ancient Egypt and the most famous monuments in the world. This plate also illustrates the Sphinx, the head of which is being inspected by some of the French savants. Half buried in sand, this world-famous monument was hewn out of limestone in the shape of a recumbent lion, the symbol of the pharaoh's might. Built for the pharaoh Khafre around 2500 BC, for millennia, the Sphinx has symbolically guarded the necropolis and with its enigmatic smile, looks eastward, where the sun rises.

Contents

126 TOP
VIEW OF THE SPHINX AND THE SECOND PYRAMID
ANTIQUITÉS, VOLUME V, PLATE 12
GIZA

This is another illustration of the Sphinx by the Commission. Cut out of a spur of limestone, the monument is about seventy meters long and twenty meters high. The Greek word 'sphinx,' which almost certainly derived from the Egyptian words *shesep ankh*, or 'living statue,' has been synonymous with a lion with a human face for millennia (in this case, the pharaoh Khafre), the living symbol of the power of the pharaoh, who was identified with the solar god Atum. In the background stands the Khafre's pyramid, the entrance of which was discovered by the Italian explorer Giovanni Battista Belzoni on March 2, 1818.

126-127 TOP
TOPOGRAPHICAL PLAN OF THE PYRAMIDS
ANTIQUITÉS, VOLUME V, PLATE 6
GIZA

This plan reproduces the topography of the area of Giza, which now forms the western suburb of Cairo, but at the time of Napoleon's expedition, it was bounded to the west by the Libyan mountains and to the east by cultivated fields. The Giza plateau was the site of the three great pyramids, the Sphinx (at right in front of Khufu's monument), a series of satellite pyramids dedicated to the queens, and numerous *mastabas* that made up the necropolis of the dignitaries from the Fourth and Fifth Dynasties (ca. 2600–2300 BC).

126-127 BOTTOM
GENERAL VIEW OF THE PYRAMIDS FROM THE SOUTHEAST
ANTIQUITÉS, VOLUME V, PLATE 7
GIZA

"Regum pecuniae otiosa ac stulta ostentatio",
"A useless and foolish display
of the sovereigns' riches."
(Pliny the Elder, 23–79 AD)
"The whole world fears time, but time
fears the Pyramids."
(Thirteenth-century Arab proverb)
"My soldiers, remember that forty
centuries are looking down at you
from the height of these Pyramids and
will applaud your victory."
(Napoleon Bonaparte, 1769–1821)
The royal tombs of mighty rulers, these
pyramids are still viewed by visitors and
tourists as gigantic mountains of stone:
the more one contemplates them, the
greater and deeper remain their mystery,
magic, and fascination. This engraving
shows the sandy plain of Giza and the
famous monuments of Khufu, Khafre, and
Menkaure. The fourth pyramid, the tomb
of a queen, is much smaller.

128
THE MAIN GALLERY IN THE PYRAMID OF KHUFU
Antiquités, Volume V, Plate 13
GIZA

This plate illustrates two ramps of the gallery of the great pyramid. In the drawing at left is the engineer Jean-Baptiste Lepère at the foot of the portable stairway he built; he observes Captain Jean-Joseph Coutelle, who enters a small chamber they have just discovered, so we see only his right leg. In the scene at right, other French scholars, aided by locals, are going up the gallery to the chamber where the sarcophagus was placed.

129
PLAN, SECTION, AND ENTRANCE OF THE GREAT PYRAMID
Antiquités, Volume V, Plate 14
GIZA

This is the section of Khufu's pyramid with the entrance, the ascending and descending corridors, the main gallery, the vestibule, the king's burial chamber, and the 'Queen's Chamber.'

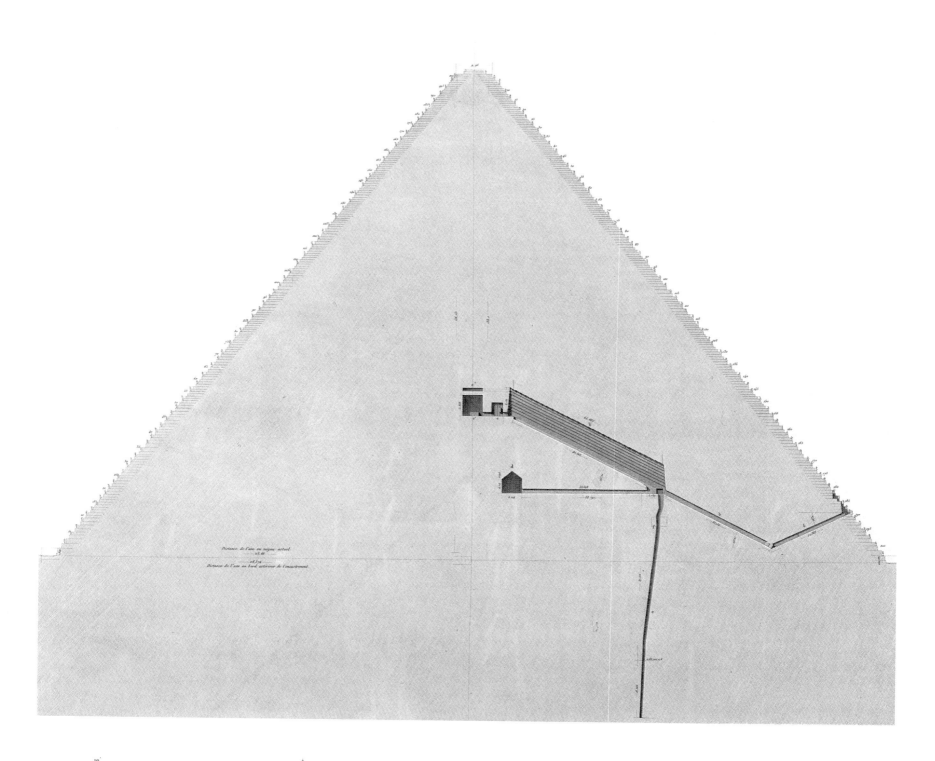

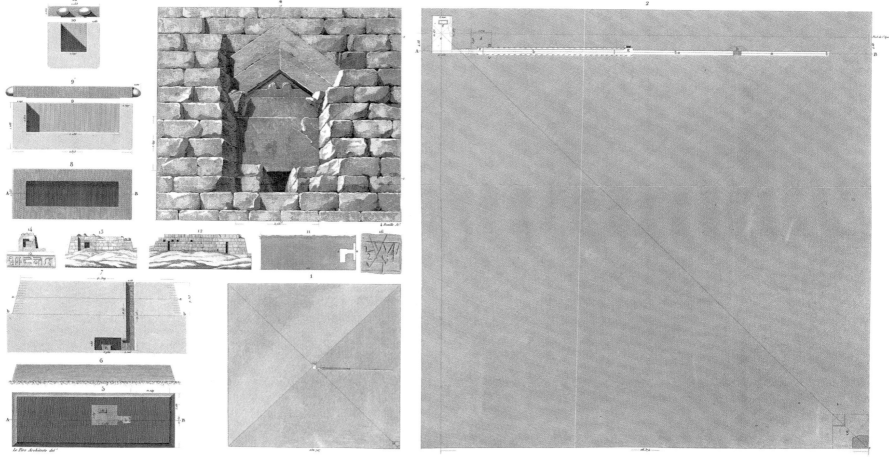

Southwest of modern Alexandria one can still admire this monument, mistakenly known as 'Pompey's Pillar.' In fact, it has nothing to do with the death of Pompey, who was killed in 48 BC on the Egyptian coast, where he had taken refuge after being defeated by Caesar. In reality, the column was built around AD 300 in honor of the emperor Diocletian. It is made of pink granite and is over twenty meters high, with a lovely Corinthian capital that probably supported an equestrian statue of the Roman emperor. In the background of this plate, beyond a canal, one see Arab houses and minarets.

Two obelisks were found near the large port of this famous city, one standing and the other lying on the ground—it had fallen in the fourteenth century and was partly buried in the sand. Known for centuries and described by many travelers as 'Cleopatra's Needles,' a curious name referring to the last queen of Egypt (51–30 BC), the two monoliths were, in fact, originally raised in Heliopolis by Thutmose III around 1470 BC. In 22 BC the Roman emperor Augustus had them transported to Alexandria and placed in front of the Caesareum, the temple Cleopatra had dedicated in honor of Antony. Today, the two obelisks are no longer in Egypt, as they were donated to Great Britain and the United States. The fallen obelisk was erected along the Thames in London in 1878, while the other was placed in Central Park, New York City, in 1881..

ANCIENT EGYPT
BY IPPOLITO ROSELLINI

Contents

133
A PHARAOH MAKING OFFERINGS
THEBES, VALLEY OF THE KINGS
HISTORIC MONUMENTS, II
PLATE XVI,
DETAIL

137
OFFERINGS TO THE GODS
THEBES, TOMB OF RAMESSES III
RELIGIOUS MONUMENTS
PLATE LXXIV,
DETAIL

134-135
THE BATTLES AND VICTORIES
OF RAMESSES II
ABU SIMBEL, GREAT TEMPLE
HISTORIC MONUMENTS, III
PLATE LXXXI

138-139
RAMESSES II WITH
THE THEBAN TRIAD
ABU SIMBEL, GREAT TEMPLE
HISTORIC MONUMENTS, III
PLATE LXXXVI

136
SETI I WITH GODS
THEBES, TOMB OF SETI I
RELIGIOUS MONUMENTS
PLATE LIX

Ippolito Rosellini
AND THE REDISCOVERY OF
ANCIENT EGYPT IN THE NINETEENTH CENTURY

140

140
PORTRAIT OF ROSELLINI
PAINTING BY GIUSEPPE ANGELELLI

In this detail from the large painting of the *Franco-Tuscan Expedition to Egypt* (1828–29), executed by Giuseppe Angelelli, the Pisan Egyptologist, Ippolito Rosellini, is shown in Oriental dress and has a long beard.

Thanks to Napoleon's campaign in Egypt (1798-1801) and above all to the scientific expedition carried out at his behest, Europe rediscovered ancient Egyptian civilization two hundred years ago. The splendid engravings in Vivant Denon's *Voyage dans la Basse et la Haute Egypte* (1802) and the two editions of the *Description de l'Egypte* (1809 and 1821) were crucial to making known, as never before, the marvels of the land of the Nile.

While all credit is due to France and the eminent scientist Jean-François Champollion for having revealed the final secret in deciphering ancient Egyptian hieroglyphs twenty years later, Italy deserves her share of glory as the birthplace of an illustrious citizen who became the pupil and spiritual heir of Champollion—Ippolito Rosellini, 'the father of Italian Egyptology.'

Ippolito Rosellini was born in Pisa on August 13, 1800, and soon revealed an aptitude for 'cultivating letters.' In fact, at the tender age of seventeen he was already devoting his energies to the study of Hebrew and the history of the Catholic Church at the local university. He earned his degree in theology in 1821 and moved to Bologna to follow the courses in Oriental languages under the famous polyglot and Orientalist, Giuseppe Mezzofanti. After returning to Pisa, Rosellini, who had just turned twenty-four, was appointed lecturer of Oriental languages and Hebrew at the University of Pisa.

When he found out about the decipherment of Egyptian hieroglyphs, illustrated by Champollion in his famous *Précis du système hiéroglyphique* which was published in 1824, he immediately devoted himself with passion to the study of this new discipline, partly in order not to remain "within the regrettable limits of mediocrity."

In the summer of 1825, almost certainly in Florence, he met the "Decipherer" (as Rosellini was fond of calling the great French scholar), who had gone to Italy the preceding year to study the Drovetti Collection at Turin and other collections of ancient Egyptian objects. "Because of that secret law of nature," he recalled, "that binds those souls who are molded in unison and carry out the same studies, we had hardly seen each other that we were already friends. I was no sooner taken into his friendship and generously informed about his secrets and discoveries, than I felt grow more sharply and deeply in my heart a love for Egypt; and I immediately determined to follow him wherever he should go."

Apropos of the decipherment of Egyptian writing, at the end of that year, the young Pisan published a paper in which he set forth (" . . . at the level of even the less educated readers") Champollion's discovery and defended the latter from his detractors, such as Lanci, Cordero di San Quintino, and Seyffarth. This work was much appreciated by the French Egyptologist for its clarity and conciseness.

In the spring of the following year Rosellini saw Champollion again, as he had returned to Italy to study more ancient Egyptian artifacts, visit other Italian cities and take possession of British Consul Henry Salt's collection, which he had already examined and which had just been purchased by the French government.

The two scholars spent four months together, which cemented their deep and sincere friendship even more. Rosellini was to become the "Decipherer's" (as Champollion was sometimes known) favorite disciple and the latter even went so far as to call him "… mon fidèle compagnon et élève… jeune homme plein d'esprit" ('my faithful companion and pupil, a young man full of spirit'). And Champollion wrote to his

brother: "I have noted (in the researches I made in Rome and Naples) the young professor's true passion for serious studies, his total devotion to science, while at the same time appreciating the winning qualities that so distinguish him. Egyptian archaeology has made a profitable acquisition with him . . . . I myself would be happy, in associating with him in my studies on Egypt, to furnish him with the means to progress in the other branches of philology he is cultivating with such enthusiasm and commitment . . . . The subject is so vast that at times I feel both the impossibility of succeeding all by myself and the need of a collaborator so devoted to science as Rosellini."

Further demonstration of Champollion's esteem for the young Pisan scholar was his request, made a few months later, to Leopold II of Tuscany, an illuminated as well as ambitious ruler, to allow Rosellini to finish his specialist studies of Oriental languages and hieroglyphs at Paris.

After being granted permission to leave (and to take a year's leave from his teaching duties), Rosellini set off for the French capital in December 1826. He stopped off at Turin on the way to meet the Orientalist Amedeo Peyron and friar Costanzo Gazzera, a lecturer in philosophy and passionate linguist. This marked the beginning of a long friendship between Gazzera and the Pisan scholar that is attested by their long correspondence, which went on from 1826 to 1840.

During his sojourn in Paris, which lasted seven months, Rosellini helped his "dear Maestro" to classify and put in order the Salt Collection and Drovetti's second collection, which had recently been purchased by the Louvre Museum.

JEAN-FRANÇOIS CHAMPOLLION
PORTRAIT BY LÉON COGNIET

A passionate student of ancient Oriental languages at an early age, Champollion took the first step in the decipherment of hieroglyphic script in 1808, when he began to study a copy of the Rosetta Stone, which Captain Bouchard had found in 1799 and is now kept in the British Museum. After years of constant devotion to his studies, thanks to his intuition and knowledge of languages, the French scholar was finally able to announce he had succeeded in interpreting ancient Egyptian script in September 1822.

He studied with unswerving passion, met some French Orientalists, and had many talks with Champollion concerning the plans for a Franco-Tuscan expedition in Egypt, whose aim was to make a scientific exploration of the ruins of that ancient civilization and gain definitive confirmation of the discovery and decipherment of hieroglyphs.

When he returned to Italy in July 1827, Rosellini presented the project to Grand Duke Leopold II, who approved it with great interest and guaranteed the necessary financing. In September, Rosellini went back to Paris to find out whether the plan had been approved by the French government, which had seemed rather averse to the scientific mission. The following month, the Pisan scholar put his sentiments before his love of Egypt and married Zenobia, the daughter of the famous composer Luigi Cherubini whom he had met the preceding year. She bore him four children, including a girl who died while still quite young.

In the early months of 1828, the last obstacles to the mission were overcome; it was finally approved and financed by King Charles X as well. The mission began its work in July of that year and ended in the autumn of 1829. The most important events in the journey to Egypt and Nubia–including comments on the research, on the discovery of various archaeological sites, and on the joint work–were noted down in the interesting travel journal written by Rosellini and published by Gabrieli in 1925.

When he returned to Pisa in January 1830, Rosellini devoted his energy to rearranging the vast scientific material he had prepared in Egypt. In July 1831 he went back to Paris to plan the publication of a work with Champollion. However, the premature death of his mentor in March 1832, plus a sort of unjustified mistrust of Rosellini on the part of Champollion's brother, known as Champollion-Figeac, prevented the results of the mission from being published together, so that two large works came out separately.

In 1834 and 1835, Rosellini–due to his outstanding merit, and for the first time in Italy–held courses in the Coptic and ancient Egyptian languages at the University of Pisa and was appointed university librarian by Grand Duke Leopold II.

Rosellini had by then become a leading figure in Egyptology, receiving recognition and testimonials from various international academies and representatives of European culture.

La Grammaire
Egyptienne

In his *Grammaire Egyptienne*, two manuscript pages of which are reproduced here, Champollion reaffirmed his conviction that hieroglyphic script was at the same time figurative, symbolic, and phonetic.

The Rosetta Stone

Champollion compared Ptolemy's cartouche, which appears several times in this famous stela, with Cleopatra's, which was carved on an obelisk found at Philae, and this provided him with the virtually definitive confirmation of his method of decipherment.

For example, in 1836 the young German scholar Richard Lepsius went to Pisa to finish his studies under Rosellini's guidance, and two years later the Dutchman Conrad Leemans, then director of the Leiden Museum, began a long and fruitful correspondence with him. Rosellini initiated an equally interesting exchange of letters, which lasted for years, with leading Italian men of letters, archaeologists such as Luigi Maria Ungarelli, and the already mentioned Gazzera and Peyron.

From 1838 to 1841, Rosellini's often frenetic efforts to finish his various work commitments and the increasingly bitter polemics that continued for years all contributed to weakening his health, which was already precarious because of lung and intestinal illnesses. Like his dear "Maestro," he also died prematurely, in Pisa, on June 4, 1843.

The Franco-Tuscan Expedition in Egypt

1828-29

144-145
THE FRANCO-TUSCAN EXPEDITION
PAINTING BY GIUSEPPE ANGELELLI

This canvas (3.47 x 2.28 m) executed by Giuseppe Angelelli ca. 1835, portrays all the members of the Franco-Tuscan expedition. The artist set the scene among the ruins of ancient Thebes, but the natural scenery in the background is for the most part imaginary. The persons portrayed–almost all of whom are in Oriental dress–are, from left to right: the French illustrator Albert Bertin (barely visible), Salvador Cherubini, Alessandro Ricci (in a red tunic), Nestor L'Hôte, and a richly attired dragoman, or interpreter. Behind L'Hôte is Angelelli, who is holding a piece of paper. Next to him are Pierre Lehoux, Giuseppe Raddi (seated, looking at some plants in his lap), and two Egyptians. In the foreground, almost lying on the ground, is the French painter Alexandre Duchesne. Standing in the middle of the painting are Rosellini, who is holding a drawing in his left hand, and behind him, his uncle Gaetano. Champollion is seated on a rock, with a thick beard, and is holding a saber that Mohammed Ali gave him; at his feet are some objects the group just found.
The bare-chested man is the foreman of the excavation laborers.
The last figure is the local sheikh, who is indicating other sites to be discovered.

145

THE EXPEDITION REGULATIONS

Some of the seventeen articles of the
regulation that the Franco-Tuscan
Expedition observed during its research.

The close friendship between Rosellini and Champollion gave birth to the idea of a common mission in the land of the pharaohs. Despite King Charles X's irresolution in this regard, the grand duke of Tuscany, Leopold II, as we have already seen, was enthusiastic about the project and promoted the first international scientific mission that aimed at the "exploration of the surviving historic monuments in Egypt."

Compared to Napoleon's expedition, this one set out not only to illustrate and describe most of the remains of ancient Egypt that could still be seen, but thanks to the newly gained ability to interpret hieroglyphic writing, also to make a targeted and systematic study of the antiquities in this recently rediscovered country.

There were fourteen members of this mission.

The French team consisted of:
• Jean-François Champollion;
• Antoine Bibent, a young architect who soon had to leave his colleagues and return to France due to illness;
• Nestor L'Hôte;
• Alexandre Duchesne;
• Albert Henry Bertin and
• Pierre François Lehoux, all of whom were illustrators.

The Tuscan team was made up of the following persons:
• Ippolito Rosellini;
• Gaetano Rosellini, Ippolito's uncle, an architect and engineer;
• Alessandro Ricci, a physician and illustrator;
• Giuseppe Angelelli, a painter and illustrator;
• Giuseppe Raddi, a naturalist;
• Gaetano Galastri, Raddi's assistant, who soon had to return to Italy because of a foot injury;
• Salvador Cherubini, an illustrator and Rosellini's brother-in-law, a naturalized Italian. Although he was officially part of the Tuscan team, he was at the disposal of both.

l'exhaussement de 6 p.ᵈ 3 p. de diametre sur 2 p.ᵈ de hauteur qui se trouve sur le tailloir du
chapiteau paroit indiquer qu'il y a eu autrefois un piedestal circulaire surmonté d'une
statue. Ce qui peut le faire presumer est un beau fragment d'une statue Colossale de
guerrier en porphire, qui se voyoit il y a quelques annéés sur le rivage de la mer
et que le C.ᵉⁿ Cassas a fait enlever pour l'ambassadeur Choiseul.

Plan du Chapiteau.
Coté de la mer.

Coté du Desert

La hauteur totale de la colonne
d'après les mesures qui ont eté
communiquées a l'auteur par le
C.ᵉⁿ Norry, est de 88. p.ᵈ 6 p. 6 L.
ce qui se trouve conforme aux
mesures determinées par le C.ᵉⁿ
Fauvel artiste francais en 1769.

il y a eu une inscription
sur cette partie du piedestal qui regarde la mer ;
elle est totalement effacée.

Des traces pratiquées au dessous
des angles du piedestal doivent
faire supposer quatre supports
qui ensemble avec celui du
milieu encore existent
soutiennent la colonne.

A.

B.

Support
de
Breche

B. partie du support de la
colonne, pris sur l'angle
ce support est de Breche
et couvert d'hierogliphes.

The Journey to Egypt and Nubia

The French corvette *Eglé* set sail from Toulon on July 31, 1828, with the fourteen original members of the mission, and after a brief stop in Sicily, arrived in Alexandria on August 18.

The first leg of the journey to Egypt, which Champollion and Rosellini in particular had set their heart on, had been reached. The first few days after landing were given over to meeting with the local authorities and European diplomats, including Carlo Rossetti, the consul general of Tuscany, and Bernardino Drovetti, who for years had been the consular delegate of France.

The stay in the city founded by Alexander the Great in 331 BC lasted for about a month, during which time the group visited the most important quarters and became acquainted with the traditions and customs of the Egyptians. The most famous monuments, which could be seen even then, were a pair of obelisks known as 'Cleopatra's Needles,' and a column called 'Pompey's Pillar.' Apropos of the first two monoliths (one of which had fallen in the fourteenth century), we know that they had been transported from Heliopolis during the Augustan age, when the city, a metropolis with 300,000 inhabitants, was the 'emporium of the world' and a brilliant cultural center. Nothing is known about when the curious name of the last queen of Egypt was given to the obelisks. Both of them left Egypt in the mid-1800s. The one that had fallen was donated to Great Britain and is now in London: it was placed along the Thames in 1878; the other, donated to the United States, was set up in Central Park in New York City in 1881.

While examining the obelisk that was still standing, Rosellini noted "excavations around the base . . . were carried out in such an irregular manner that one is led to believe attempts were made to knock it down." The name given to 'Pompey's Pillar' has no historical basis. It was connected to the memory of the death of Pompey, who was killed in 48 BC along the Egyptian coast, to which he had fled after being defeated by Caesar. In reality the column, which is over twenty-one meters high and has a Corinthian capital, was erected in the late third century AD in honor of Emperor Diocletian.

Egypt at the Time of the Franco-Tuscan Expedition

At the dawn of the nineteenth century, Egypt was a huge province of the Ottoman Empire that for some time had been weakened by internal strife and a very weak economy, and seemed to be stagnating in a sort of medieval limbo. With Napoleon's expedition the country came into contact with new institutions that triggered hope for renewal and the rise of a new era. And, in fact, a political and social turning point came about with the man considered the founder of modern Egypt, Mohammed Ali.

Bold and courageous as well as unscrupulous and cruel, this leader initiated a vast reform program in all fields. Well aware of the importance of Western civilization, Mohammed Ali did not hesitate to make use of European experts and advisers. As a result, in the early decades of the nineteenth century, travelers, technicians, explorers, and adventurers poured into the country in search of antiquities. As far as the field of archaeology is concerned, several foreign diplomats devoted all their energy to the search for finds to be set on display in the museums and collections of their respective countries. This sort of antiquities hunt was not always characterized by fair play, to say the least; in fact, it was sometimes accompanied by gunshots.

On September 14, after managing to get the necessary *firmans*, or decrees, authorizing them to travel and carry out digs and research in the different localities of Egypt, the members of the mission set off for Cairo in two boats. Because of a painful sore on his foot, the young Galastri could not continue the journey and was forced to return to Italy.

They navigated for one week among villages and thick vegetation. "The shores of the Nile," Rosellini wrote, "continue to delight one because of the crops and luxuriant greenery that covers them. Cotton, hemp, and other plants grow most beautifully . . . . Tamarisk and Nilotic mimosa are quite abundant." And again: "The Nile persists in being charming and green on both banks, which have many villages. The people are distrustful and afraid of us at first . . . but they soon realize our intentions and all the children gather around us to watch us with curiosity, or with the hope of getting a para [coin]."

On September 20, the mission members disembarked at Boulaq, at that time a river port of Cairo, and went to the nearby metropolis, which, in that season, was quite lively because of the important feast in honor of the birth of the Prophet. "The overall view of Cairo has nothing in common with our life," we read in Rosellini. He continues: "The broad expanse of the square was filled with people: voices crying out, bagpipes and fifes playing . . . the cry of acrobats who entertain large circles of people with their clever tricks and with the dances of the *cynocephali*, a large and lovely species of baboon, which was a sacred animal in ancient Egypt. The constant to and fro of small donkeys, camels, dromedaries, and horses that knock their way through the crowd, amid the shouts of the muleteers, riders, and the people; the clothes, voices, words–in short, everything is new, bizarre, and indescribable."

The time spent at Cairo was used to observe other ceremonies and visit the various parts of the city, with its characteristic bazaars, mosques, and the tombs of the caliphs, which at the time were fine examples of Islamic architecture.

Rosellini's note regarding the vile slave market, which continued to thrive in Egypt until the mid-nineteenth century, is quite moving: "In one of those large square houses," he observes, "are the male and female slaves that are sold in Cairo. There is a great number of them and the sight is at once pitiful and interesting . . . ."

148
THE FOUNTAIN OF TUSUN PASHA
ENGRAVING BY ROBERT HAY

The fountain of Tusun Pasha, dating from the early nineteenth century, in an engraving reproduced from Robert Hay's *Illustrations of Cairo* (1840).

149
FOUNTAIN OF NAFISA
ENGRAVING BY ROBERT HAY

This fountain is a typical example of Islamic art and architecture. The illustration is again by Robert Hay, the British traveler and illustrator (1799-1869) who visited Egypt several times between 1818 and 1838. Among his assistants, Owen Browne Carter and Charles Laver are particularly worthy of mention.

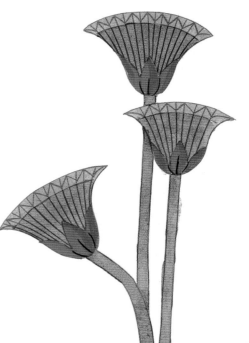

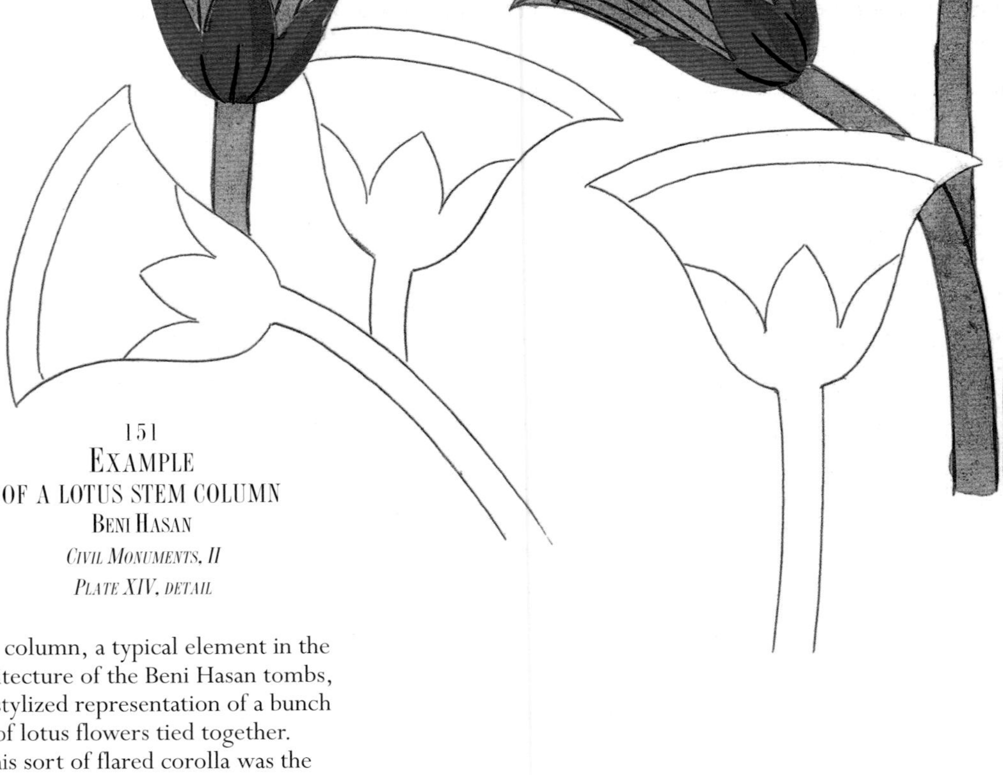

150 TOP LEFT
QUEEN ISIS
HISTORIC MONUMENTS, I
PLATE VIII, detail

This drawing shows Queen Isis,
Ramesses VI's mother, whose tomb lies
in the Valley of the Queens.

150 BOTTOM RIGHT
BIRDS AMONG PAPYRUS PLANTS
BENI HASAN
CIVIL MONUMENTS, I
PLATE XIV, detail

This is a drawing of a nest of ibises
among papyrus plants.

150-151
**VIEW OF THE NECROPOLIS
OF BENI HASAN**
CIVIL MONUMENTS, I
PLATE I, detail

This drawing is a view of the important
Middle Kingdom (2000–1800 BC)
archaeological site about 299
kilometers south of Cairo.

151
**EXAMPLE
OF A LOTUS STEM COLUMN**
BENI HASAN
CIVIL MONUMENTS, II
PLATE XIV, detail

This column, a typical element in the
architecture of the Beni Hasan tombs,
is a stylized representation of a bunch
of lotus flowers tied together.
This sort of flared corolla was the
capital of the column.

After a few days spent in Memphis, which bore hardly any traces of its former grandeur and which a dismayed Rosellini described as "now in a heap of scraps," the mission camped in nearby Saqqara to visit the site so rich in Old Kingdom tombs and pyramids, copy the sculptures and paintings, and carry out digs with the aid of young locals.

After passing through illness and indisposition caused by the fatigue and conditions of life (which were often quite difficult by European standards), the mission rode on camels and donkeys to Giza, the plateau with the pyramids and the Sphinx, which at that time was half buried in the sand.

These famous monuments, described and drawn by hundreds of travelers, impressed the mission members, who did not hesitate to go up to the top of the Pyramid of Khufu (or Cheops), from where they could admire the plain where the famous battle between Napoleon and the Mamluks had taken place thirty years earlier.

With these recollections, which were rounded off by their first archaeological experience and with interesting drawings executed, on October 11, 1828, the group resumed navigation southward and on October 22 reached a locality in Middle Egypt known as Beni Hasan. When they landed, the travelers began to inspect the surrounding area, which was delimited by hills or average-sized mountains. "The Arab mountain, cut vertically," the *Journal* says, "for a long stretch consists of rock-hewn caves, which we climbed up to visit and found more beautiful than any others we had seen till then."

Instead of staying one day as planned, the expedition remained there two weeks. In fact, there were many extremely interesting tombs of local governors, such as those of Amenemhet and Khnumhotep. For the most part cut out of the limestone rock, and aligned with a type of column that Champollion called "Proto-Doric," the tombs enraptured all the members of the group, who worked ceaselessly to copy the wall paintings, "true tempera paintings, remarkable for the delicacy and beauty of their draughtmanship" (Champollion).

The many scenes of domestic and civic life, which were reproduced in four hundred drawings, were the most beautiful the scholars had seen so far in Egypt: agriculture, livestock breeding, arts and crafts, games, music, dance—all flowed before their eyes, together with a series of figures and animals made vivid by colors which were still fresh and lovely in the early nineteenth century, but which now have been either ruined or have disappeared.

After their visit to Beni Hasan and other nearby localities, the expedition ventured a few miles further to see Antinoopolis, once the lovely city of the emperor Hadrian, and Hermopolis, which is another important archaeological site. According to Rosellini, both places, however, were reduced to rubble, "because of the devastating barbarism of the government and inhabitants."

They landed a little farther southward and found "an unknown city" which interested them but could not be identified: it was Tell al-Amarna, the city of Akhenaten, the 'heretic' pharaoh.

As was only natural, during the journey, some days were busier than others. They would land to buy supplies, visit villages or take part in dinners or parties organized by the *kashef*s (district inspectors) during which smoking the typical narghile pipes and watching dances by the local beauties were part of the routine.

152-153 TOP
GYMNASTIC-MILITARY SCENES
TOMBS AT BENI HASAN AND ASYUT
CIVIL MONUMENTS, III
PLATE CXVII, DETAIL

Soldiers armed with clubs, bows, arrows, and shields drilling in attack and defense.

On November 16, after visiting villages or towns on either side of the Nile, such as Asyut and Akhmim, the expedition arrived at Dendera, a place the French and Italian travelers had often heard about. They made their first excursion to see the ruins of the ancient city at night. After walking a few miles, the group came within sight of a large temple which, on the left-hand bank of the Nile, was illuminated by moonlight. "The appearance of the sky, the silence of the night, and the presence of these plants, so varied and beautiful (dum palms, sycamores, and so on), made for a wholly singular scene"–this was the first impression noted down by Rosellini in his travel journal. "Further on we caught sight of the large gate that afforded access to the vast precinct of the great temple . . . . We were struck with deep admiration for such an elegant structure and such harmonious lines . . . . 'How lovely it is!' we all said in unison.

152-153 BOTTOM
A JOURNEY DOWN THE NILE
TOMB IN BENI HASAN
CIVIL MONUMENTS, III
PLATE CIX, DETAIL

152-153 CENTER
DUCK HUNT
THEBAN TOMB
CIVIL MONUMENTS, I
PLATE IV, DETAIL

The scene shows a large hexagonal net stretched out in a lake and secured with a pole and rope. A man, hidden among the plants, is signaling when the rope should be pulled to catch the birds. The captured birds (left) are taken to a hut where they are killed, plucked, salted, and placed in large jars.

An illustration of a boat with twelve rowers who are busy mooring. Inside the cabin are the women of the harem.

And we set out to the temple near at hand that loomed so immensely in front of us . . . . Such was our surprise, amazement, astonishment, that we were speechless at that moment. The night and the lights made an impression that human language could not describe."

The following day was lovely and sunny and the group returned to admire the temple of the goddess Hathor. The monument was begun under the last Ptolemaic rulers in the first century BC and was finished in the Roman period, so it is one of the last artistic manifestations of ancient Egyptian civilization.

A favorable wind made the short trip to legendary Thebes even easier. The group arrived there on November 20, remaining only one week for an initial reconnaissance of the ruins of the ancient site, which now includes the famous localities of Luxor and Karnak. The good weather conditions of this season made it imperative to go to Nubia first; they would make a much longer stay at Thebes on their return trip.

The mission resumed its journey, visiting other interesting archaeological sites such as ancient Hermonthis, with the ruins of a temple, and then Esna, called Latopolis by the Greeks. After visiting the large Roman-period temple, which was still mostly buried in the sand, the group decided to make an excursion to the ruins of a locality called Contra-Lato on the left-hand bank of the Nile just opposite Esna. "The French Commission," Rosellini wrote, "had already drawn the small temple with Contra-Lato [*a city given this name because it lay opposite Latopolis*], and we went to see it."

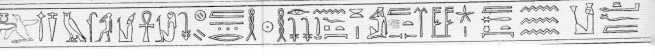

After following several rough paths, ferrying on a boat, and a long walk through the fields, almost all the members of the mission reached the indicated spot, but they did not see anything. "We made inquiries of an old Arab who protected the *durra* [a variety of sorghum] from the birds," Rosellini wrote in his *Journal*, "and, pointing to a pile of whitish scraps, he told us that it had been destroyed a few days earlier at the behest of the *nádir* [local governor]. Our indignation and anger were all the stronger because we could not know or understand the reason for this. Now we already knew that the Turkish leaders often destroyed ancient monuments made of limestone in order to make lime mortar, but the temple at Contra-Lato was made of sandstone, which could not serve this purpose . . . . Therefore, only because of age-old barbarism, ever more ruthless and resurgent, was this temple destroyed."

With Rosellini's bitter comment in mind, let us continue the description of the journey. At the end of November, the mission reached Edfu, a village known for the temple dedicated to the god Horus. After seeing the monument, begun in 327 BC under Ptolemy III and completed in the first decades of the Christian era, the Pisan scholar noted that it was "one of best preserved in all Egypt . . . ," but most of it was buried in the sand. Furthermore, "the Arabs have encumbered all this large edifice by building their miserable Nilotic mud huts inside and outside it."

Still going up the Nile, the mission stopped off at Gebel al-Silsila to visit the sandstone quarries and then at Kom Ombo, a place known for another Ptolemaic-age temple. On December 4, 1828, it arrived at Aswan, an important locality in Nubia, the gateway to black Africa.

illustrations, many of them in color, fourteen volumes of notes and hieroglyphic inscriptions, as well as about a thousand objects—most of them small—that had been either found or purchased in Egypt. Well aware of the value of this mission, which would certainly give a great boost to the burgeoning discipline of Egyptology, the Pisan scholar, with his characteristic honesty, could not but mention the passion and competence of his colleagues and express his gratitude to them: "I have been fortunate beyond all expectations to have had my Tuscan colleagues," he concluded, "to whom I owe the greatest part of the meager praise that may accrue to me from our undertaking."

But given the great recognition European scholars and various Italian and foreign academies heaped upon him, Rosellini deserved more than "meager praise." To conclude this memorial—and in doing so, taking up Gabrieli's thought—it is only right to say that for his total dedication to the study of the new discipline and his great virtues as a historian, philologist, and researcher, Rosellini deserves to stand alongside Champollion and Lepsius as one of the three founders of modern Egyptology.

*C*hampollion and Rosellini returned to their respective countries in early 1830 and saw each other again in the summer of the following year to carry out what they had planned: ". . . a work in common which, by producing great fruits for the science of antiquity, would honor France and Tuscany in equal measure . . . ."

As was mentioned above, the death of Champollion prevented their plan from being realized. Therefore, Rosellini, with his "Maestro" in mind, but also feeling his obligation to Grand Duke Leopold and science, threw himself headlong into the task of finishing "the long and fatiguing work" by himself. For eleven years, from 1832 until his death, Rosellini devoted all his energies to his work, struggling against numerous difficulties, not the least of which were illness and envious detractors.

The huge work is divided into three parts—Monumenti Storici ('Historic Monuments,' five volumes), Monumenti Civili ('Civil Monuments,' three volumes), and Monumenti del Culto ('Religious Monuments,' one volume)—and includes three in folio Atlases, one for each section. A French edition was published in 1835 with the same title, Monuments de l'Egypte et de la Nubie, but with somewhat different criteria.

Rosellini's volumes (the last of which was published posthumously)—which deal with the history of Egyptian civilization under the different ruling dynasties as well as the various aspects of its everyday life and religion—display great erudition and are an exemplary comment on the illustrations. The Atlases consist of 390 plates, 110 of which are in color. They are still an example of rare graphic excellence and help make Rosellini's work one of the most significant 'monuments' of Egyptology.

Historic

166 LEFT
KINGS AND QUEENS OF EGYPT
THEBES, VALLEY OF THE KINGS, TOMB OF RAMESSES III
VOLUME II, PLATE XVI, DETAIL

In this plate, Ramesses III is depicted wearing a splendid headdress with the *atef* crown. The illustration was copied from the pharaoh's tomb.

166 BOTTOM RIGHT
RULERS OF EGYPT
THEBES, VALLEY OF THE KINGS
VOLUME II, PLATE XVIII

This plate shows five pharaohs and one prince (the last figure at bottom right). Above, from left to right, are portraits of Ramesses VII, Ramesses IV, and Ramesses IX, who all belonged to the Twentieth Dynasty. Below, from left to right, are Amenmesse (Nineteenth Dynasty), Nectanebo I (Thirtieth Dynasty), and one of Ramesses IX's sons. The splendid colors bring out their rich attire.

Monuments

167 LEFT
RULERS OF EGYPT
THEBES, VALLEY OF THE KINGS
VOLUME II, PLATE XVII

167 RIGHT
A QUEEN OF EGYPT
THEBES, VALLEY OF THE QUEENS
VOLUME II, PLATE XIX, DETAIL

These illustrations are of pharaohs in the act of making offerings and were taken from their tombs.
Thanks to the cartouches, which were copied meticulously by the members of the expedition, we can identify, from above left: Amenophis II, Ramesses I, Merneptah, Seti II (making offerings to Ma'at), Setnakhte, and Ramesses VI.

This is a portrait of an Egyptian queen of the New Kingdom making offerings. She cannot be identified because of the lack of a cartouche. Noteworthy features are her elaborate clothing and ornaments. The queen is holding a neckband, the symbol of joy, and a sistrum, the musical instrument sacred to the goddess Hathor.

GROUP OF ASIATIC NOMADS
BENI HASAN, TOMB OF KHNUMHOTEP,
TWELFTH DYNASTY
VOLUME IV, PLATES XXVII AND XXVIII

The procession comprises thirteen figures, including women and children, as well as men with pointed beards and armed with bows, arrows, and cudgels. All of them have typical hooked noses and are wearing colorful clothes and sandals or leather footwear. The physiognomy, dress, bow, and the stringed instrument similar to the Greek lyre suggested to Champollion that these people were "Ionic Greeks or a people from Asia Minor . . . ."

168 BOTTOM AND 169 BOTTOM
GROUP OF ASIATIC NOMADS
BENI HASAN, TOMB OF KHNUMHOTEP,
TWELFTH DYNASTY
VOLUME IV, PLATE XXVI, DETAIL

One of the most interesting scenes in the main hall of this tomb is the one depicting the arrival in Egypt of a caravan of Bedouin from the eastern regions led by their chief, Abisha (seen below right), who is bowing respectfully while offering a pair of gazelles to the governor Khnumhotep (not depicted).

169 LEFT
GROUP OF ASIATIC NOMADS
BENI HASAN, TOMB OF KHNUMHOTEP,
TWELFTH DYNASTY
VOLUME IV, PLATES XXVII AND XXVIII

The figure on the extreme left of this page accompanies the plates showing Asiatic nomads (perhaps Syrians). She is the goddess of hunting, Satet of Elephantine, wearing a white crown and gazelle horns.

THE MILITARY CAMPAIGNS OF RAMESSES II IN AFRICA
TEMPLE OF BEIT AL-WALI, NUBIA
VOLUME III, PLATE LXIV

The scene is set in the small Nubian temple dedicated to Amun-Ra that Ramesses II had built during his long reign. "Ramesses II strikes a black man, the emblem of the people of Cush [Ethiopians]" (Rosellini). Like other temples in Nubia, in the 1970s this one was dismantled, removed, and rebuilt about half a mile south of the Aswan High Dam so that it would not be flooded by the waters of Lake Nasser.

170-171
THE BATTLES AND VICTORIES
OF RAMESSES II
ABU SIMBEL, GREAT TEMPLE
VOLUME III, PLATE LXXIX

This is the first of eight plates
illustrating a series of scenes copied

from the low reliefs in the pronaos of
the rock-cut temple of Ramesses II.
The pharaoh is depicted smiting
a group of prisoners of different
peoples in the presence of the
god Amun-Ra, who in turn is
offering the characteristic Egyptian
sword to Ramesses.

172

THE BATTLES AND VICTORIES
OF RAMESSES II
ABU SIMBEL, GREAT TEMPLE
VOLUME III, PLATE LXXX

A Syrian fortress on the top of a
cliff is being attacked by the pharaoh.
While the defenders are being killed
by the Egyptian archers, a woman at
the top of the fort is holding a child
aloft to arouse the pharaoh's pity.
Below, a Syrian flees with his herd.

173

THE BATTLES AND VICTORIES
OF RAMESSES II
ABU SIMBEL, GREAT TEMPLE
VOLUME III, PLATE LXXXII

This is the last scene of the battle,
depicting three princes, the pharaoh's
sons, who can be identified by the
lock of hair they wear at the side of
their heads. They stand on their
chariots, protected by the shield
bearers; in one hand they hold a bow
and, in the other, the reins of the
horses elegantly decorated with
multicolored materials.

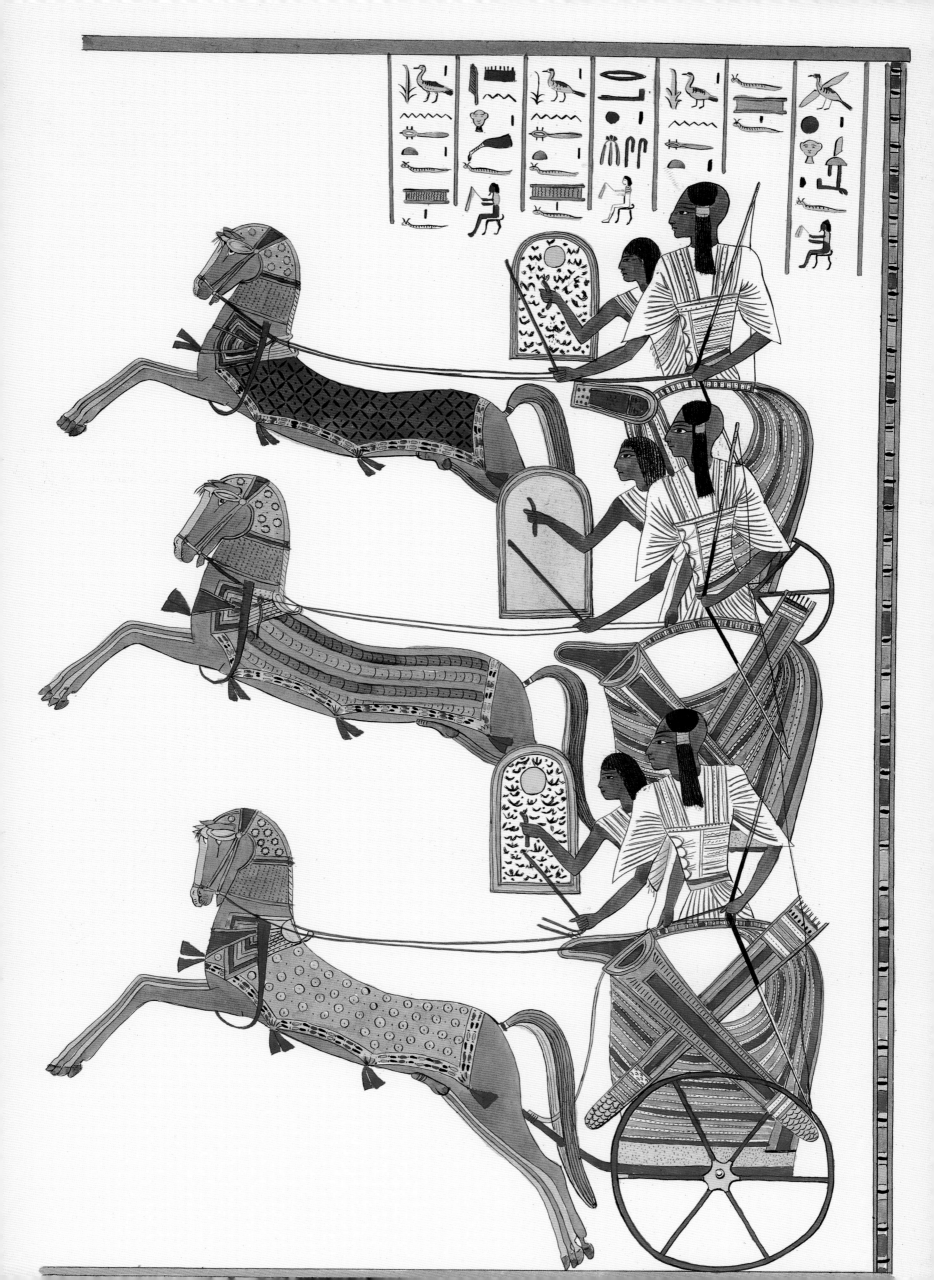

174-175
THE BATTLES AND VICTORIES
OF RAMESSES II
ABU SIMBEL, GREAT TEMPLE
VOLUME III, PLATE LXXXIII

This plate and the following ones
continue the self-glorification
of the pharaoh. A recurring
iconographic motif shows him
crushing a hapless enemy leader
and lancing another, both of whom
are thought to be Libyans.
Here the artist has ignored the canons
of perspective and, in order not
to cover Ramesses II's face,
has rendered the lance in an
unnatural manner so that it
passes behind the head and left arm
of the pharaoh.

175
THE BATTLES AND VICTORIES OF RAMESSES II
ABU SIMBEL, GREAT TEMPLE
VOLUME III, PLATE LXXXV

Here we have two groups of war prisoners, Ethiopians and Nubians. The prisoners wear animal skins and are bound by the neck and arms, who attest once again the famous ruler's victories over various African peoples. The gait of the figures (almost a mixture of dance steps) reveal how the Egyptian artists succeeded in lending a sense of movement to the entire scene.

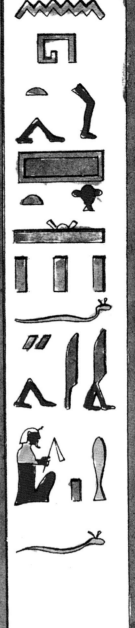

176-177
VICTORIES OF RAMESSES II
ABU SIMBEL, GREAT TEMPLE
VOLUME III, PLATE LXXXIV

Taken from the south wall of the
pronaos, the scene depicts
the pharaoh in triumph.
Preceded by an archer, Ramesses II,

with a blue crown and a bow in his
left hand, is drawn in his war
chariot by a pair of elegantly
harnessed horses.

178-179 TOP
THE BATTLE OF KADESH
ABU SIMBEL, GREAT TEMPLE
VOLUME III, PLATE LXXXVII

This plate is a small-scale, summary reproduction of a large scene that covers the entire north wall of the pronaos in the temple at Abu Simbel.

It is divided into two parts. The upper register represents the pharaoh attacking a citadel near a river with his chariots. The lower one shows the army of chariots and foot soldiers in battle formation, the camp and the pharaoh's tent, the pharaoh in person receiving an ambassador and, lastly, a chariot battle.

This is the representation of the famous Battle of Kadesh, at the river Orontes in Syria, which Ramesses II fought against the Hittites around 1275 BC. In reality, neither side won the battle, but the ambitious Egyptian sovereign had the event propagandized as a sort of personal triumph.

179 BOTTOM LEFT
THE BATTLE OF KADESH
ABU SIMBEL, GREAT TEMPLE
VOLUME III, PLATE LXXXVII, DETAIL

This scene shows the perfectly aligned Egyptian footmen who are protected by chariots with archers and cuirassiers.

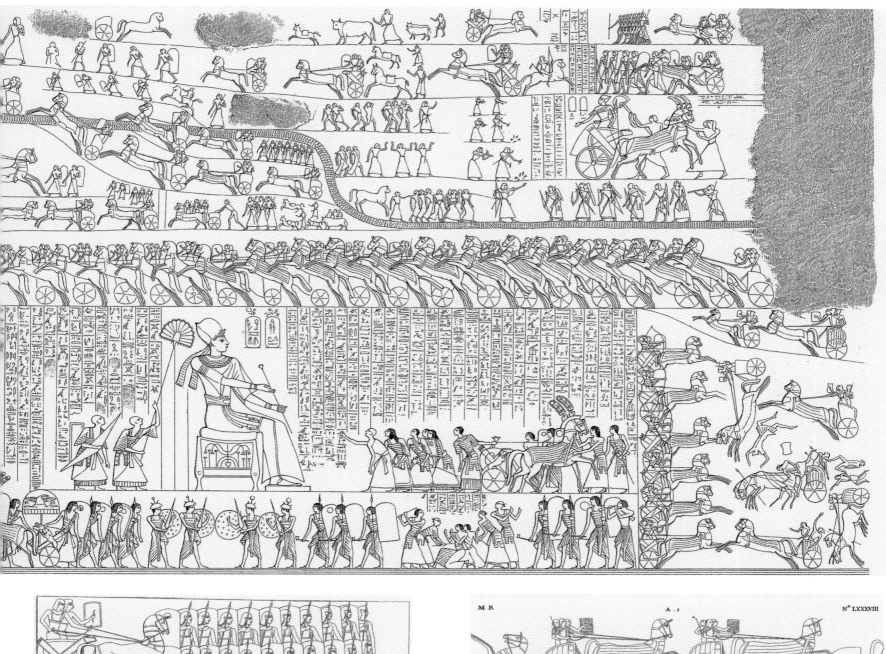

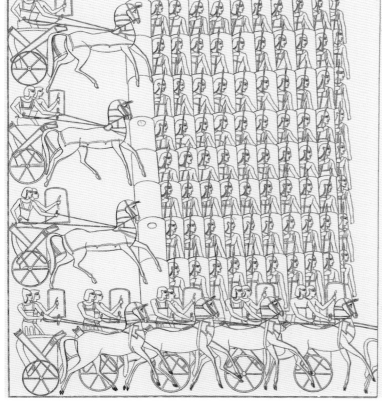

179 BOTTOM RIGHT
THE BATTLE OF KADESH
ABU SIMBEL, GREAT TEMPLE
VOLUME III, PLATE LXXXVII, detail

Ramesses II (right), shooting
an arrow from his chariot,
throws his enemies into disarray.

180 and 181
THE BATTLE OF KADESH
ABU SIMBEL, GREAT TEMPLE
VOLUME III, PLATES C AND CI

The Battle of Kadesh, narrated in the low reliefs in the Great Temple of Abu Simbel, was copied masterfully by the Franco-Tuscan mission artists in January 1829. Of the sixteen plates published in Rosellini's work, in this page and the following ones are reproductions of the last four, which stand out for their superb and colorful images.

In the illustration at left, the pharaoh, seated and in military dress, is being informed of the enemy's imminent attack. Below are the Egyptian forces, among whom are various foreigners, ready for battle. In the scene at right, two servants (above) are holding Ramesses II's flabellum and his bow in its case; below are soldiers armed with axes and lances, protected by their breastplates. The long hieroglyphic inscription contains part of the so-called "Pentaur Poem," an account of the battle, which the great pharaoh also had carved on the walls of other temples.

182
THE BATTLE OF KADESH
ABU SIMBEL, GREAT TEMPLE
VOLUME III, PLATE CII

This plate is the conclusion of the preceding scene. Kneeling before Ramesses II (not portrayed), officers talk among themselves, while the servants try to calm down the horses. In the lower register, two Hittite spies are being beaten so that they will reveal the location of their army. Note the trumpeter among the Egyptian soldiers.

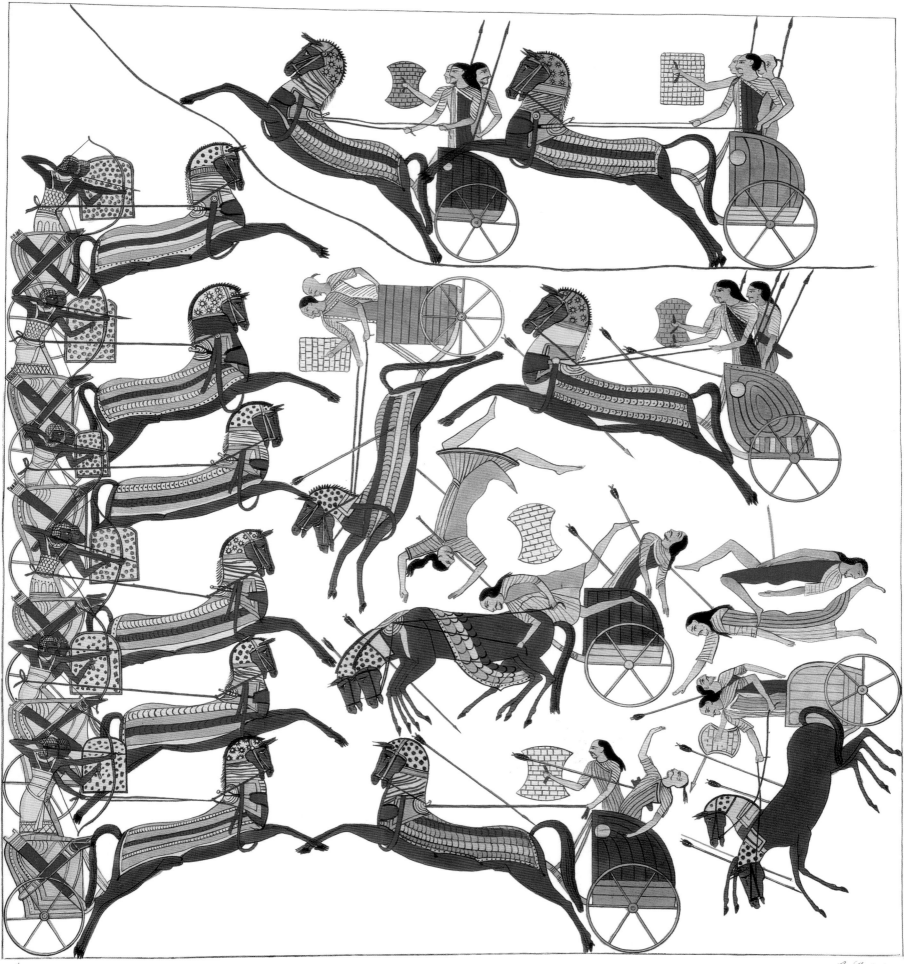

G. Lasinio scul.

183
THE BATTLE OF KADESH
ABU SIMBEL, GREAT TEMPLE
VOLUME III, PLATE CIII

This is the last of the sixteen plates
illustrating the famous event
immortalized in the Nubian temple.

Angelelli's beautiful polychrome
drawing shows, at left, the aligned
light Egyptian chariots with
two soldiers each. At right
are the heavier Hittite chariots,
which carry three soldiers; they are
fleeing, since both the soldiers
and horses have been struck by

Egyptian arrows. A typical feature
of Egyptian art is the lack of
perspective: the figures,
all of equal size, are 'staggered
vertically,' that is, one over
the other, and not on the same plane,
which lends a lack of depth
to the entire composition.

184-185
The Battle of Kadesh
West Thebes, Ramesseum
Volume III, Plate CIX

This is another representation of the battle in Syria as it was rendered in low relief on the right-hand pylon of the funerary temple of Ramesses II. Once again, in keeping with classical Egyptian iconographical canons, the pharaoh is depicted on his chariot as he shoots an arrow, while the battlefield is covered with the bodies of the dead and wounded enemy.

186 bottom
HUNTING LIONS
MEDINET HABU, TEMPLE OF RAMESSES III
VOLUME III, PLATE CXXIX

Scenes of military prowess and courage are depicted in the temple that Ramesses III had built around 1200 BC. Besides showing a part of the Egyptian army, this plate illustrates the pharaoh hunting lions.

187
THE PHARAOH AND A GOD
THEBES, TOMB OF MERNEPTAH
VOLUME III, PLATE CXVIII

This plate shows the son of Ramesses II in splendid dress wearing the *atef* crown while receiving the gifts of stability and peace from the god Ra-Horakhty, the symbols of which are in his left and right hands.

186 top
THE PHARAOH MAKING OFFERINGS
THEBES, TOMB OF MERNEPTAH
VOLUME III, PLATE LXIX

On both sides of the image on the upper register, Merneptah, the son and successor of Ramesses II, is represented while offering vases of wine to various divinities. This act is repeated in the scene below left, while in the last scene the two symbolic personifications of the Nile seem to be taking gifts to the pharaoh's cartouche.

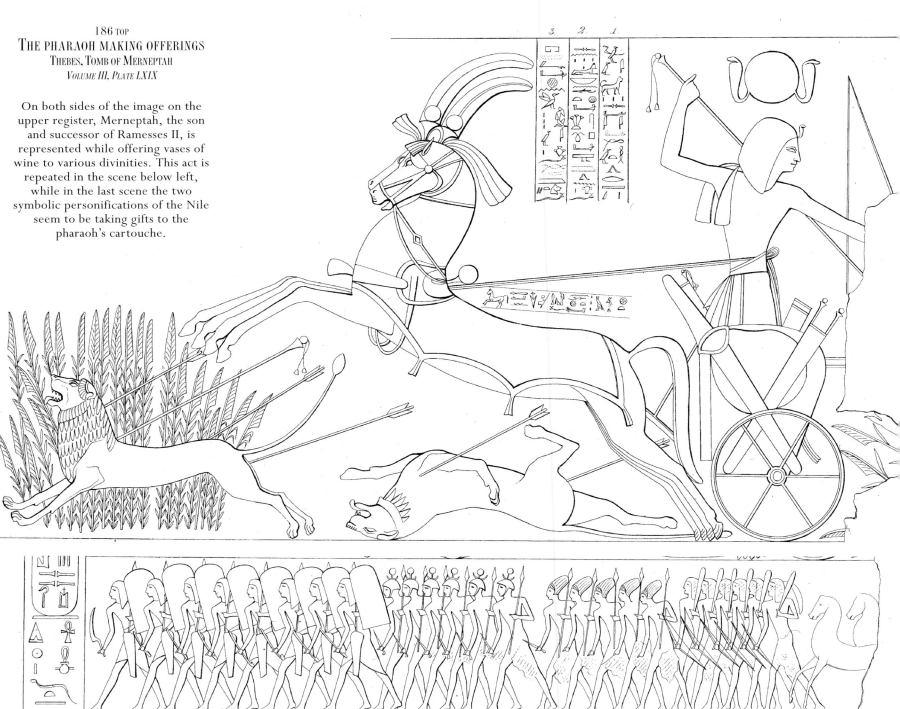

NAVAL BATTLE
MEDINET HABU, TEMPLE OF RAMESSES III
VOLUME III, PLATE CXXXI

This scene narrates the attempt to invade Egypt by the 'Sea Peoples,' populations from the Mediterranean and Asia Minor who were active in the region in the thirteenth-eleventh centuries BC.

The are thought to have been Etruscans, Achaeans, Sardinians, and Lycians. Around 1180 BC, they were driven away by Ramesses III in a battle that may have been decisive for the independence of his country. The plate shows the Egyptians in battle on land and sea; their adversaries can be recognized by their feathered headdresses and round shields.

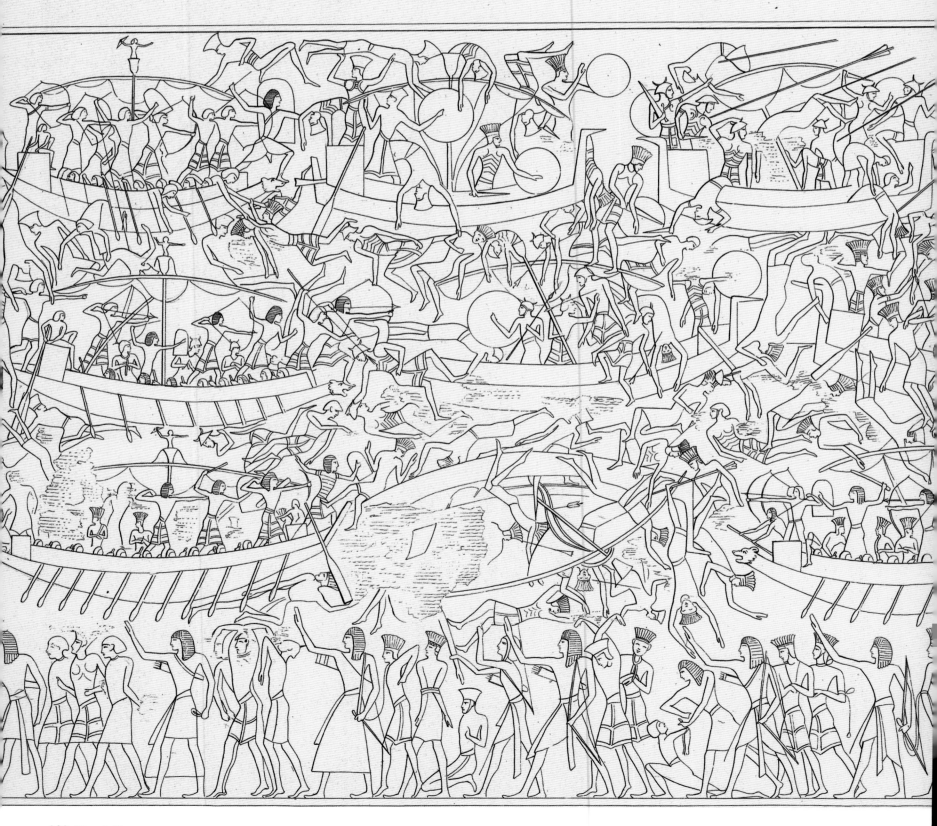

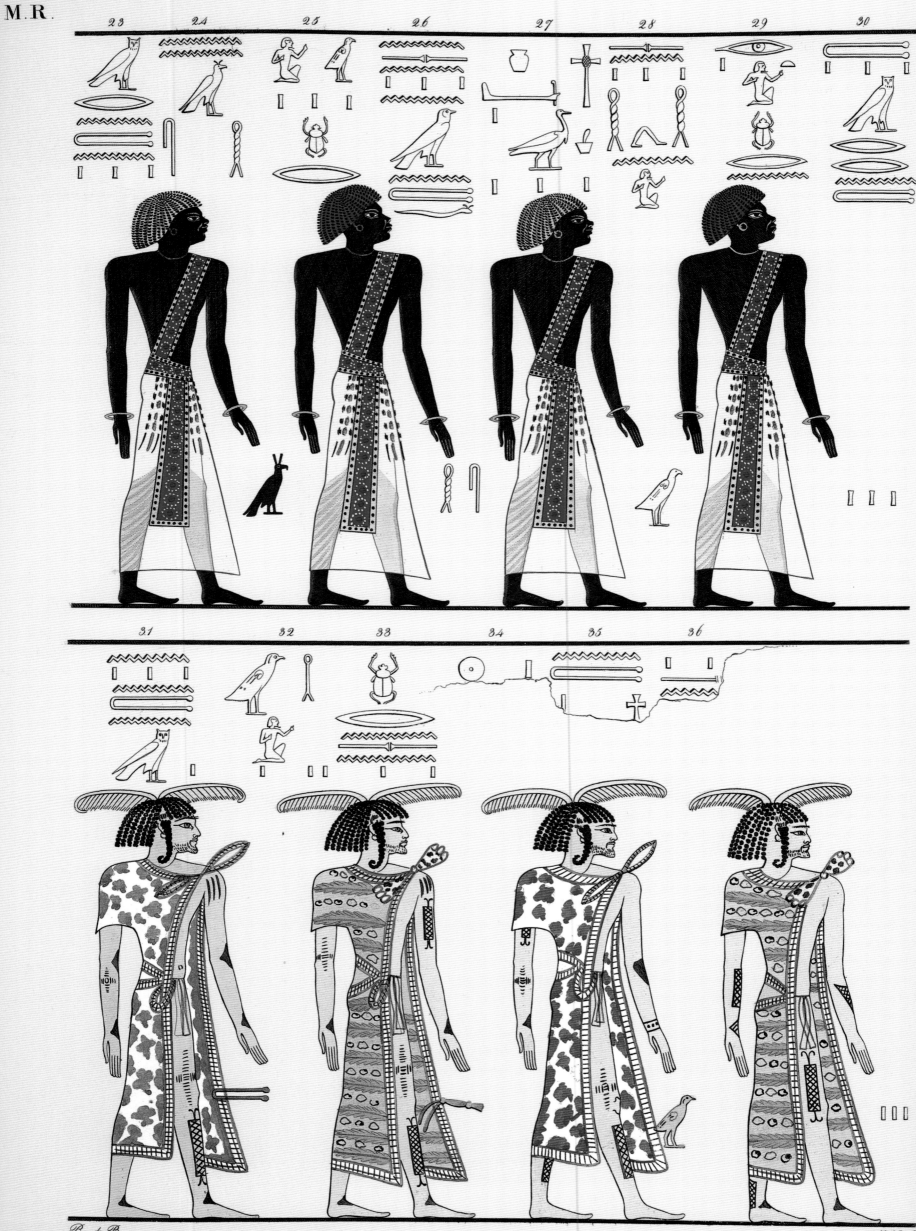

190
Procession of Egyptians and Foreigners
Thebes, Tomb of Seti I
Volume IV, Plate CLVI

These are portrayals of representatives of some foreign populations who came into contact with the ancient Egyptians. The four Nubians in this upper section are easily recognizable: true black Africans with their dark skin and kinky hair, wearing long garments and bracelets on their wrists. Below are four other figures with light skin, straight noses, feathers in their hair and a sort of mantle wrapped around their left shoulder. They have been identified as Libyans.

191
Prisoners of War
West Thebes, Ramesseum
Volume III, Plate CXLI

Two prisoners, an African and an Asian, on their knees with their necks and arms tied, represent another testimony to Ramesses II's victories.

192 AND 193
OTHER FOREIGNERS
THEBES, TOMB OF SETI I AND OTHER TOMBS
VOLUME IV, PLATES CLVII, CLVIII, AND CLIX

In the three plates reproduced here, there are "various figures of foreign men represented on the monuments of Egypt . . ." (Rosellini): Libyans, Africans, Assyrians, Asians, and members of Aegean populations.

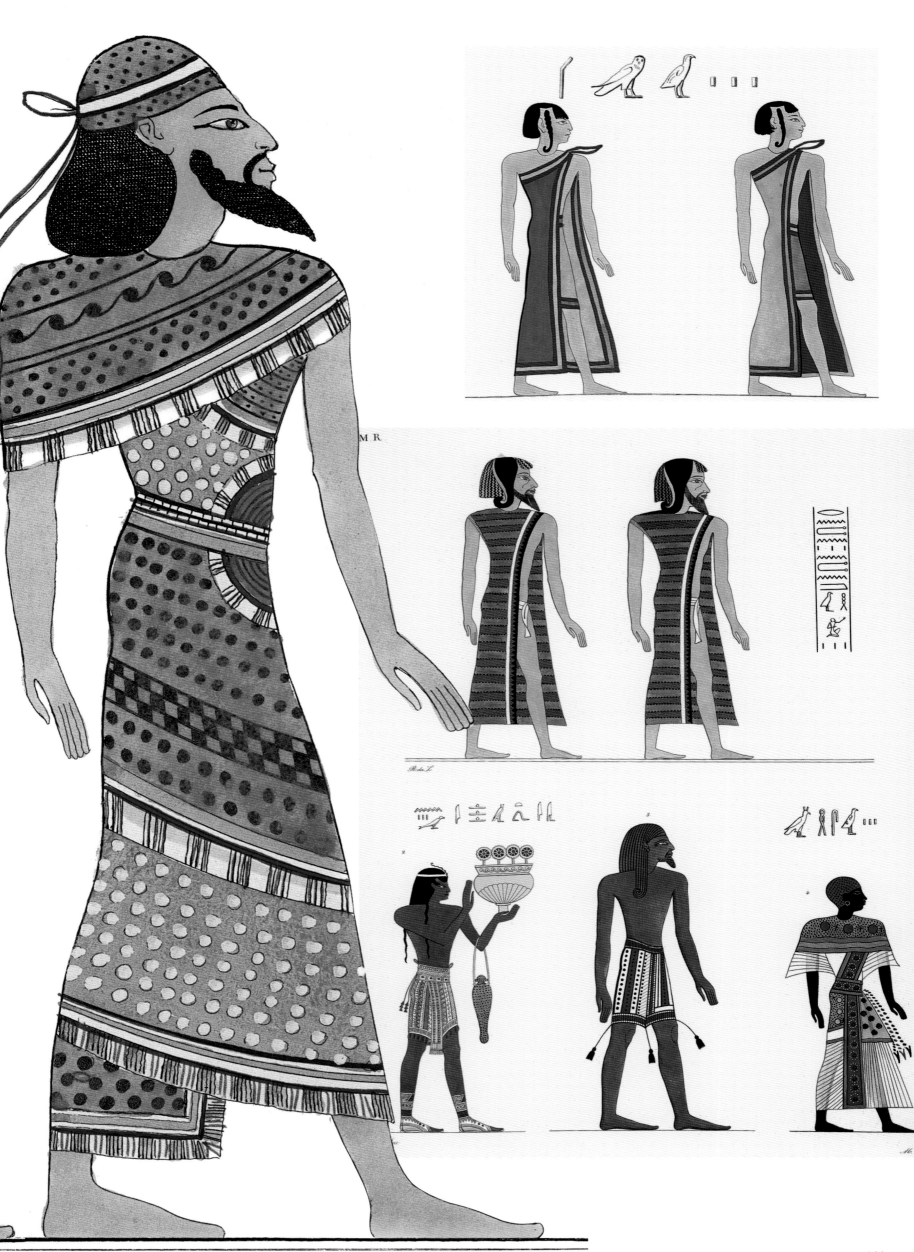

194-195
HEADS OF FOREIGNERS
ABU SIMBEL AND THE TOMB OF SETI I
VOLUME IV, PLATE CLX

The plate is a synthesis of the physical features of some ethnic groups already described above. They include the heads of three Asians (figures 1, 2, 3), one Libyan (figure 4), and a Nubian (figure 5).

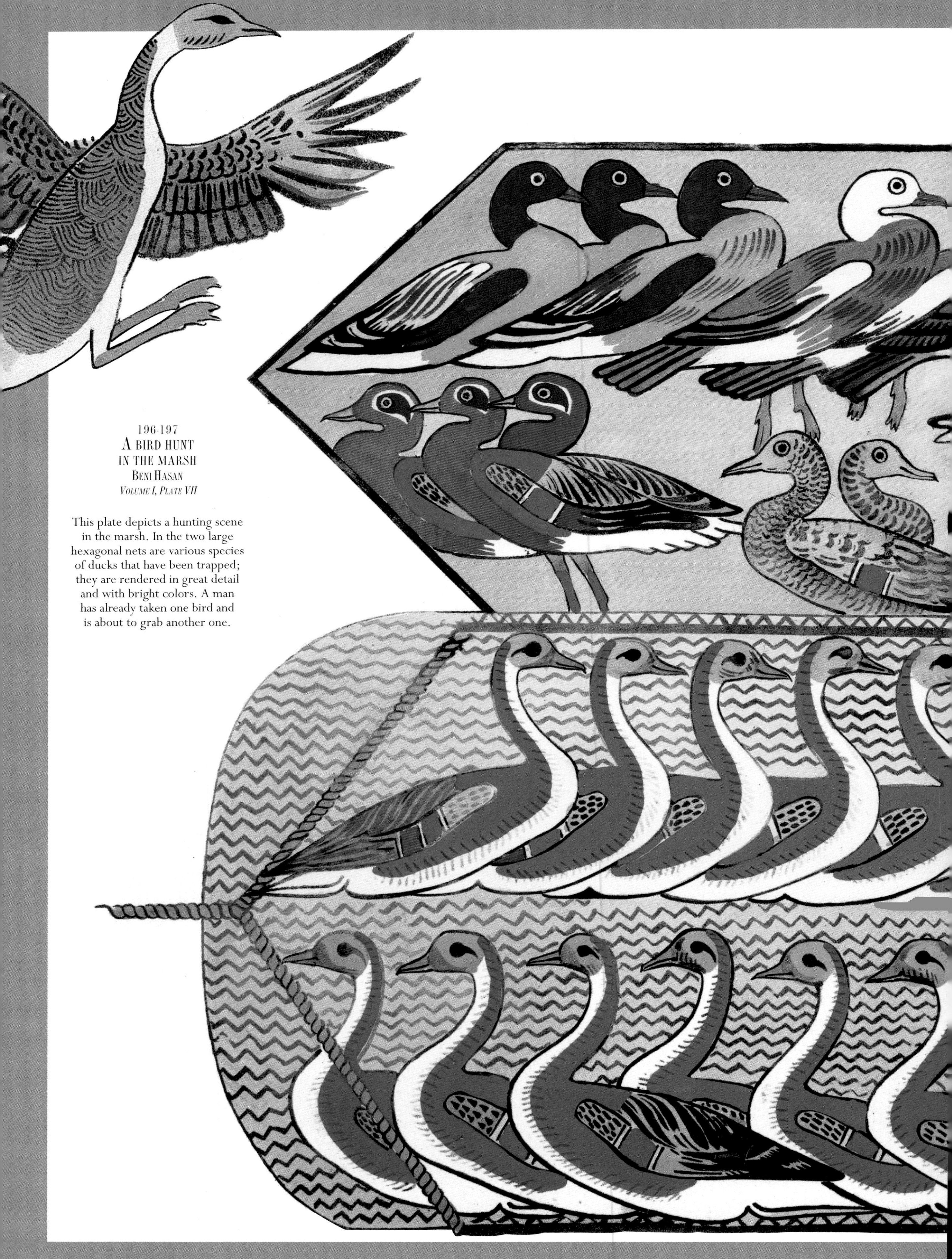

196-197
A BIRD HUNT
IN THE MARSH
BENI HASAN
Volume I, Plate VII

This plate depicts a hunting scene
in the marsh. In the two large
hexagonal nets are various species
of ducks that have been trapped;
they are rendered in great detail
and with bright colors. A man
has already taken one bird and
is about to grab another one.

198 TOP
VARIOUS SPECIES OF EXOTIC ANIMALS
THEBES, TOMB OF THE VIZIER REKHMIRA
VOLUME I, PLATE XXII

The animals depicted here are quadrupeds not native to Egypt, and are for the most part associated with foreigners who are perhaps in the act of bearing tributes. From above left: a giraffe with a cute monkey on his neck, is tied down by two Nubians; a lion with particular markings, a bear-like animal (figure 5) and a small elephant (figure 3) are being led by what appear to be Syrians, given their attire and beards. In the middle is an Ethiopian holding either a leopard or a cheetah by a leash and carrying a trunk of highly prized ebony on his shoulders.

198-199 BOTTOM
VARIOUS SPECIES OF QUADRUPEDS
BENI HASAN
VOLUME I, PLATE XX

From left to right are a dog with a spiral tail, an Asian bull with a large lotus-shaped collar, and a small carnivore climbing up a papyrus plant. This last animal was widespread in ancient Egypt and was called *Viverra zibetta* (a species of civet cat) by Rosellini.

199 TOP

FANTASTIC ANIMALS
BENI HASAN AND A THEBAN TOMB
VOLUME I, PLATE XXIII

Besides a greyhound and a cheetah
(figures 1 and 3), which Rosellini calls
a "hunter tiger," this illustration has
some species of chimeras or griffins,
which are probably the fruit of the
tomb painters' imaginations.

200 TOP
VARIOUS SPECIES
OF AQUATIC BIRDS
BENI HASAN, TOMB OF KHNUMHOTEP
VOLUME I, PLATE XIII

Some species of ducks and geese are
rendered quite accurately and in
detail. There are also two ibises,
which were considered sacred by
the ancient Egyptians.

200 BOTTOM AND 201 BOTTOM
VARIOUS SPECIES OF BIRDS
BENI HASAN
VOLUME I, PLATE XI

These illustrations, once again copied from a tomb at Beni Hasan, depict other species of birds, most of which are aquatic, rendered with bright colors, among which a splendid heron on a flower stands out.

200-201 TOP
VARIOUS SPECIES OF BIRDS
BENI HASAN, TOMB OF KHNUMHOTEP
VOLUME I, PLATE VIII

The charming birds illustrated here are also depicted with lovely colors. Among them are a hoopoe and a shrike perched on a small branch of a Nilotic mimosa, and a jay in flight.

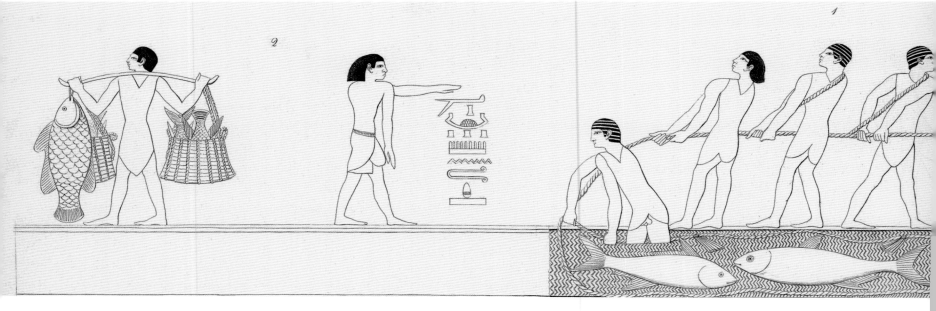

This plate features a scene of spear fishing and representations of various species of fish, all drawn in detail and with subtle color nuances. Above right, a man is cutting a fish and preparing it to be preserved.

Different Egyptian fishing techniques are illustrated here. In the pictures copied from the walls of the Beni Hasan tombs, some men are fishing from the shore with a trawl net and others with a hook and line, while the scene at top right, copied from a tomb at Kom al-Ahmar, illustrates the use of a harpoon to catch crocodiles from a typical papyrus boat.

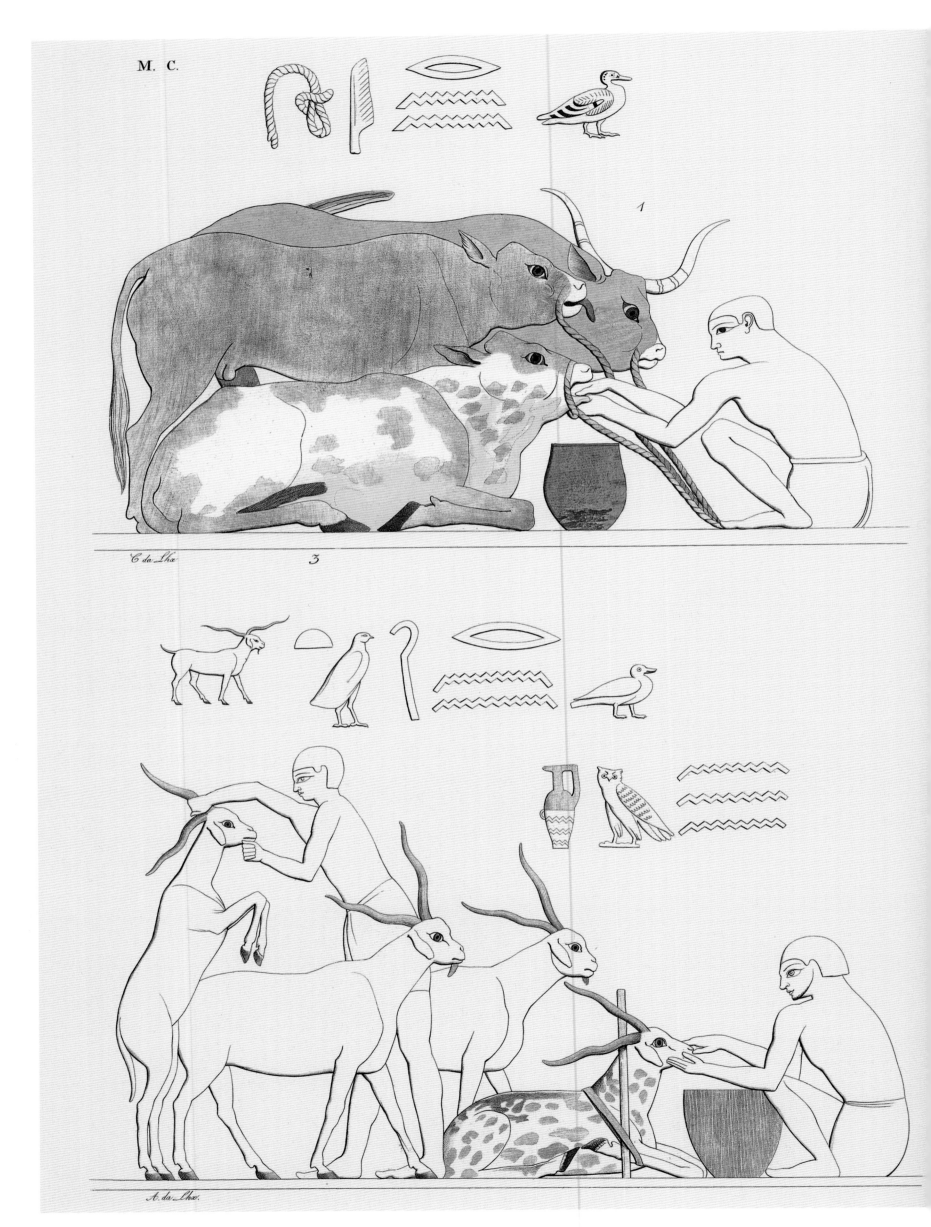

M. C.

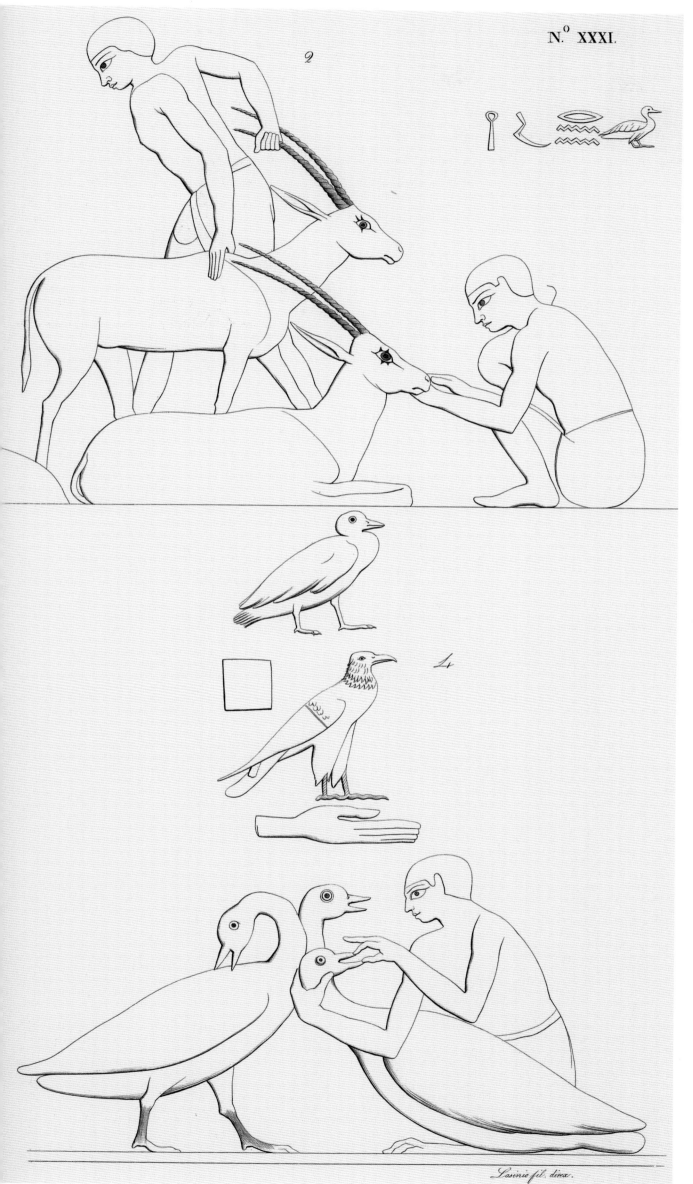

204-205
LIVESTOCK RAISING
BENI HASAN
VOLUME I, PLATE XXXI

Although Rosellini considered this a "veterinarian" scene, it more likely depicts the forced feeding of animals. In effect, the men seem to be forcefully putting food in the mouths of the oxen, gazelles, goats, and geese.

206-207
WINE-MAKING SCENES
GIZA, BENI HASAN, AND THEBES
CIVIL MONUMENTS, PLATE XXXVII

Viniculture in Egypt was carried out in very ancient times and developed mostly in the Nile Delta. Wine was drunk almost exclusively by the upper classes, while beer, made mostly from barley, was very widespread and was always on the tables of common people. After the harvest, the grapes were trodden; in order not to slip in the vat, the men shown here are holding on to a support. More pressing was then done with the aid of a bag. The juice dripped into a tub and was then poured in earthen amphorae to age. The ancient Egyptians wrote the quantity as well as the provenance, the name of the landowner, and the vintage year on the amphorae—much like a modern-day wine label. A scribe, with a quill behind his ear, is noting down the amount of wine.

206 LEFT AND BOTTOM
FARM SCENES
BENI HASAN AND AL-KAB
VOLUME I, PLATE XXXIV

The various phases of the wheat harvest included winnowing, measuring, transporting, and storing wheat under the watchful gaze of the scribe (center). Below, the grain is transported and then preserved in a two-story silo with several compartments, on each of which the harvest yield is indicated.

207 BOTTOM
FARM SCENES
BENI HASAN AND THE THEBES AREA
PLATE XXXVI, DETAIL

The upper scene depicts, from left to
right: flax being harvested, and durra,
a grain sorghum used as food, being
cut and then transported. The lower
scene shows the threshing of the harvest
carried out by oxen, as well as two men
who have just cut a number of papyrus
stems. The fibers of this plant were
used, among other things, for making
writing material.

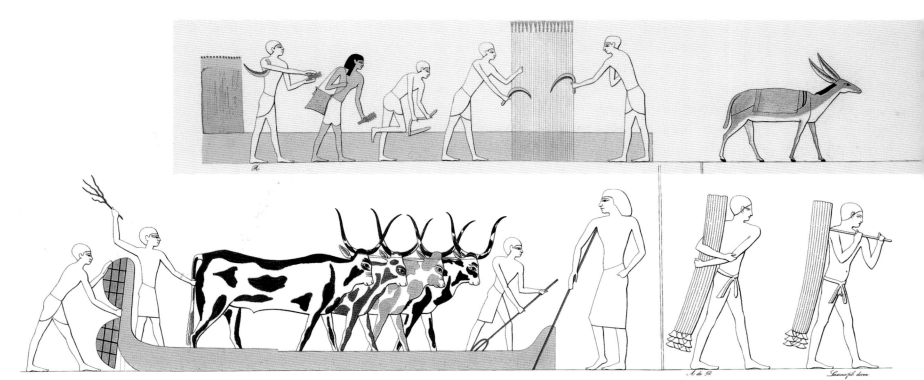

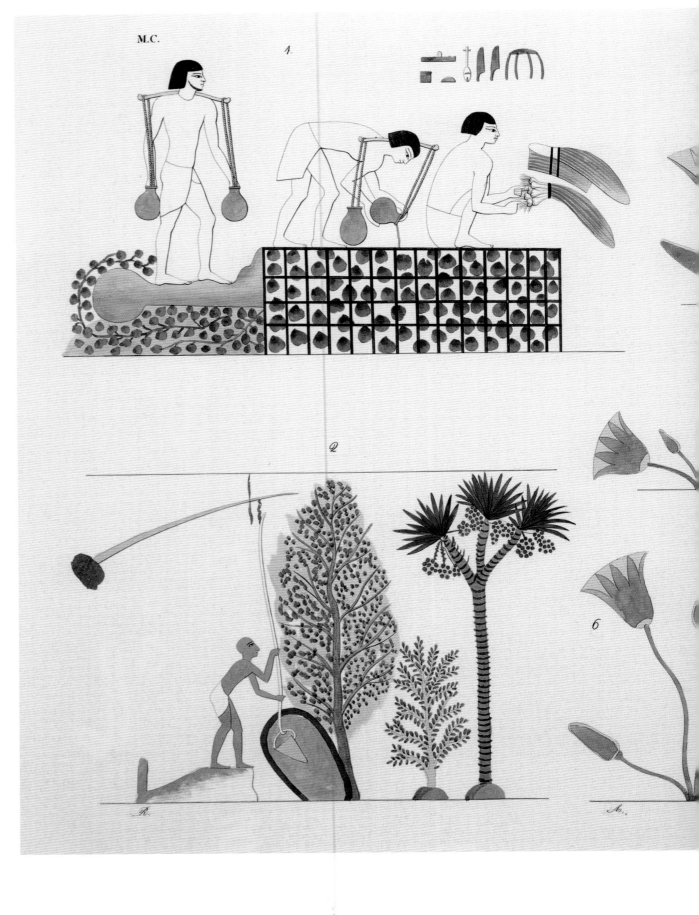

208-209
CULTIVATION AND IRRIGATION
BENI HASAN
VOLUME I, PLATE XL

This plate illustrates the two most common methods of irrigating crops and gardens in ancient Egypt. The manual system, consisting of people carrying vessels filled with water on their shoulders and then pouring the water into the different plots of land is illustrated above; below, the mechanical system, which made use of the *shaduf*, a suspended rod with a weight at one end and a bucket at the other which was used to raise water from the Nile or the many canals. The plate also has drawings of vegetables and fruit, as well as a date palm.

208 BOTTOM
FARMING
VARIOUS TOMBS
VOLUME I, PLATE XXXII, DETAIL

This scene, which is probably taking place in a field along a canal, depicts plowing, which in ancient Egypt was carried out with the aid of oxen. The scene continues with a farmer sowing the newly plowed land.

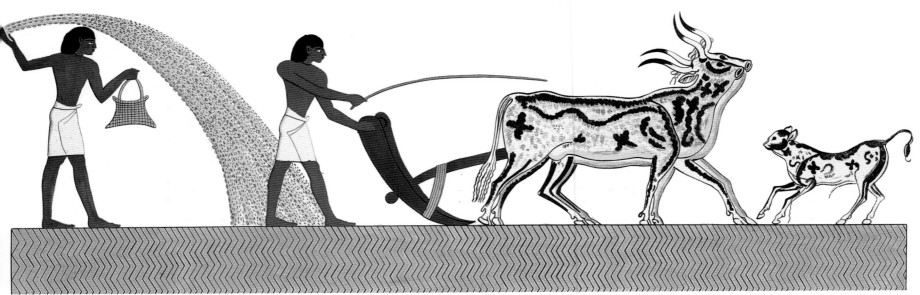

This charming scene depicts figs being picked by two people while monkeys are absorbed in eating the sweet fruit. According to Rosellini, in the other scene these peasants are gathering okra, an edible vegetable of the hibiscus family.

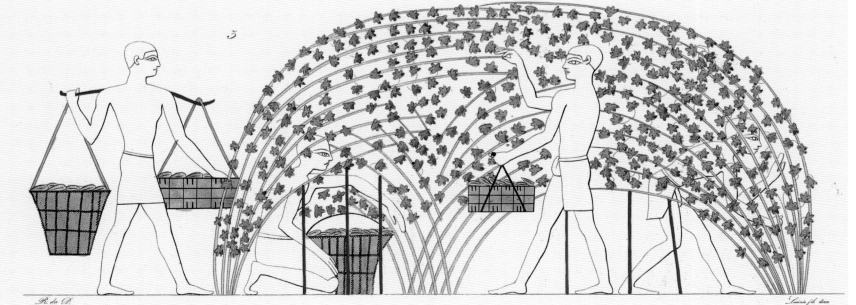

210 top and bottom, **211** right and bottom
Spinning and Weaving
Volume II, Plate XLI, detail

The only fiber worked by the ancient
Egyptians to produce fabrics was
flax, which had been used since the
Neolithic era. The first two registers
(bottom left) show the different
phases of soaking the flax, beating
it with wooden mallets, and preparing
the yarn. In the third and fourth
registers (next page, bottom),
some men are weaving on horizontal
looms, while in the last scene
(top right) two women are working
with a vertical loom.

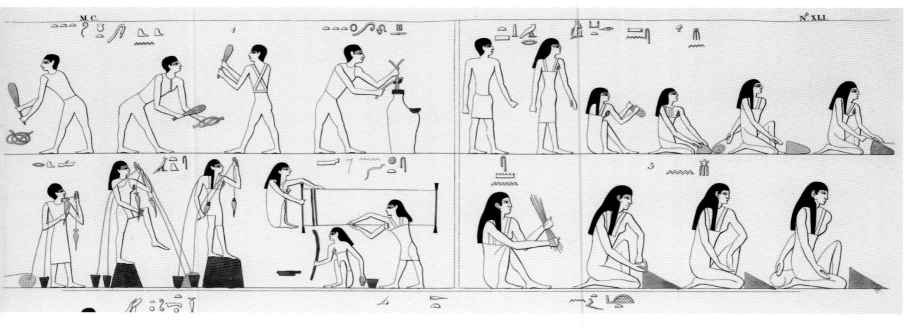

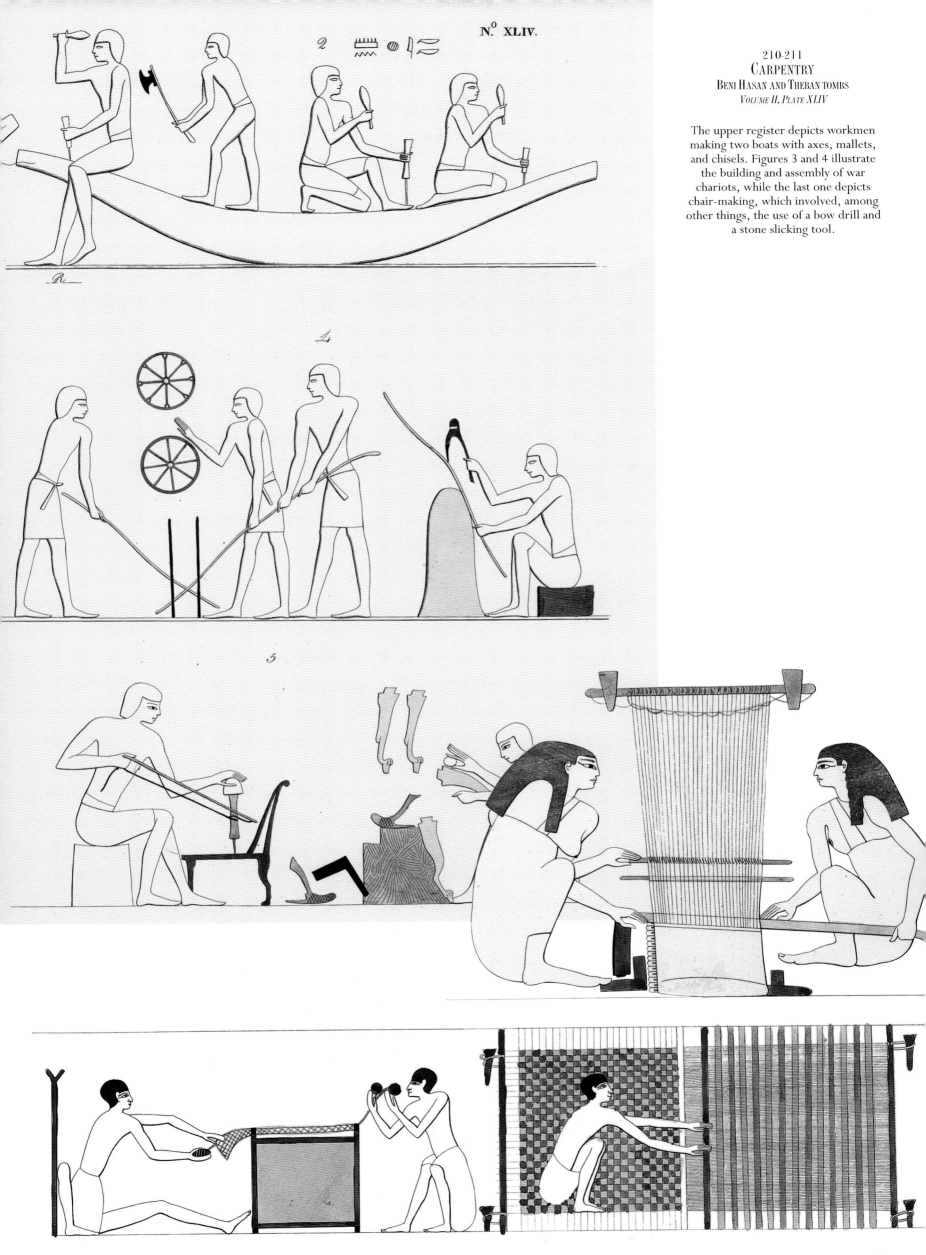

210-211
CARPENTRY
BENI HASAN AND THEBAN TOMBS
VOLUME II, PLATE XLIV

The upper register depicts workmen
making two boats with axes, mallets,
and chisels. Figures 3 and 4 illustrate
the building and assembly of war
chariots, while the last one depicts
chair-making, which involved, among
other things, the use of a bow drill and
a stone slicking tool.

212-213
THE ART OF SCULPTING
THEBAN TOMBS, INCLUDING THE TOMB OF REKHMIRA
VOLUME II, PLATE XLVII

The plate first illustrates the art of sculpting a statue of a lion and a sphinx (figures on the left). This is followed by several artisans giving the final touches to two large red granite statues representing a standing pharaoh and a pharaoh on his throne (from Rekhmira's tomb in Thebes). The scenes below illustrate the transport of a wooden trunk and a block of stone.

212 BOTTOM
TRANSPORTING A COLOSSUS
TOMBS IN MIDDLE EGYPT
VOLUME II, PLATE XLVIII, detail

This plate shows a famous scene taken from a tomb in Deir al-Bersha. A huge statue is being transported: it is tied to a sledge and dragged by eight rows of men. The person on the colossus' knee is beating time with his hands in order to synchronize the movement of the laborers. One workman is pouring water on the sand so that the sledge will slide better, while below him three water bearers stand ready to help him.

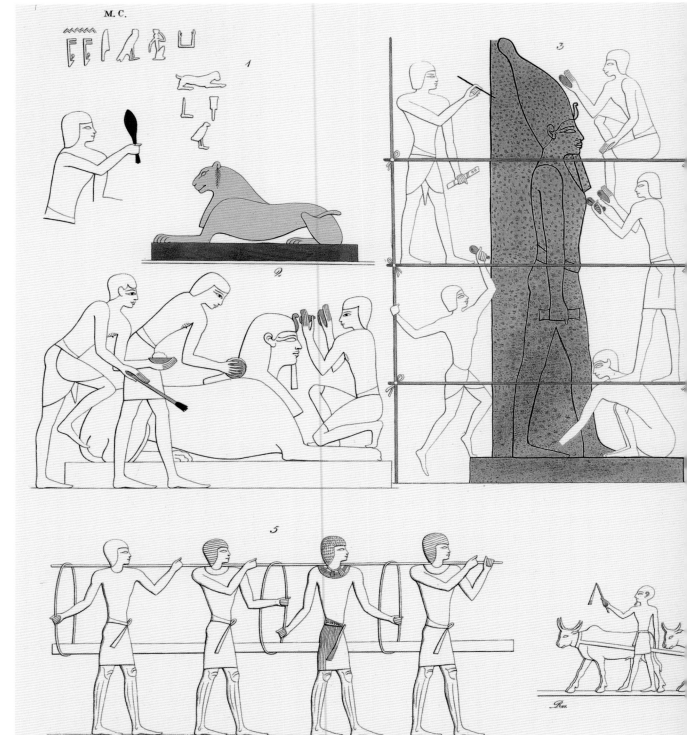

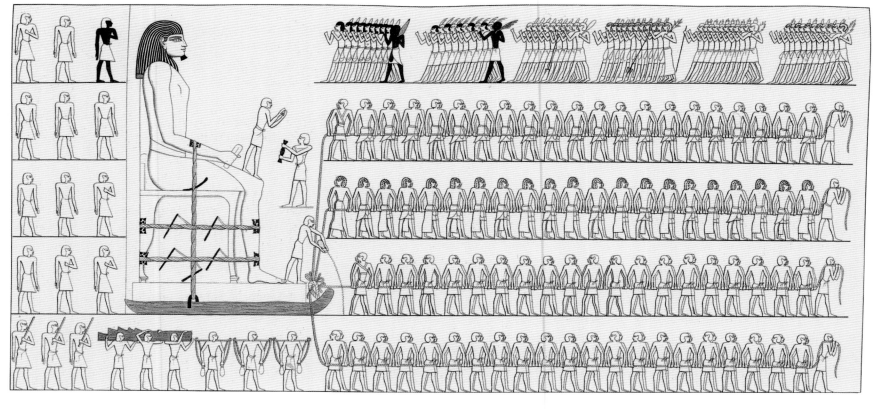

213 TOP
CARPENTRY
BENI HASAN AND THEBAN TOMBS
VOLUME II, PLATE XLV

The upper register depicts artisans making furniture and various wooden objects, including a chest, a bed, and a casket. The illustration in the middle shows the construction of a wooden papyrus column, while the other drawings are of models of religious and mortuary decorative art, such as mummiform statues, canopic jars, a *djed* pilaster, and a sphinx presenting offerings.

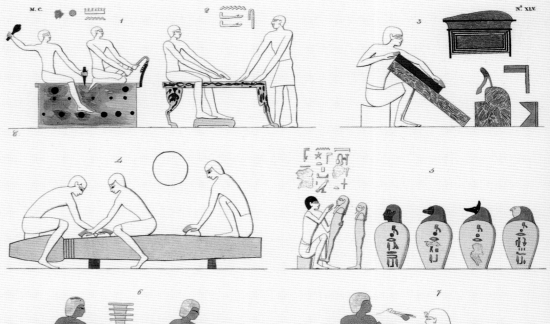

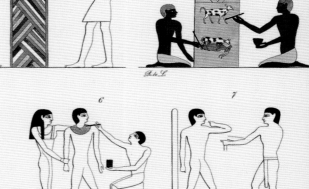

213 CENTER AND BOTTOM
DYERS AND PAINTERS
BENI HASAN AND THEBAN TOMBS
VOLUME II, PLATE XLVI

The upper register has three scenes depicting the grinding and preparation of colors, and then decorators varnishing wooden caskets.
The scenes in the lower register depict examples of sculpting, which involved the use of chisels and mallets as well as polishing and decorating the pieces with ornaments.

214-215
MASONRY
THEBES, TOMB OF REKHMIRA
VOLUME II, PLATE XLIX

The scenes above and below left illustrate the process of making mud bricks in rectangular molds and then transporting them: note the darker color of the dried bricks compared to those just molded. Figures on the right show painters and sculptors working on vases and statues. The different physical features—such as the color of the skin, the beard, and the hair—led Rosellini to think the workmen were Jews, but it is more likely that they were Syrians.

214 BOTTOM, 215 TOP RIGHT AND BOTTOM
METALLURGY
BENI HASAN AND THEBES
VOLUME II, PLATE L

In these illustrations, which are copies of decorations in an Eighteenth Dynasty Theban tomb, we see phases of the melting and filtering of gold, which was mined in Nubia and the eastern zone of Egypt. Using foot-operated bellows, the artisans stoke the fire, melt the gold, and pour it into small receptacles of the same size. The scene at top right, from a tomb at Beni Hasan, depicts potters at work: after kneading the clay with their feet, they then shaped the vessels at the potter's wheel, fired them in cylindrical ovens, and transported them. Terracotta was the most common material used for pottery, but the ancient Egyptians also used stones such as limestone, granite, and alabaster.

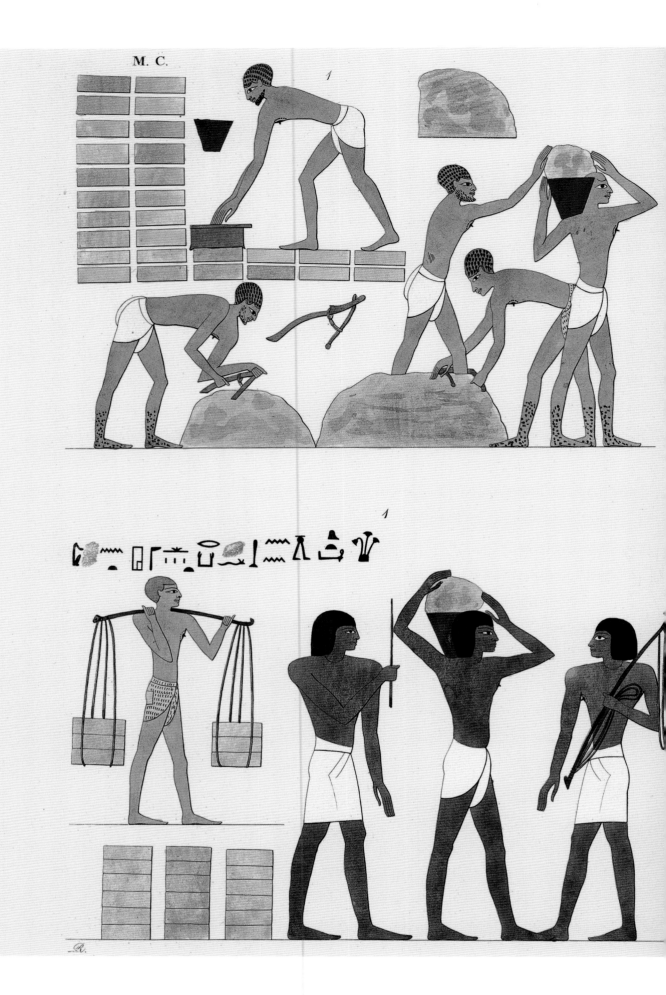

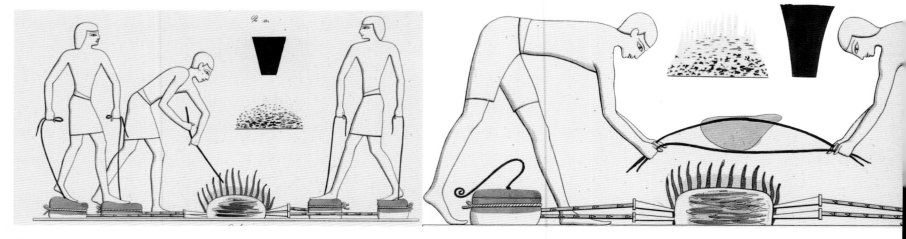

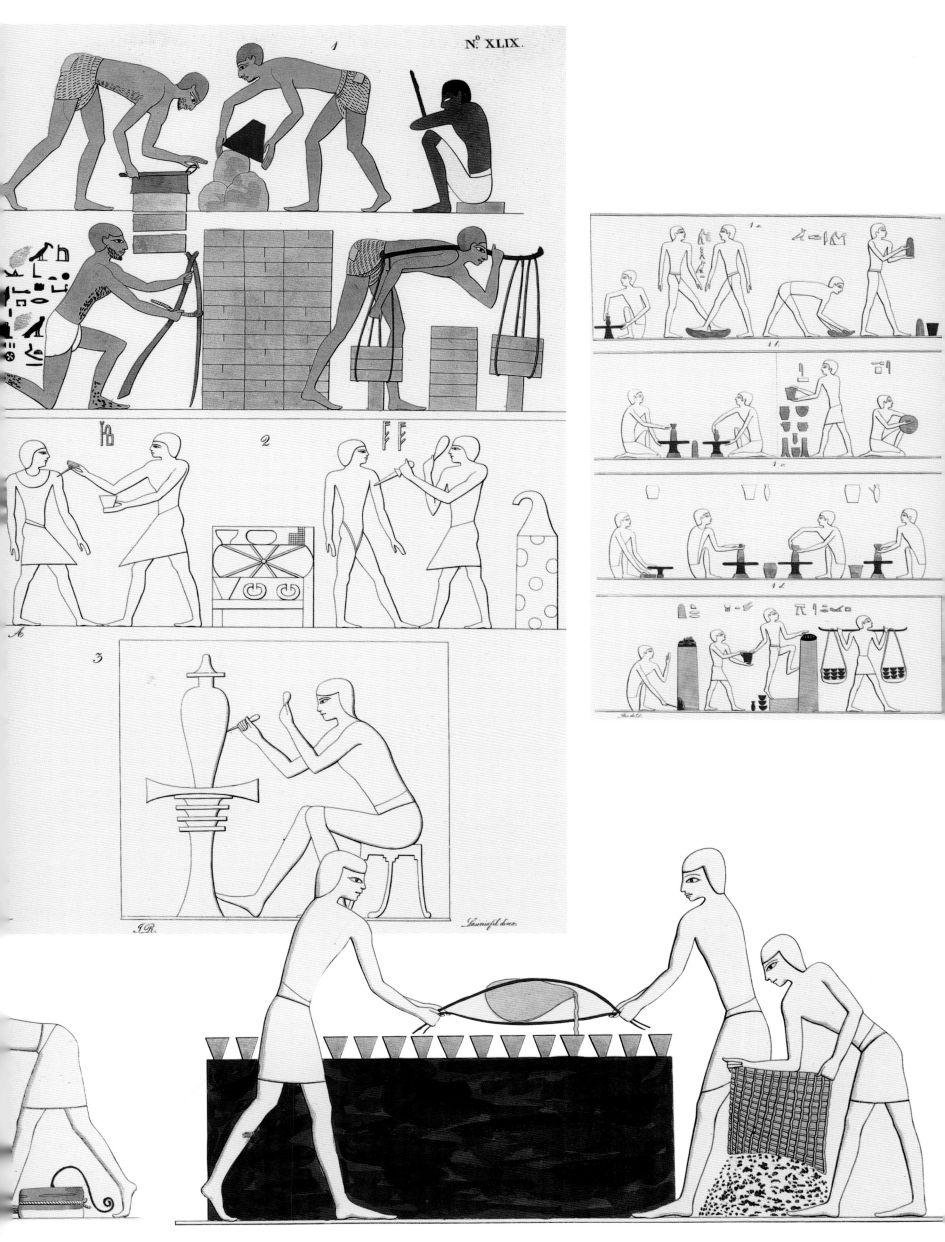

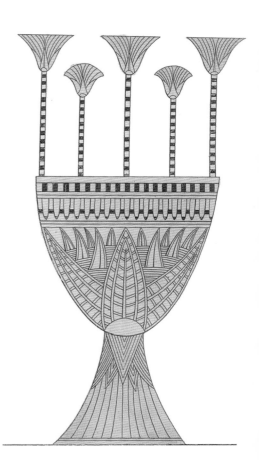

216 TOP
OTHER TYPES OF VASES
THEBAN TOMBS AND BENI HASAN
VOLUME II, PLATE LX

In this plate are illustrated vases and
vessels with different shapes. They are
made of enamel, gold, and other
materials and sometimes have supports
beneath them. The drawing below
depicts three unusual small vases
decorated with lotus flowers.

216 BOTTOM
VASES AND DIFFERENT VESSELS
THEBAN TOMBS
VOLUME II, PLATE LXII, DETAIL

Here we have more illustrations
of vases and other vessels that
are finely decorated with depictions
of lotus and papyrus flowers.
The objects were made of precious
or semiprecious metal that was
enameled or gilded.

217
GOLDEN VASES
THEBES, TOMB OF NEBAMUN
VOLUME II, PLATE LVIII

Different types of amphorae and vases
"of gold and enamel" (Rosellini) are
illustrated here. All of them are
elaborately decorated and have handles
and lids depicting animals or gods.
These extremely elegant objects
"preceded the beautiful production of
Greek art by a thousand years"
(Champollion).

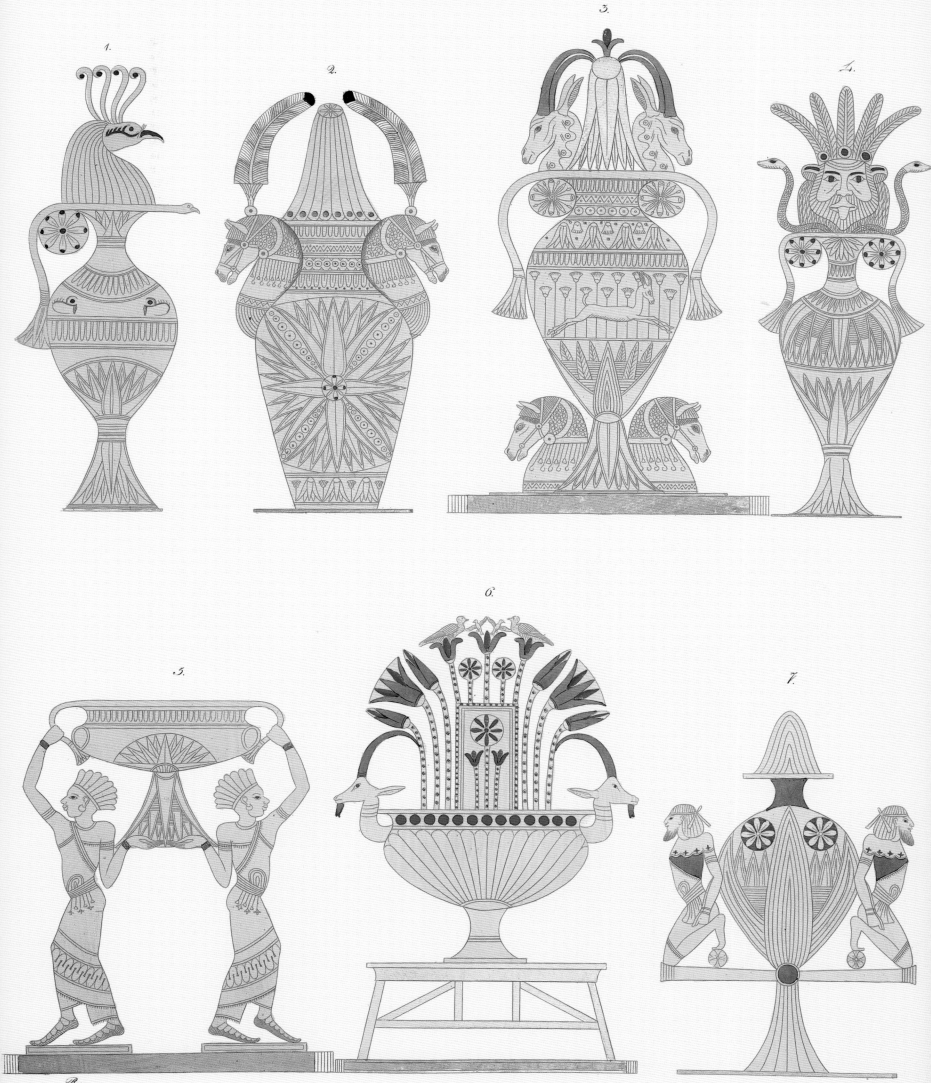

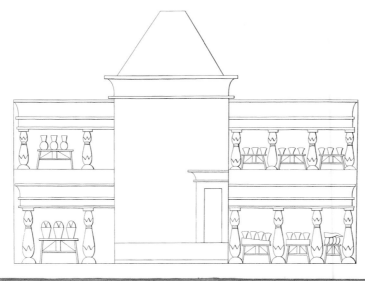

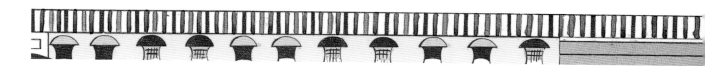

218-219
Scenes of Domestic Life
Theban tomb
Volume II, Plate LXVIII

Here is Rosellini's description of this scene: "The exterior of a house" (top figure) and "Inner courtyard of a house with garden, where a feast is taking place" (left figure). The owner is entering with his two children and a maidservant, preceded by some women and a man bearing food and fresh water (bottom left). A large amount of food and drink is seen in the middle of the scene, which may be a rather uncommon example from private life in ancient Egypt.

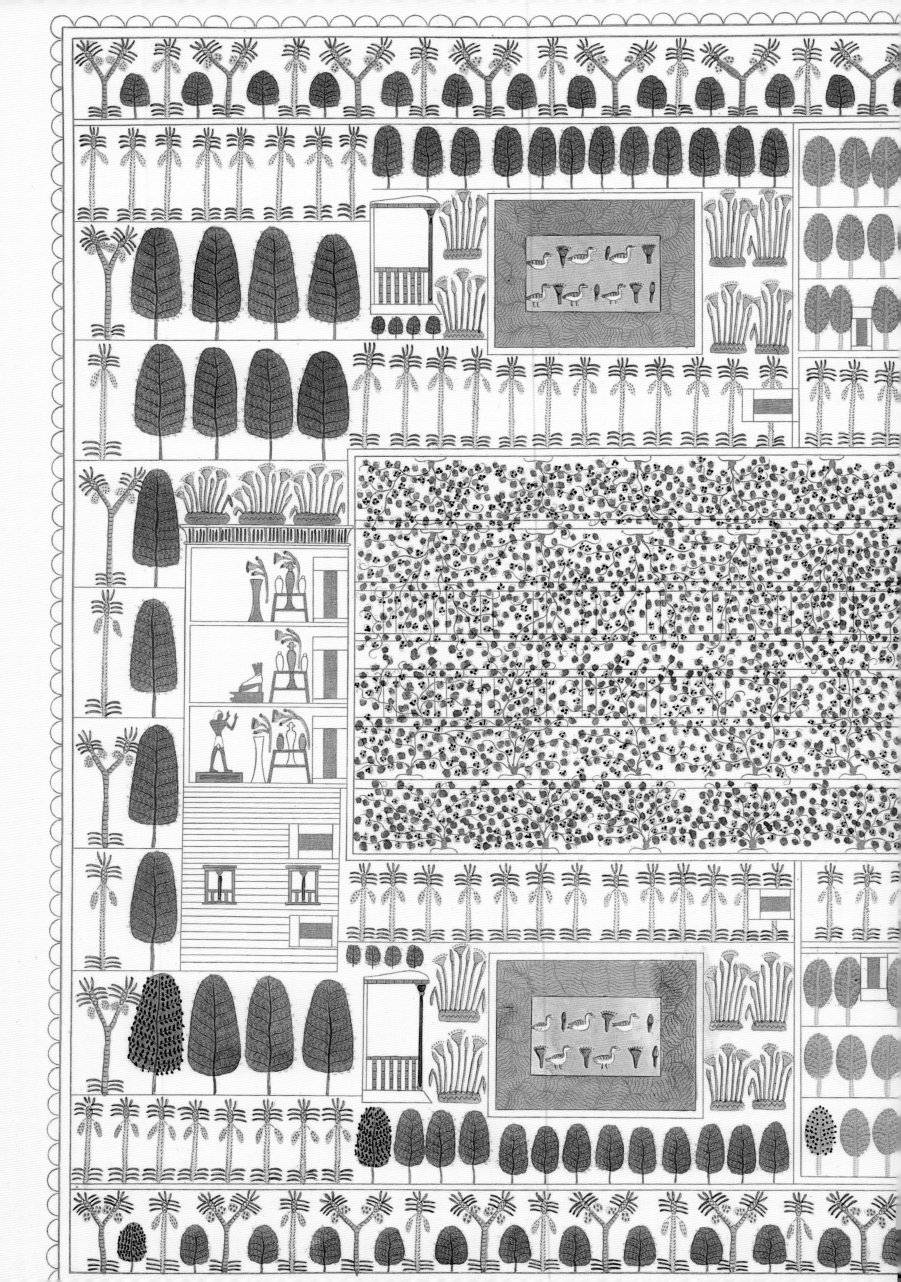

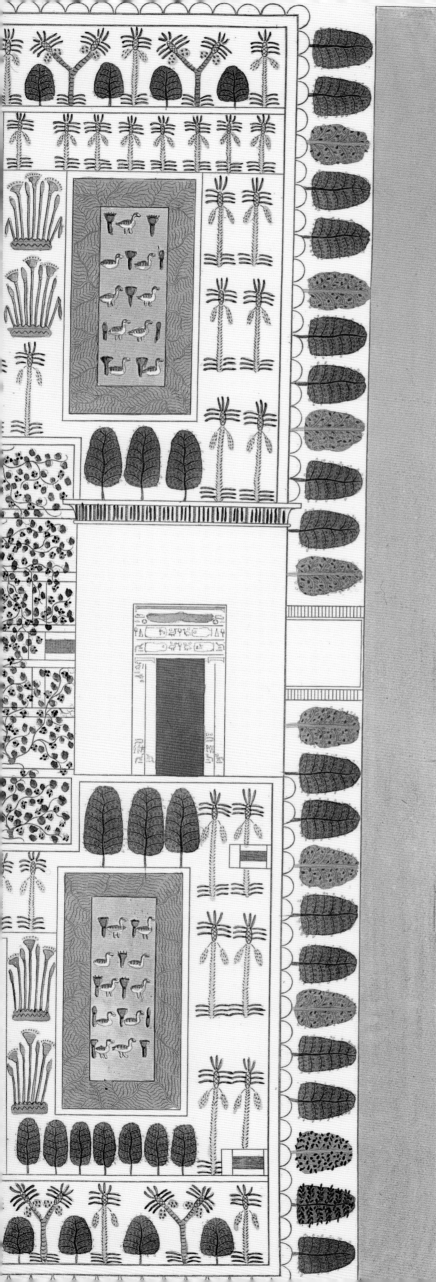

This scene is the only evidence
of what remains of the 'Garden
of Amun,' which was drawn in a
nobleman's tomb. In fact, the scene
no longer exists, because it was
either removed or destroyed after the
Franco-Tuscan expedition.
The entire garden is illustrated
with plan and elevation drawings, in
keeping with the particular canons
of Egyptian painting. In the middle
is a vineyard, while all around there
are paths lined with palm and
sycamore trees. Papyrus plants and
pools in which ducks are swimming
elegantly round off this bucolic scene.

This plate has examples of polychrome decoration and ornaments on the walls and ceilings of tombs, royal palaces, and private mansions. Besides the geometric and plant motifs, there is a marked preference for stylized plants or flowers. The spiral shown above and in the middle, on the other hand, is a feature typical of the Aegean civilization and was adopted by Egyptian art in the Middle Kingdom. Note the motif of the star-studded ceiling so common to many tombs.

M.C.

Here are other examples of friezes and decoration on the vaults and floors of tombs, temples, and private houses.

The latter were often decorated with checkered geometric motifs or with birds in flight. The different motifs drew inspiration from the patterns on the fabric usually used to conceal the beams that supported the ceilings in patrician houses.

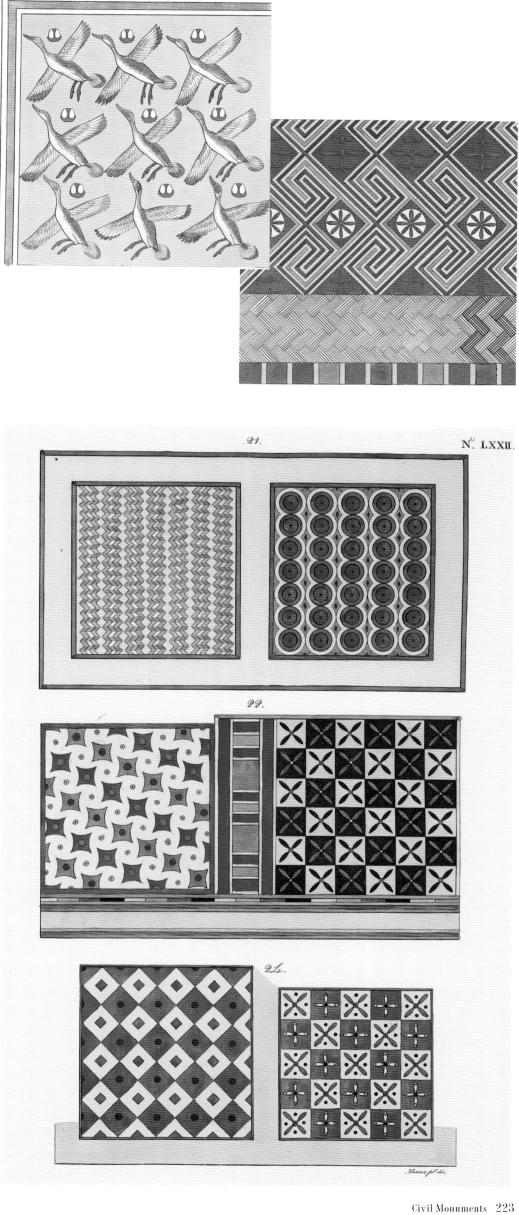

224-225
EXAMPLES OF DECORATIVE ART
THEBAN TOMBS
VOLUME II, PLATE LXXIII

Further examples of ancient
Egyptian decorative art: in the
upper register, checkered, floral,
or geometric decorative motifs
in aristocratic homes; below,
three flower-shaped and plant-shaped
wall socles.

224 BOTTOM AND 225 BOTTOM AND RIGHT
FURNITURE AND ORNAMENTS
THEBAN TOMBS
VOLUME II, PLATE LXXIV

Besides some ornamental motifs
similar to those described in the
preceding plate, here is an interesting
range of furniture, including a wooden
folding chair whose legs end in
duck heads, and a bed or divan with
a lion's head and paws.

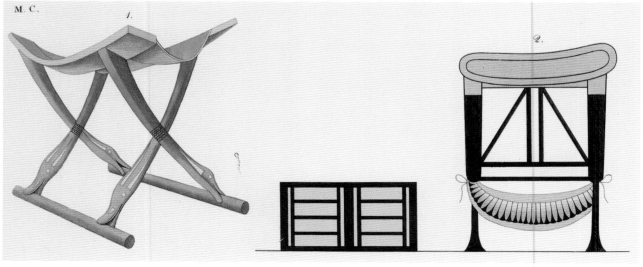

226-227
FURNITURE AND ORNAMENTS
THEBAN TOMBS
VOLUME II, PLATE LXXV

This plate shows furnishings used in religious and royal circles.
At top left, a royal bed with four incense burners, the figure of the pharaoh making offerings, and two figures of the goddess Merhyt; on the pedestal is a series of cartouches with the names and prenomen of Ramesses IX. These are followed by a sedan chair with a statuette of the pharaoh, the goddess Isis who is protecting him with her wings, and the goddess Nekhbet in the guise of a vulture. The upper register ends with a tiger pelt used as a rug. Below left are a cedar wood naos or shrine, a granite sphinx, and two cubic thrones.

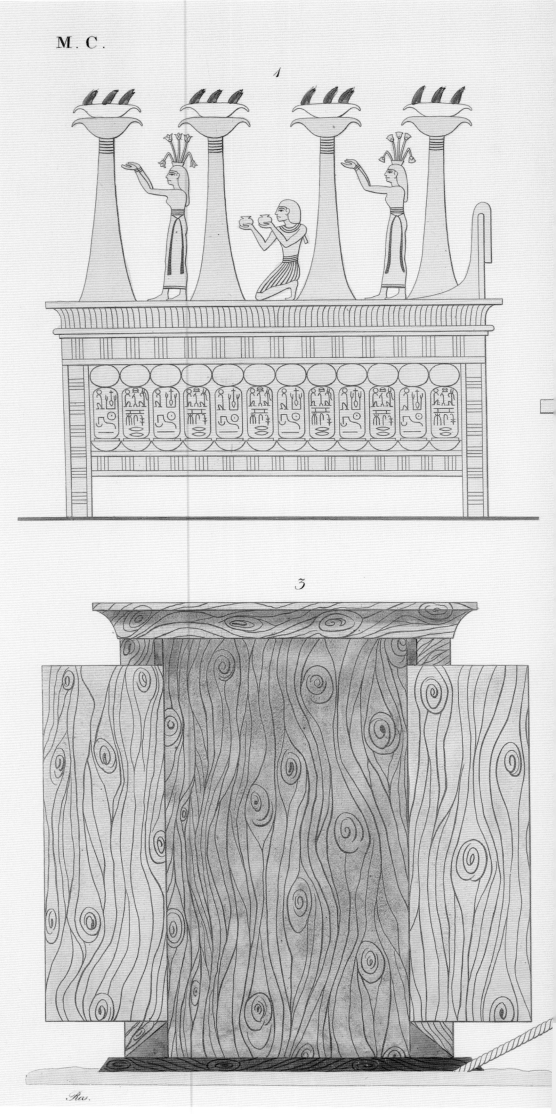

1.

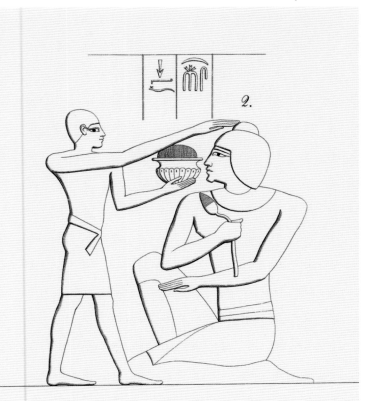

2.

3.

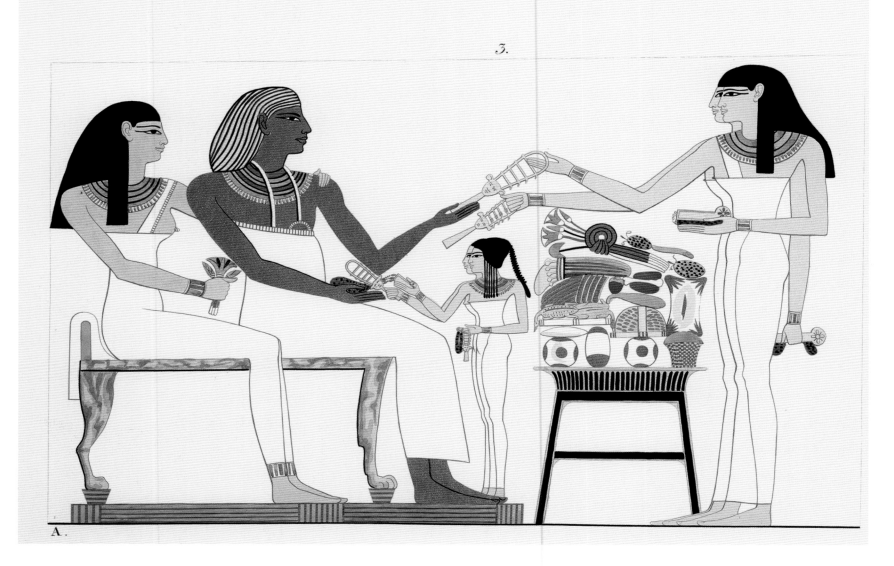

A.

228
FUNERARY OFFERINGS
TOMBS IN AL-KAB AND THEBES
VOLUME II, PLATE LXXVIII

Above, a servant is offering his lord a bowl and is putting a bar of perfumed fat on his head. Below, in front of a richly laid table of offerings, the deceased couple receive sistra and necklaces from their daughters.

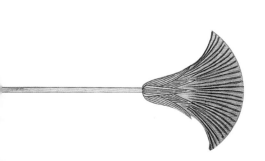

229
JEWELS AND FLABELLA
THEBAN TOMBS
VOLUME II, PLATE LXXX

These are illustrations of pectorals, necklaces, and bracelets, generally made of gold and embellished with semiprecious stones or enamel. These are followed by a series of flabella–large fans that were usually made in the shape of a papyrus

and with ostrich feathers. In almost all cultures jewels have always had a particular fascination. The ancient Egyptians also attached great importance to various kinds of jewelry, which they usually wore both as ornaments and for their powers to ward off evil: the luxurious funerary equipment in the tombs of some pharaohs are examples of this latter function.

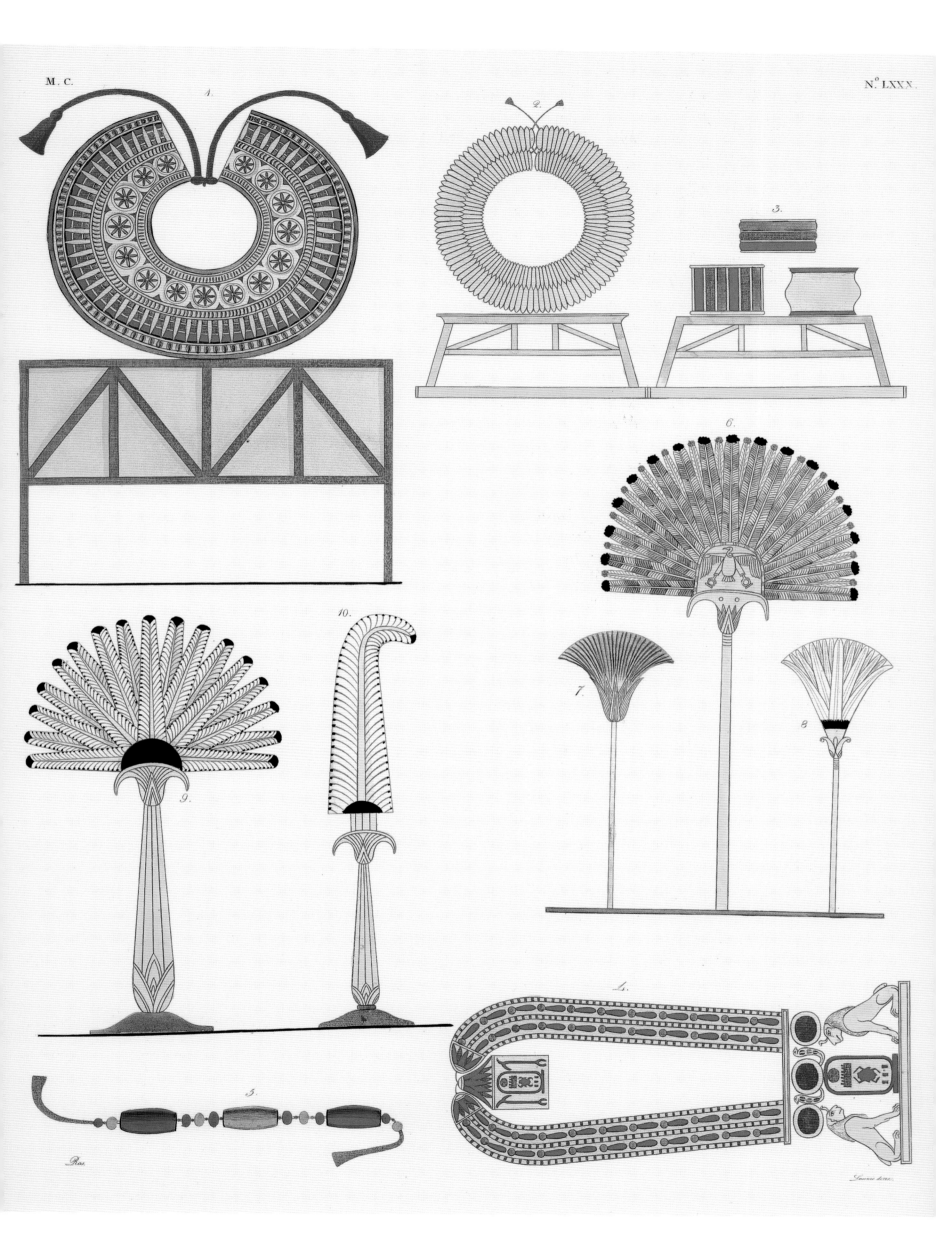

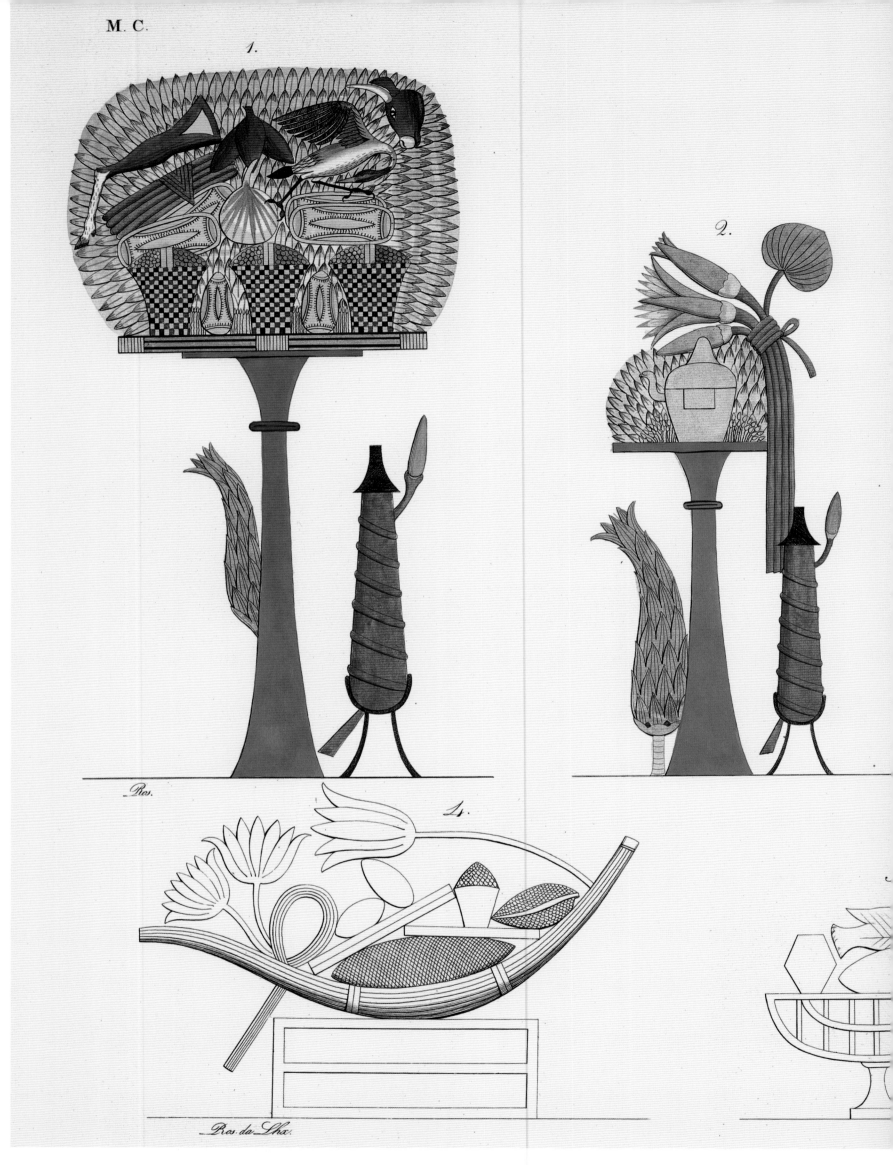

1.

2.

Ros.

4.

Ros. da Dha.

230-231
FOOD OFFERINGS
THEBES, VALLEY OF THE KINGS
VOLUME II, PLATE LXXXVIII

The funerary equipment the ancient Egyptians placed inside the tombs also included food and drink, which were needed to guarantee the survival of the deceased in the afterlife. According to their religious beliefs, mural paintings of food offerings would assure—magically and eternally—the continuation of earthly existence. Among the drawings copied from royal tombs, are these two tables of offerings from a tomb at Biban al-Muluk: in the first (figure 1), among

3.

R.

6.

Ros.

vegetable leaves, are baskets
filled with fruit, some bread or sweets,
an ox's leg and head, and a duck.
The second table (figure 2) has
a jug and lotus buds.

Both tables have slender amphorae
beside them made more lovely by a
charming lotus bud that
is still closed. The next scene is
quite different in that it is not a

still-life: while one man is making
an offering of parts of an ox,
another is fanning the flames of two
perfume burners which are probably
consecrated to the deceased.

232 LEFT
DIFFERENT KINDS OF BEDS
THEBES, TOMB OF RAMESSES III
VOLUME II, PLATE XCII

This plate presents drawings of wooden beds (figures 4, 5, 6, and 7), for both domestic and funerary use whose legs rest on lions' paws. The funerary beds (figures 1, 2, and 3) are more richly decorated and elegant, and call to mind the cow-headed goddess Mehet-Weret, the hippopotamus-headed goddess Taweret, and the goddess Isis-Mehet in the guise of a lioness. The first two beds have mirrors with handles in the shape of a papyrus and lotus flower next to them.

232-233 TOP AND 233 CENTER
FURNITURE
THEBAN TOMBS
VOLUME II, PLATE XC

Examples of chairs and thrones are illustrated here. The chair with a low back (figure 1) and the round offering table (figure 7) date from the Old and Middle Kingdom respectively. The chairs with tall backs and lion's feet and the folding stool (figures 2, 3, and 4) mostly date from the New Kingdom. The plate also depicts a cube-shaped throne decorated with different geometric motifs.

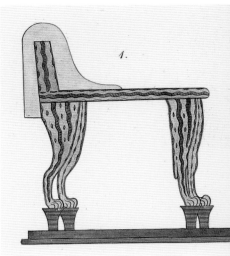

232-233 BOTTOM
ROYAL THRONES
THEBES, TOMB OF RAMESSES III
VOLUME II, PLATE XCI

These thrones have the same shape as the table in the preceding plate, and their elegance is heightened by the precious cloth upholstery. The side panels are covered with symbolic decoration in gold, semiprecious stones, or ivory.

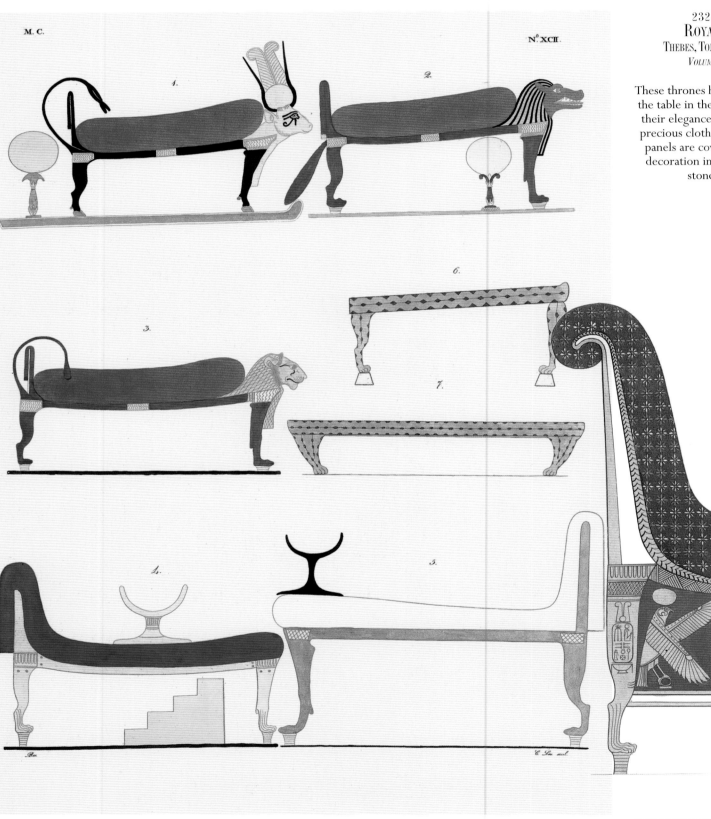

234-235
HARPISTS
Thebes, Tomb of Ramesses III
Volume III, Plate XCVII

These are the famous images of two blind harpists, who were perhaps priests. With shaven heads and long pleated gowns, they are holding two large, beautifully colored harps whose sound boxes are decorated with the image of the pharaoh; he is shown wearing the red crown of Lower Egypt (left) and the double crown, the symbol of Upper and Lower Egypt (right). The tomb of Ramesses III was discovered in 1768 by the Scottish explorer James Bruce and the Italian Luigi Balugani during their adventurous and dramatic journey to present-day Ethiopia in search of the source of the Nile.

236 AND 237
WOMEN MUSICIANS AND DANCERS
THEBAN TOMBS
VOLUME III, PLATE XCVIII

A group of women with shaven heads
are playing and dancing to the rhythm of
a lute and quadrangular drum (top left).
Below are women playing stringed and
wind instruments. Note the harps,
which have different shapes and from
three to thirteen strings. Music and
dance were widespread art forms
in ancient Egypt.

238-239
WOMEN MUSICIANS AND DANCERS
THEBES, TOMB OF NEBAMUN,
AND BENI HASAN
Volume III, Plate XCIX

This beautiful drawing shows the
famous fragment of wall painting
which, during Rosellini's time, was in
the tomb of Nebamun, and is now kept
in the British Museum, London. The
extremely rare frontal rendering of the
musicians shows that the artist was
trying to surpass the limits of
conventional ancient Egyptian
iconography, which called for portraits
only in profile. While the woman at
right is playing the double flute, the
others—splendidly dressed and with the
characteristic perfumed cone on their
heads—accompany her by clapping their
hands and perhaps singing.

238 TOP AND 239 TOP
MUSICIANS AND DANCERS
THEBES, TOMB OF NEBAMUN,
AND BENI HASAN
Volume III, Plate XCIX

In the upper pictures, women rehearse
dance steps while others move to the
rhythm of drums.

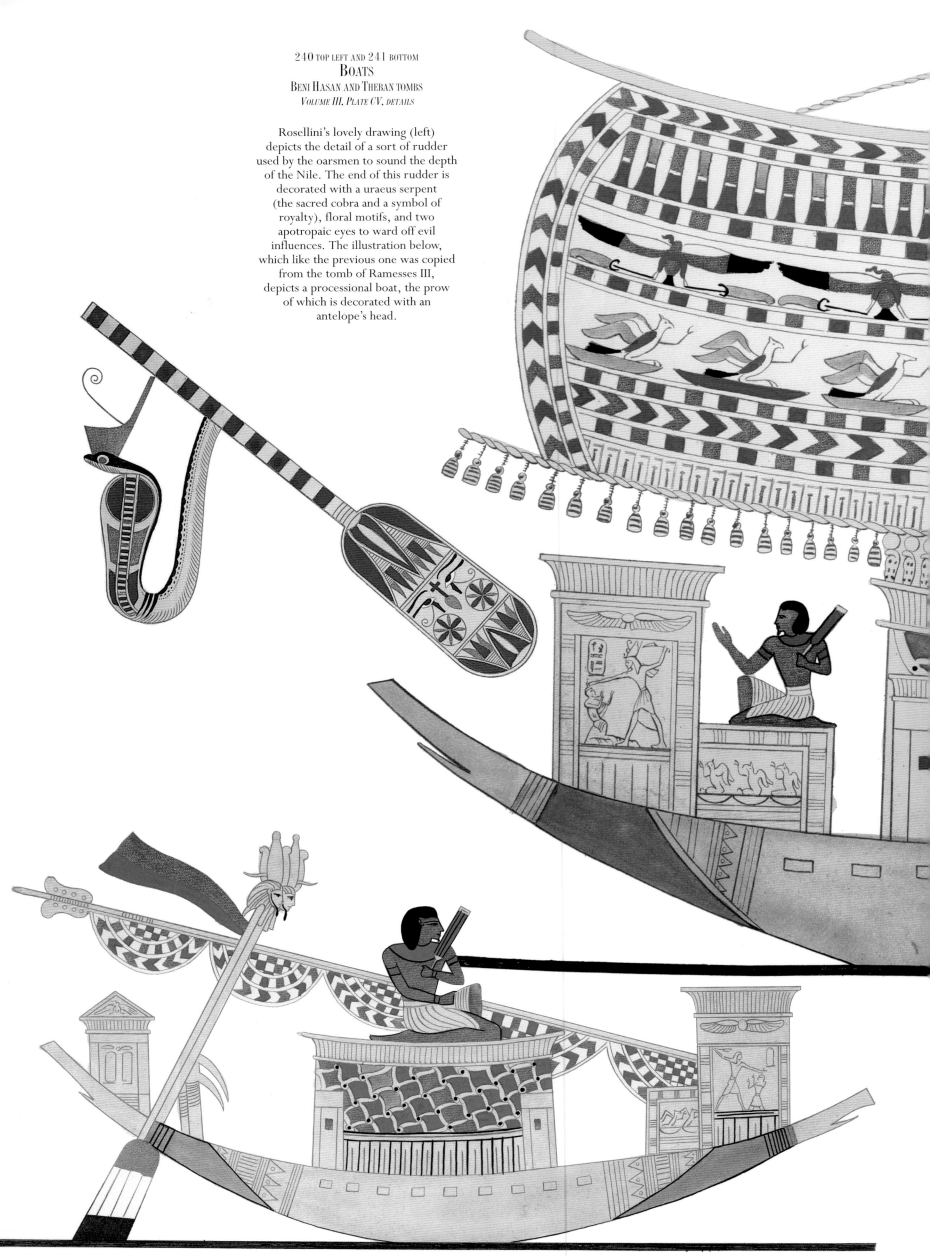

Rosellini's lovely drawing (left)
depicts the detail of a sort of rudder
used by the oarsmen to sound the depth
of the Nile. The end of this rudder is
decorated with a uraeus serpent
(the sacred cobra and a symbol of
royalty), floral motifs, and two
apotropaic eyes to ward off evil
influences. The illustration below,
which like the previous one was copied
from the tomb of Ramesses III,
depicts a processional boat, the prow
of which is decorated with an
antelope's head.

240 bottom and 240-241
ROYAL BOATS
THEBES, TOMB OF RAMESSES III
VOLUME III, PLATE CVII

Since the Nile was the only major means of communication in ancient Egypt, the most common means of transport had to be boats. Though they were skilful in river navigation, the Egyptians were never great navigators and were easily outdone by other peoples, including the Phoenicians, who were known as the 'carters of the sea.' Small- or medium-sized Egyptian boats were made of acacia or sycamore, since tall trees such as pine or cedar did not grow in ancient Egypt. However, cedar was imported from Lebanon to build large ships or those used by the pharaohs. This plate shows two royal sailboats with spacious central cabins protected by mats and smaller cabins at the prow and stern. Both boats, watched over by guards, have large sails and are painted with brightly colored geometric motifs. Symbols and trimming decorate the oars, which have heads with royal crowns.

242-243
ROYAL BOATS
THEBES, TOMB OF RAMESSES III
PLATE CVIII

In the illustration at left,
"two boats, driven by the wind"
(Rosellini, III, 146) and with their sails
unfurled, "proceed in convoy"
(Champollion, III, 3); in the
illustration at right, the boat, complete
with a royal throne and royal symbols,
sails down the river. In the latter,
there is a seated guard holding
a *herep* scepter, the "insignia of
that office."

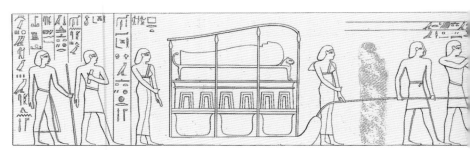

244-245 top and center
FUNERARY SCENES
TOMBS IN THEBES AND AL-KAB
VOLUME III, PLATE CXXVII

The upper representation, copied from the tomb of Amenemope, depicts the mummy which, after the propitiatory rituals carried out by one of the deceased's two sons, is about to be placed in a naos, then put on a boat pulled by cows. A woman, perhaps his wife, is weeping. In the other two figures, copied from tombs at al-Kab, the mummy is being transported toward its burial site.

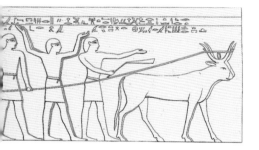

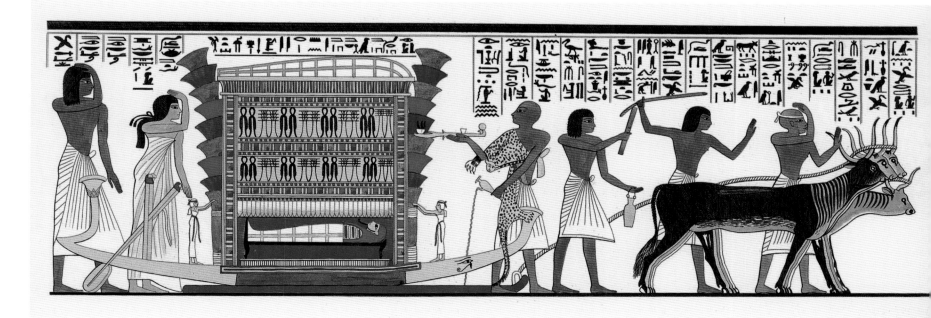

244 BOTTOM AND 245 BOTTOM
FUNERARY SCENES
THEBAN TOMB
VOLUME III, PLATE CXXVIII

The scene at right shows a mummy being transported. Placed first in a naos on a boat, it is then gently put on a sled pulled by four heifers. A priest, wearing the typical panther pelt, offers incense and carries out purification rituals. At left, among the grieving persons and the group of professional mourners, four men are bearing the chest, surmounted by the figure of Anubis in the guise of a jackal, that held the canopic jars containing the deceased's viscera.

246-247
FUNERARY SCENES
THEBAN TOMB
Volume III, Plate CXXIX

This plate depicts the conclusion
of the funeral ceremony. Besides
the mourning scene (above), there
is the priest carrying out the 'opening
of the mouth' funerary ritual,
which guaranteed the continuation
of life in the hereafter. Anubis, the
jackal-headed god of mummification,
sees to the final details of embalming
the deceased, who is on a sort
of catafalque, under which the
four canopic jars containing the
deceased's viscera can be seen.
The goddesses Isis (left) and Nephthys
(right) watch over the ceremony.

248 top
FUNERARY BOATS
BENI HASAN
VOLUME III, PLATE CXXX

This plate depicts two boats used
for the burial ritual. Both have
a chamber adorned with latticework
matting. Above, men and women mourn.

248 center and bottom
FUNERARY BOATS
BENI HASAN
VOLUME III, PLATE CXXXI

More illustrations of boats used in
the burial ritual. The two upper scenes
depict the transport of funerary goods,
while below women grieve before
the mummy of the deceased.

249
FUNERARY SCENES
THEBAN TOMBS
VOLUME III, PLATE CXXXIV

The goddess of the sycamore tree
(top and right) offers fruit to the dead
couple. The scene below, similar to
the one already described in plate
CXXIX, shows the god Anubis next
to the deceased. The latter's *ba*, or soul,
depicted as a human-headed bird,
flies over the deceased and places
near his nose a sailboat and a
scepter–symbols of the vital breath
indispensable to guarantee rebirth.

250
SETI I AMONG GODS
THEBES, TOMB OF SETI I
PLATE LIX

In this scene the pharaoh is presented by the god Horus to Osiris, the principal god in the domain of the dead, who is here seated on the throne in mummy wrapping. Behind Osiris is Amentet, the goddess of the West, who is ready to receive the dead. This beautiful drawing by Nestor L'Hôte is completed by multicolored friezes and inscriptions, among which are the pharaoh's names in the two cartouches.

251
SETI I AND HATHOR
THEBES, TOMB OF SETI I
PLATE LVIII

This plate illustrates a relief that is now kept in the National Archaeological Museum in Florence but which at the time of the Franco-Tuscan expedition was in Seti I's burial chamber. The pharaoh, in a rich transparent robe, is received by the goddess Hathor, who offers him her necklace, which will guarantee him protection and prosperity. The tomb, discovered by Belzoni, is considered the most beautiful in the Valley of the Kings.

The scene, enclosed among the signs
of the firmament and mountain
(the latter is a symbol of the western
necropolis), is a double portrait of
Ramesses X, the penultimate Twentieth

Dynasty pharaoh, who is kneeling while offering the eye of Horus to the sun-god Ra. The latter is represented as a disk containing the beetle Khepri, a form of Ra as the rising sun, and the ram-headed god Atum as the setting sun. The scene is completed with the goddesses Isis (left) and Nephthys (right).

This vast scene is a variation
of the 'weighing of the heart.'
Osiris is seated on his throne, holding
his scepter and the symbol of life,
and is about to receive nine persons
(the souls of nine dead people) whom
he is going to judge. A balance,
carried by a mummiform spirit,
is ready to weigh these individuals'
deeds on Earth.
The souls that are judged to be
guilty return in animal guise,
that is to say, they are sent back
to Earth in the form of animals,
which were considered symbols
of various sins. According to
Champollion, the image of the sow,
which is on a boat between two baboons,
represents the sin of greediness.
The jackal-headed god Anubis
and four mortuary genii with
gazelle heads, are witnessing
the judgment of the dead.

256 top
THE COURSE OF THE SUN
IN THE AFTERLIFE
THEBES, TOMB OF TAUSERT/SETNAKHTE
PLATE LXX

This is a symbolic scene regarding the birth of the sun-god Ra, who emerges from the waters of the underworld through a narrow passageway, first in the guise of a boy sucking on his finger, then as a beetle with a ram's head, and lastly as a solar disk. The lower register illustrates a ram-headed vulture with outspread wings, which completes the theological conceptions concerning the course of the sun in the domain of the dead and its rebirth, that is to say, the birth of a new day.

256 bottom and 257
OFFERINGS TO THE GODS
THEBES, TOMB OF RAMESSES III
PLATE LXXIV

This splendid procession of men and women personifying the Nile and some of the forty-two provinces of Egypt, completes this selection of illustrations from Rosellini's *Religious Monuments*. Among all the symbolic images bearing offerings of flowers, fruit, and birds to the various divinities, mention should be made of the manifestation of the Nile, the god Hapi: a hermaphroditic figure with drooping breasts and a swollen belly, he has a sort of headdress made of papyrus, which bears the plant which is his symbol (top left).

EXPLORERS AND ARTISTS
IN THE VALLEY OF THE KINGS

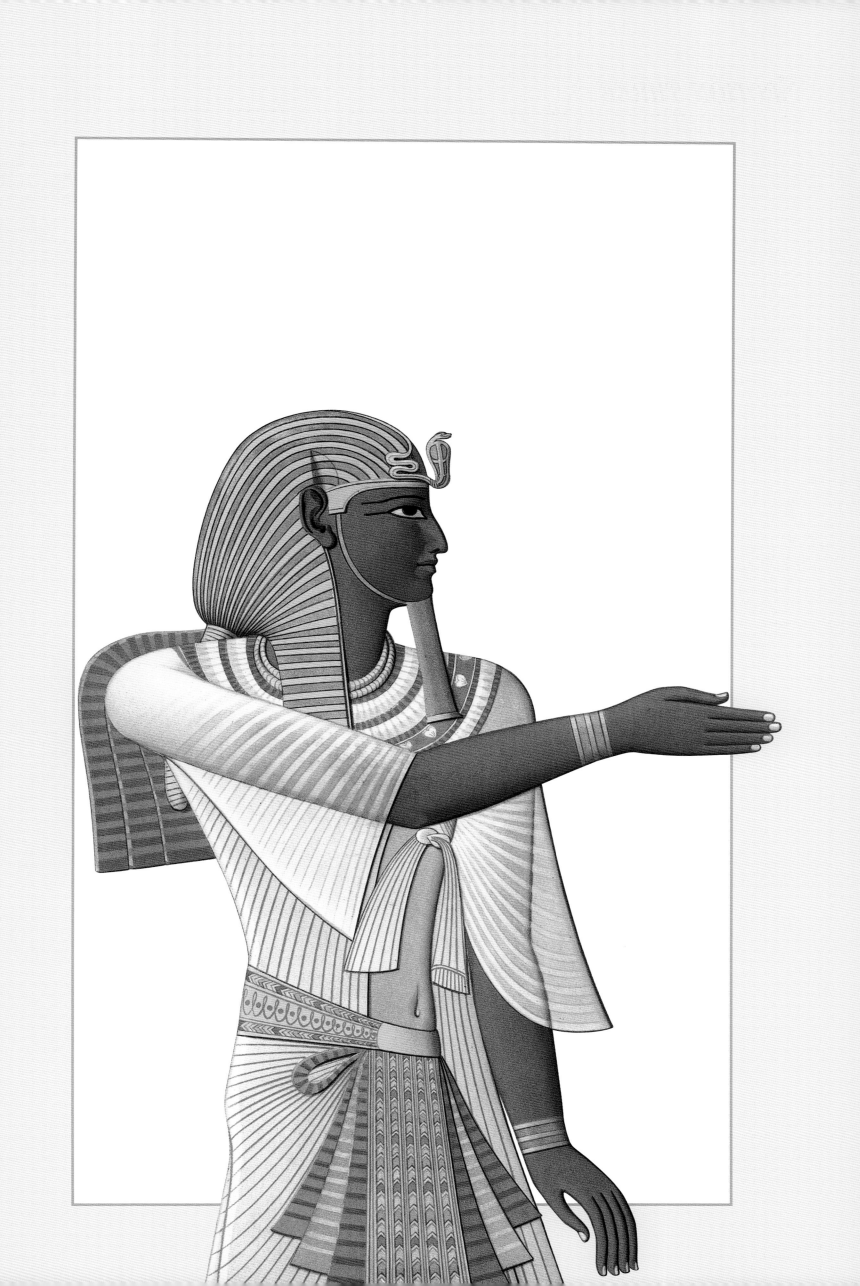

Foreword

The nineteenth century was a busy time in Thebes. Ancient Egyptian art and architecture were all the rage in Europe, and scores of travelers were making their way up the Nile to see firsthand what everyone agreed was one of the world's most fascinating sites. Among those visitors was a number of highly skilled artists who sought to record in sketches and watercolors the landscape of Thebes and the hundreds of beautifully decorated monuments that lay there. Sometimes their drawings were made as aides-memoire in personal journals or as contributions to scholarly surveys of Egyptian culture. Some were intended for interior designers back in Europe who catered to the Egyptomania sweeping the continent. Whatever their motivation, these adventurous and talented artists left behind brilliant records of the monuments of Thebes as they were over a century ago.

In many cases, these records are all we have. Many of the monuments they recorded have since been destroyed by erosion, water, vandalism, and theft, and the modern-day Egyptologist must rely heavily on these nineteenth-century paintings to reconstruct badly damaged tomb and temple walls. The paintings have proved essential to our knowledge of ancient Egypt. But they can be appreciated in their own right, too: they are not only accurate records, they are also works of art, elegant testimonials to their artist's keen eye and aesthetic sensibility.

No less fascinating than the images are the stories of the artists who made them. Always colorful and often downright eccentric, these dedicated men worked in arduous conditions, often threatened by violence and disease. Their lives are told in fascinating detail in this volume, and certainly justify the high regard in which they are held by modern scholars. It is no exaggeration to claim that Egyptology today would be much the poorer were it not for the works of the nineteenth-century explorers and artists described in this book. Their work is every bit as important to our field of study as that of modern epigraphers and photographers. It proudly stands as one of the pillars of our discipline.

Kent R. Weeks
Director
Theban Mapping Project

Contents

259
MERENPTAH
BY E.P. D'AVENNES

260-261
THEBAN TOMB
CIVIL MONUMENTS
IPPOLITO ROSELLINI

262-263
BERNARDINO DROVETTI
VOYAGE DANS LE LEVANT
BY L.N.P.A. FORBIN

263
ILLUSTRATION
CULT MONUMENTS
IPPOLITO ROSELLINI

Introduction

Among the earliest tourists to western Thebes were the Egyptians themselves. In the early Eighteenth Dynasty (ca. 1500-1450 B.C.), scribes visited an offering chapel that had been dedicated by the vizier Antefoker to his mother Senet. This brightly painted rock-cut chapel was already 500 years old, having been carved in the early Twelfth Dynasty, during the reign of Senwosret I (ca. 1950 B.C.). Some of the visitors just wrote their names—"the scribe Siamen came to see this tomb." Others included a funerary offering to the dead, and a few commented on the tombs beauty—"He found it like heaven in its interior," "They found it exceedingly pleasant in their hearts."

More than a thousand years later, Greek and Roman travelers left their names on the temples, tombs and statues of the western plain. To these visitors, the already ancient city on the east bank of the Nile—called *Waset* by the Egyptians—was known as the hundred-gated Thebes, a designation first recorded in Homer's Iliad. One of the most popular attractions was the Valley of the Kings where fourteen tombs contain more than 2000 Greek and Latin graffiti. By far the favorite, with nearly one thousand graffiti, was the tomb of Ramesses VI (KV 9 - ca. 1140 B.C.). Located in the center of the Valley, this huge rock-cut tomb is decorated with graphic funerary texts and vignettes that must have seemed as strange to

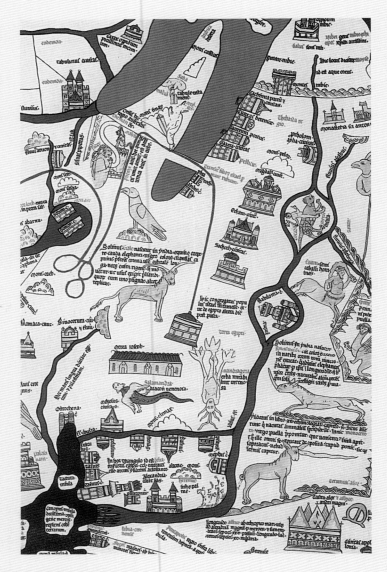

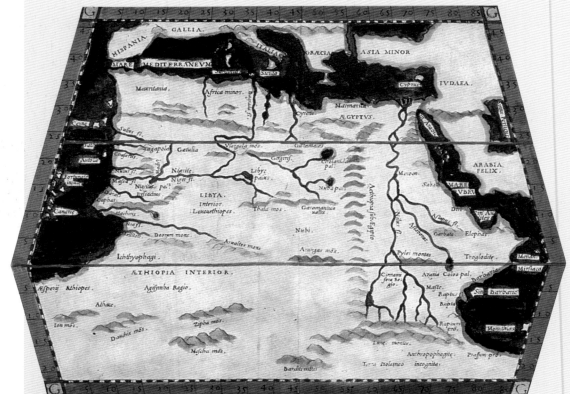

264 TOP

In this detail from the Mappa Mundi, drawn by Richard of Haldingham in 1290, the word "Thebaidea", a term applied to a large portion of Upper Egypt, is written in red between the Red Sea town of Berenice and the Nile, below the mountains separating Egypt from Nubia to the south.

264 BOTTOM

This sixteenth century map, drawn by Jacopo Gastaldi, is based on one drawn by Claudius Ptolemaeus, who lived in the second century. At that time, the kingdom of Meroe, whose capital is prominently indicated along the Nile, was a powerful rival to Roman control of Egypt.

265

This detail of a map, copied in the eleventh century from one dating to the eighth century, shows how little was known of Africa, which has been reduced to Libya, Egypt, and Ethiopia. The "island of Meroe," surrounded here by the Nile and included within Egypt, is actually a huge region in southern Sudan.

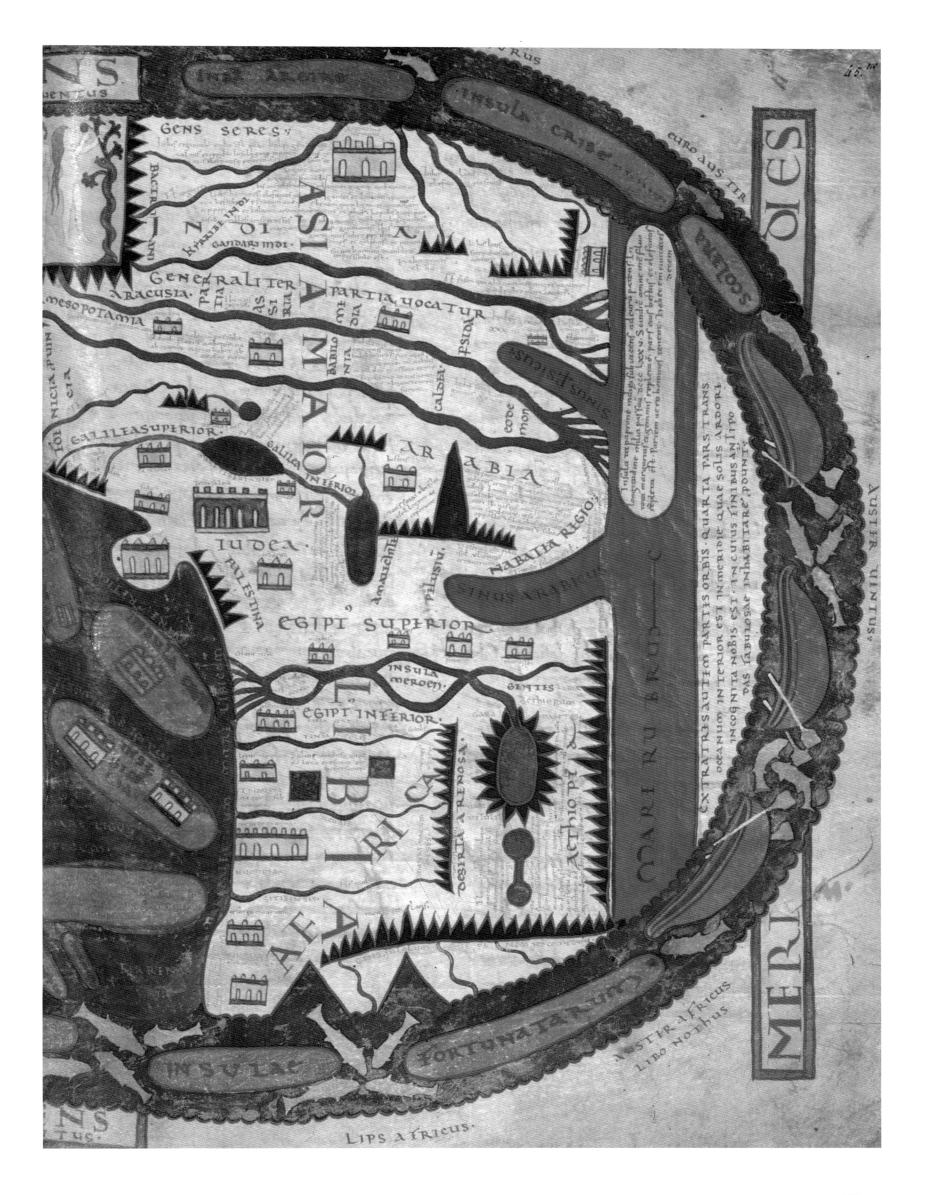

these early western tourists as they did to the European travelers who arrived more than a thousand years later. In Roman times, the tomb was identified as belonging to Memnon, a mythical king of Ethiopia, who had fought in the Trojan war and been killed by Achilles.

Another popular stopping place was in the flood plain where two colossal statues, measuring more than fifteen meters (fifty feet) in height, dominate the landscape.

Dozens of classical graffiti cover the base and ankles of the northern colossus, identifying it as an image of Memnon. This statue had been damaged in such a way that it emitted a strange sound at sunrise. Since Memnon was the son of Eos, goddess of the dawn, the sound was interpreted as Memnon greeting his mother. Among the visitors who waited to hear the statue speak was the emperor Hadrian (A.D. 130). In reality, these seated quartzite giants (still called the colossi of Memnon) once flanked the entrance to the mortuary temple of Amenhotep III (ca. 1375 B.C.). Amenhotep had built the largest temple in western Thebes, but the great entrance pylon was of mud-brick which eventually melted away with the encroachment of the annual Nile flood. The reliefs, statues, and

Perhaps the most famous of the ancient visitors to Egypt was Herodotus. In the mid-fifth century B.C., Egypt was under Persian rule, but the Greek historian seems to have traveled freely, sailing up the Nile as far as Aswan. The information he gathered from priests and his own observations filled book II of his *History*, which was a popular resource for later European travelers.

Another important Classical source was written by Diodorus Siculus, a scholar of Greek descent living in Sicily in the time of Julius Caesar. The first book of his history of the world was devoted to Egypt and includes a number of descriptions of western Thebes, many of them based on earlier literary references. For example, Diodorus paraphrases a description by Hecataeus of a monument belonging to King Ozymandias. This seems to be the mortuary temple of Ramesses II (identified as the Memnonium by early European travelers, but now called the Ramesseum) and includes the fallen colossus of the king, whose throne name, Usermaatra, is probably the source of the name Ozymandias. This statue was reported to have a completely mythical inscription that was later reinterpreted by the British poet, Percy Shelley "My name is

Ozymandias, King of Kings: Look on my works, ye Mighty, and despair!"

In regard to the Valley of the Kings, Diodorus states that: "...the priests claim to find records of forty-seven royal tombs, but they say that by the reign of Ptolemy son of Lagus only seventeen remained; and many of these were in ruins at the time of our visit..." (Book I, 46; trans. Murphy).

Not long after Diodorus, the geographer Strabo visited western Thebes: "Here are two colossal figures near one another, each consisting of a single stone. One is entire; the upper parts of the other, from the chair, are fallen down, the effect, it is said, of an earthquake. It is believed, that once a day a noise as of a slight blow issues from the part of the statue which remains in the seat and on its base. When I was at those places ... I heard a noise at the first hour (of the day), but whether proceeding from the base or from the colossus, or produced on purpose by some of those standing around the base, I cannot confidently assert." (Book XVII, Chapter I, paragraph 46; trans. Hamilton).

With the Arab conquest of Egypt, in the seventh century, access to ancient Thebes became restricted to Europeans, though Alexandria and

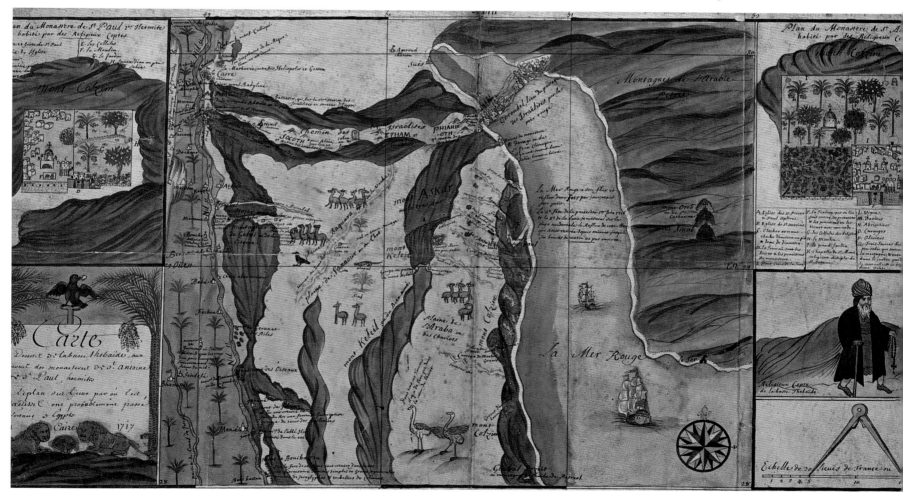

columns, made of sandstone or limestone, were reused in other structures, or were left to disintegrate over thousands of years in the damp soil. But traces of the column bases and statues were still visible to Richard Pococke, a British cleric who visited Thebes in January of 1738 and was one of the first European travelers to leave both drawings and descriptions of what he saw.

266
This map, by the Dutch cartographer Abraham Ortelius, first published in 1570, is far more detailed than earlier maps, and more accurate than many later ones. Thebes may be seen on the east bank just south of the large bend in the river. On the west bank, Ortelius has placed one of the principal monuments mentioned by Classical authors, the Memnonium.

267
The French Jesuit, Claude Sicard, traveled extensively in Egypt in the early eighteenth century. On his map of the country, he located dozens of ancient sites, including Thebes.

Cairo were still open to traders and pilgrims to the Holy Lands. As a result, although the pyramids at Giza and other northern sites were known to Europeans even in the middle ages, little was known about Egypt or the ancient monuments south of Cairo, a fact that is evident in early maps.

Beginning in the eighteenth century, however, a few intrepid travelers ventured farther up the Nile valley. One of the first was Claude Sicard (1677-1726) who had joined the Jesuits in 1692. In 1700, he had become a missionary to Syria and in 1707, he was sent to the Jesuit mission in Cairo and remained in Egypt until his death. Fluent in Arabic, and with a thorough knowledge of the classical writers, he is credited with being the first European in modern times to recognize the contemporary town of Luxor as the site of ancient Thebes. His purpose for being in Egypt was to bring the Coptic church under the authority of Rome, but he was also asked by Philippe d'Orleans, the French Regent, to make a record of the ancient monuments. Sicard eventually drew a map of Egypt on which he located 24 temples, 50 decorated tombs, and 20 pyramids.

Less than two decades after Sicard's death,

side, solitude, aridity, desolation, and death; on the other, temples, palaces, a beautiful river, vegetation, cultivated fields, herds, people, and all the movement of living nature."

The early nineteenth century also brought individuals such as Giovanni Belzoni and Jean Jacques Rifaud, who came not as tourists or scholars, but as the agents of the European consuls to Egypt, who had become avid collectors of Egyptian antiquities. These men invariably spent time in Thebes, one of the richest archaeological sites in the world. Belzoni's description of the impression created by the monuments is eloquent: "The most sublime ideas, that can be formed from the most magnificent specimens of our present architecture, would give a very incorrect picture of these ruins: for such is the difference, not only in magnitude, but in form, proportion, and construction, that even the pencil can convey but a faint idea of the whole. It appeared to me like entering a city of giants, who, after a long conflict, were all destroyed, leaving the ruins of their various temples as the only proofs of their former existence."

By the middle of the nineteenth century, the ancient Egyptian language had been deciphered, and dozens of individual travelers,

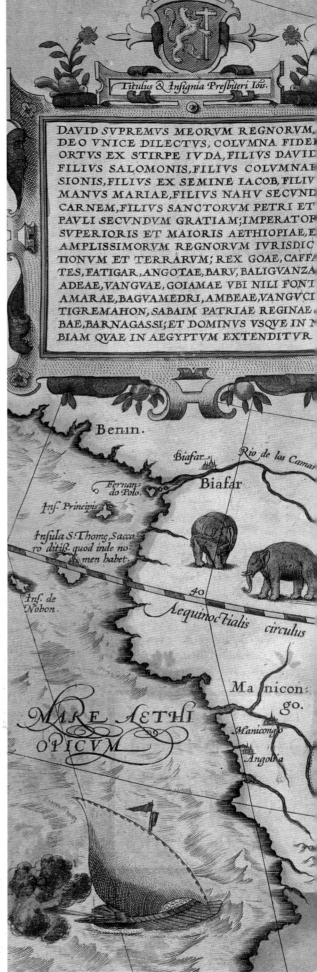

Richard Pococke and Ludwig Norden, traveling separately, journeyed up the Nile and returned home to publish illustrated accounts of their travels in Egypt. More than half a century later, the first of the great scientific expeditions arrived in Egypt with Napoleon's invading army. Their scholarly efforts, published as the multi-volumed *Description de l'Égypte* provided Europeans with the first comprehensive view of the monuments of Western Thebes.

While exploring the Valley of the Kings, a small group climbed to the top of the cliffs that separate this desert wadi from the western plain of the Nile valley. Perhaps the first Europeans to see this remarkable view, one of them (M. Costaz) described it thus: "It is impossible to imagine a contrast more striking than that presented by the two scenes that we had before our eyes: on one

scholars, adventurers, artists, and two more great scientific expeditions had explored and published volumes on the ruins of western Thebes. But even Richard Lepsius, leader of the Prussian expedition, was inspired to comment in a letter dated February 25, 1845: "Thebes...has been more explored than any other place by travelers and expeditions ... and we have only compared and supplied deficiencies in their labors, not done them afresh. We are also very far from imagining that we have exhausted the immense monumental riches to be found here. They who come after us with fresh information, and with the results of science further extended, will find new treasures in the same monuments, and obtain more instruction from them" (trans. Mackenzie). After a century and a half of further exploration, and discoveries, these observations remain valid today.

268
Between 1815 and 1819, the British antiquarian, W.J. Bankes traveled in Egypt and the Near East. During this journey, Bankes visited the temple of Philae, south of Aswan, and hired Giovanni Belzoni to transport an obelisk from there back to England. Bankes commissioned this view of the Giza pyramids and sphinx with Cairo in the distance.

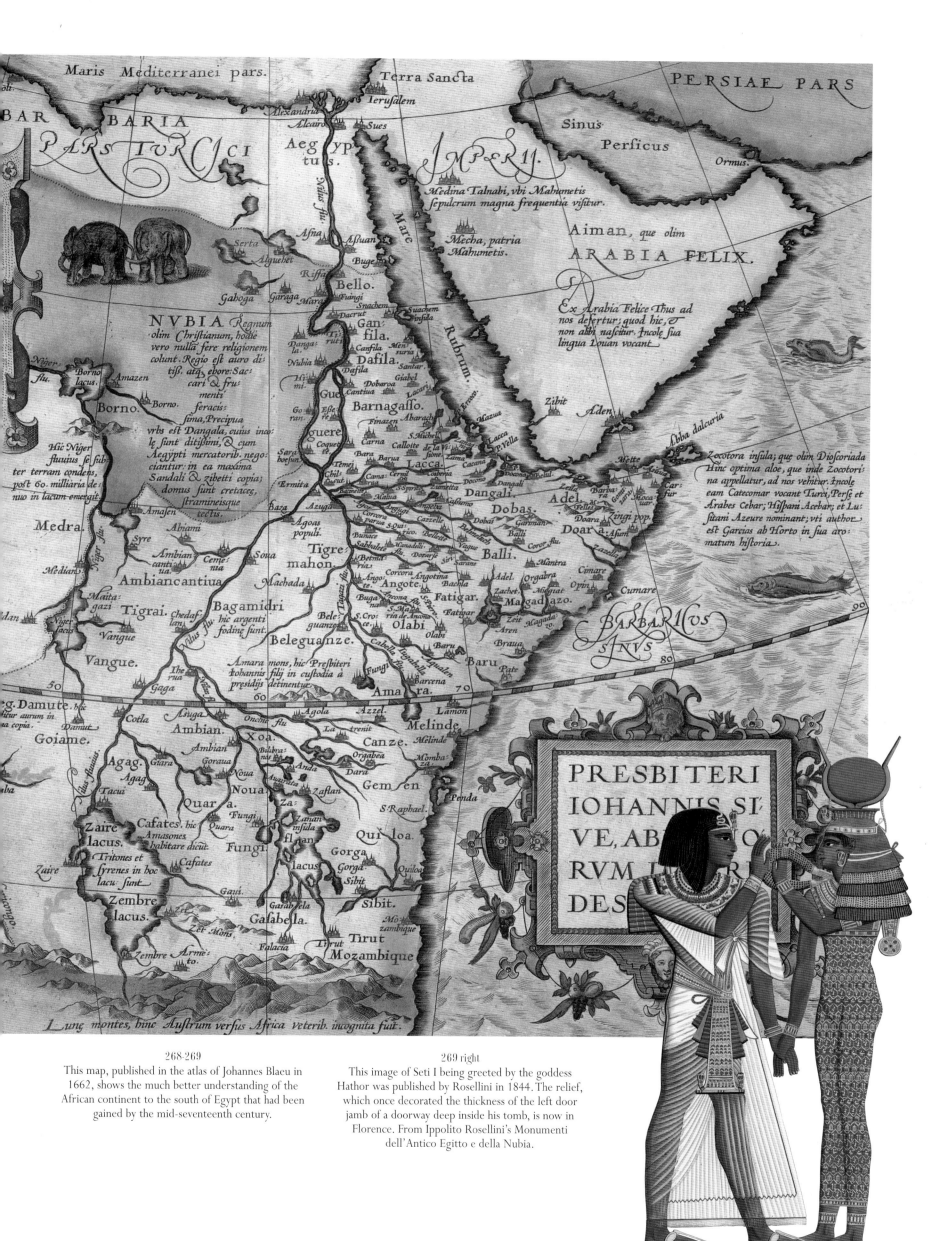

Maris Mediterranei pars.

Terra Sancta

PERSIAE PARS

Ierusalem

BAR · BARIA

Alexandria

Alcairo

Sues

Sinus

Persicus

Ormus.

PARS TVRCICI

Aegyptus.

IMPERII.

Medina Talnabi, vbi Mahumetis
sepulcrum magna frequentia visitur.

Serta

Alguehet

Asna

Assuan

Buge

Riffa

Mare

Mecha, patria
Mahumetis.

Aiman, que olim
ARABIA FELIX.

Bello.

Fiangi

Snachem

Suachem insula.

Ex Arabia Felice Thus ad
nos defertur; quod hic, &
non alibi nascitur. Incole sua
lingua Louan vocant

Gahoga

Garaga

Miara

Danga-
la.

Tiruti

Dacrit

Ganfila.

Menfuria

NVBIA Regnum
olim Christianum, hodie
vero nulla fere religionem
colunt. Regio est auro di-
tiss. atq; ebore: Sac-
cari & fru-
menti
feracis-
fima, Precipua
vrbs est Dangala, cuius incole sunt ditissimi, & cum
Aegypti mercatorib. nego-
ciantur: in ea maxima
Sandali & zibetti copia;
domus sunt cretaceq,
stramineisque
tectis.

Borno
lacus.

Amazen

Borno.

Borno

Dafila.

Canfila

Santar

Dafila

Guere

Dobaroa

Giabel

Lacari

Barnagasso.

Finazen

Abarach

S.Michel

Callote de la Vi-
sione

Lacca

P. Vella

Zibit

Aden

Abba dalcuria

Zocotora insula; que olim Dioscoriada
Hinc optima aloe, que inde Zocotori-
na appellatur, ad nos vehitur. Incole
eam Catecomar vocant Turci, Persæ et
Arabes Cebar; Hispani Acebar; et Lu-
sitani Azeure nominant; vti author
est Garcias ab Horto in sua aro-
matum historia.

Go
ran.

Esse
re

Hic Niger
fluuius se sub-
ter terram condens,
post 60. milliaria de-
nuo in lacum emergit.

Niger
flu.

Medra.

Syre

Ambian
canti-
ua

Ceme
nua

Sova

Maita-
gazi

Tigrai.

chedaf
lien

Bagamidri.
hic argenti
fodine sunt.

Ambiancantiua

Machada

Tigre-
mahon.

Sara
boesen

Ermita

Azuga

Agoas
populi.

Amasen

Abiami

Median

Niger flu.

Vangue

Niger
lacus.

Vangue.

Medra.

chedaf
lien

Bele
guanze

Beleguanze.

Temei

Chils
cucut

Bara

Barua

Cama

Cernil

Malua

Barnelit

Corcora
parua

S.Qui-
rico

S.Spiritus

Angeba

Cazelle

Bunace

Sabbalete

Betma-
rias

Ango-
te

Ancona
te

Carna

Callote de la Vi-
sione

Zama

Cacana

Docono

Dangali

Dangali.

Dobas.

Doar a.

Adel.

Ringi pop.

Adel

Balli.

Balli.

Garinman

Coror flu.

Vague

Sirt

Sarane

Amara mons, hic Presbiteri
Iohannis filij in custodia à
presidijs detinentur.

Ihe
rua

Gaga

Nilus flu.

Amara

Azzel

Damute. hic
itur aurum in
a copia.

Goiame.

Cotla

Asuga

Onchit flu.

Agola

La trenit

Melinde.

Melinde

Ambian.

Xoa

Canze.

Orgabea

Momba
za.

Ambian

Goraua

Noua

Anda

Auranta

Dara

Gemen

S.Raphael.

Agag.

Ghara

Quar
a.

Noua.

Za-

Zaflan

Penda

Agag

Tacui

Fungi

Quara

Zaman
insula

fl. nan

Quiloa.

Qui loa.

Zaire
lacus.

Cafates. hic
Amasones
habitare dicut.

Cafates

Gorga

Gorga.

Sibit

Tritones et
syrenes in hoc
lacu sunt

Gaui.

Sibit.

Zembre
lacus.

Zet Mons.

Gasabela

Galabella.

Mo
zambique

Tirut

Tirut
Mozambique

Zembre Arme
to.

Falacia

Lune montes, hinc Austrum versus Africa veterib. incognita fuit.

BARBARICVS
SINVS

PRESBITERI
IOHANNIS SI-
VE, AB...O-
RVM I...RI
DES...

268-269
This map, published in the atlas of Johannes Blaeu in
1662, shows the much better understanding of the
African continent to the south of Egypt that had been
gained by the mid-seventeenth century.

269 right
This image of Seti I being greeted by the goddess
Hathor was published by Rosellini in 1844. The relief,
which once decorated the thickness of the left door
jamb of a doorway deep inside his tomb, is now in
Florence. From Ippolito Rosellini's Monumenti
dell'Antico Egitto e della Nubia.

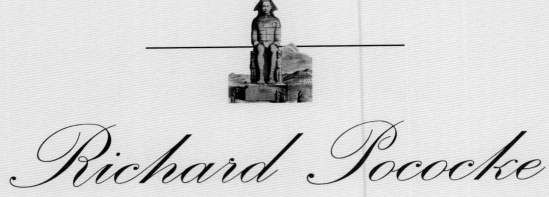

Richard Pococke

In 1737, the Reverend Richard Pococke (1704-1765) embarked on a journey that took him to archaeological sites of Egypt, western Asia, the Aegean islands and Greece. Having studied religion at Oxford, Pococke was familiar with the classical authors whose descriptions of the ancient sites he used as a guide for his own travels. Pococke arrived in Egypt in late September 1737. After exploring Lower Egypt, he sailed south from Cairo in early December, finally arriving in the Luxor area in mid-January 1738.

270
Pococke's view of western Thebes, though not precise, gives an impression of the magnificent landscape, and generally locates the sites mentioned in his text. A, Qurna village; B & C, tombs of New Kingdom officials; D, the Ramesseum; I, el-Qurn—the highest point on the west bank that also dominates the Valley of the Kings; K, "various other temples" (perhaps around the Valley of the Queens); L, Medinet Habu; M & N, the Colossi of Memnon; O & P, statues and column bases from the temple of Amenhotep III that were still visible in Pococke's day; Q, the wadi leading to the Valley of the Kings.

271
Though far from being an accurate plan of the site, Pococke's birds-eye view of the Valley of the Kings captures the rugged topography of this royal cemetery, dominated by the Qurn, which appears to be a pyramidal peek from this vantage point.

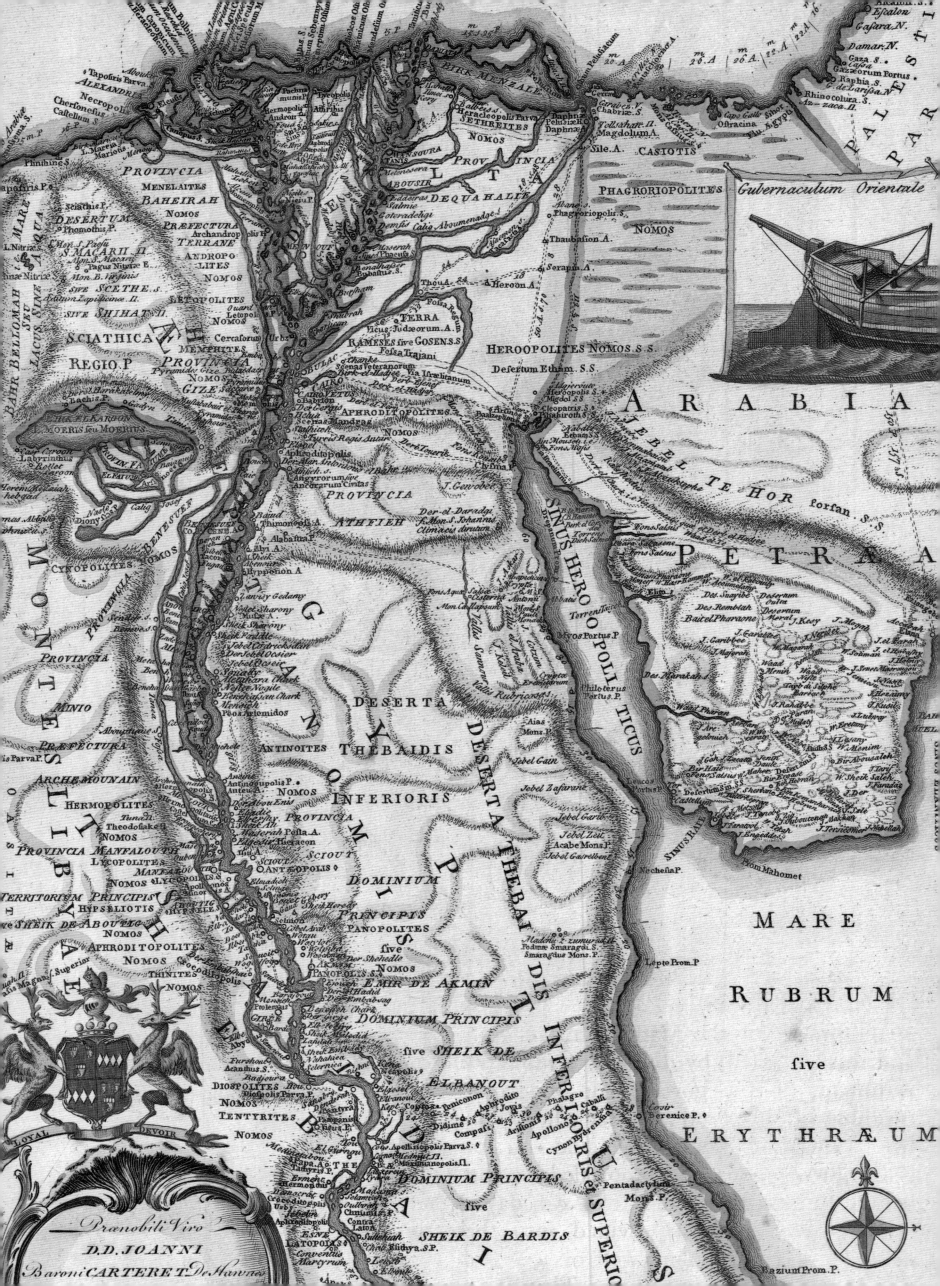

In the eighteenth century, travel in Egypt was a risky undertaking for European travelers, and before embarking on his jounrey up the Nile, Pococke had obtained letters of introduction to the local sheikhs and took along a variety of goods to present as gifts. These preparations allowed him relatively easy access to the antiquities on both banks of the river. After his arrival at Thebes, Pococke spent several days documenting the temples of Karnak. Then, on January 16th, he set out to explore western Thebes, having already sent his letter of introduction to the sheikh of Qurna, who provided him with horses for his journey to the Valley of the Kings. This was a trek of some 8 kilometers (5 miles) round-trip up the same rugged desert wadi that had seen the funerary processions of the New Kingdom pharaohs 3000 years before. In the royal cemetery, Pococke identified 18 tombs of which nine were accessible. His plans of these tombs are quite recognizable, though two were reversed in the printing process. The next day, January 17th, Pococke visited the Ramesseum and the colossi of Memnon. On his return trip from Aswan, he finally saw Medinet Habu temple, which he incorrectly identified as the Memnonium of the classical authors. Pococke's drawings and the account of his travels in Egypt appeared in 1743 as *A description of the East and some other countries.*

272
This is the map of Egypt that Pococke published in his Description of the East in 1743.

273
These drawings of the northern colossus of Memnon are quite fanciful. Although they are actually clothed in clinging pleated gowns, Pococke's drawing makes the small female figures appear naked, as perhaps they did to a British cleric of the mid-eighteenth century.

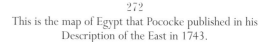

Frederik Ludvig Norden

Frederik Ludvig Norden (1708-42), an officer in the Danish navy, was educated in mathematics, architecture, and draftsmanship. On the orders of his sovereign, Christian VI, he was sent to Egypt in 1737 on a mission that included documentation of the ancient monuments. Unlike Pococke, who was in Egypt at the same time, Norden ignored the customs of the country in which he was traveling. He did not provide himself with letters of introduction, nor did he carry gifts to smooth his way. Instead, as a military officer, his methods of dealing with the local population included threats and the show of arms. As a result, he met with constant resistance and was unable to visit a number of sites, including the Valley of the Kings. Norden caught his first glimpse of the ruins of ancient Thebes in the late afternoon of

December 11. Unable to persuade the captain to set him ashore on the east bank, he spent the rest of the day sketching what he could see from the boat. On the following morning, he and some companions set off to explore the west bank using as their guide two colossal statues (the colossi of Memnon) that were visible in the distance. Because of canals and other obstacles, it took them three hours to reach the statues, which Norden spent some time sketching. He then moved on to the Ramesseum, which was visible in the distance and which he identified as the palace of Memnon. Here he made a skillful drawing of the ruins, indicating several fallen statues, including a huge overturned figure that he thought, because of its immense size, must be the colossus of Memnon described by the classical authors.

274 TOP AND BOTTOM
Norden's drawing of the Ramesseum shows the two types of columns used in the clerestory construction of the hypostyle hall.

274 CENTER
Norden's drawing of the colossi of Memnon shows the Ramesseum in the background. He mistakenly thought that the two statues represented a man and a woman. Nordens party was challenged by the local sheikh when they visited western Thebes, an event that is probably alluded to here.

275 LEFT
The inaccuracies of the maps Norden took on his voyage up the Nile affected his understanding of Theban geography and he perpetuated the errors on his own map, placing the east bank sites from Medinet Habu to Arment opposite Karnak (Carnac). In fact, Medinet Habu is nearly opposite Luxor temple and Arment is some kilometers to the south.

275 RIGHT
Although Norden and Pococke traveled in Egypt at the same time, they first met in 1841, as fellow members of Londons Egyptian Society. Norden's Travels in Egypt and Nubia, which included his drawings and descriptions of the monuments, was published in both French and English in the 1850s, more than a decade after his death.

THE IMAGES REPRODUCED IN THIS SECTION ARE TAKEN FROM *VOYAGE D'EGYPTE ET DE NUBIE*, BY FREDERIK LUDWIG NORDEN (COPENHAGEN 1755).

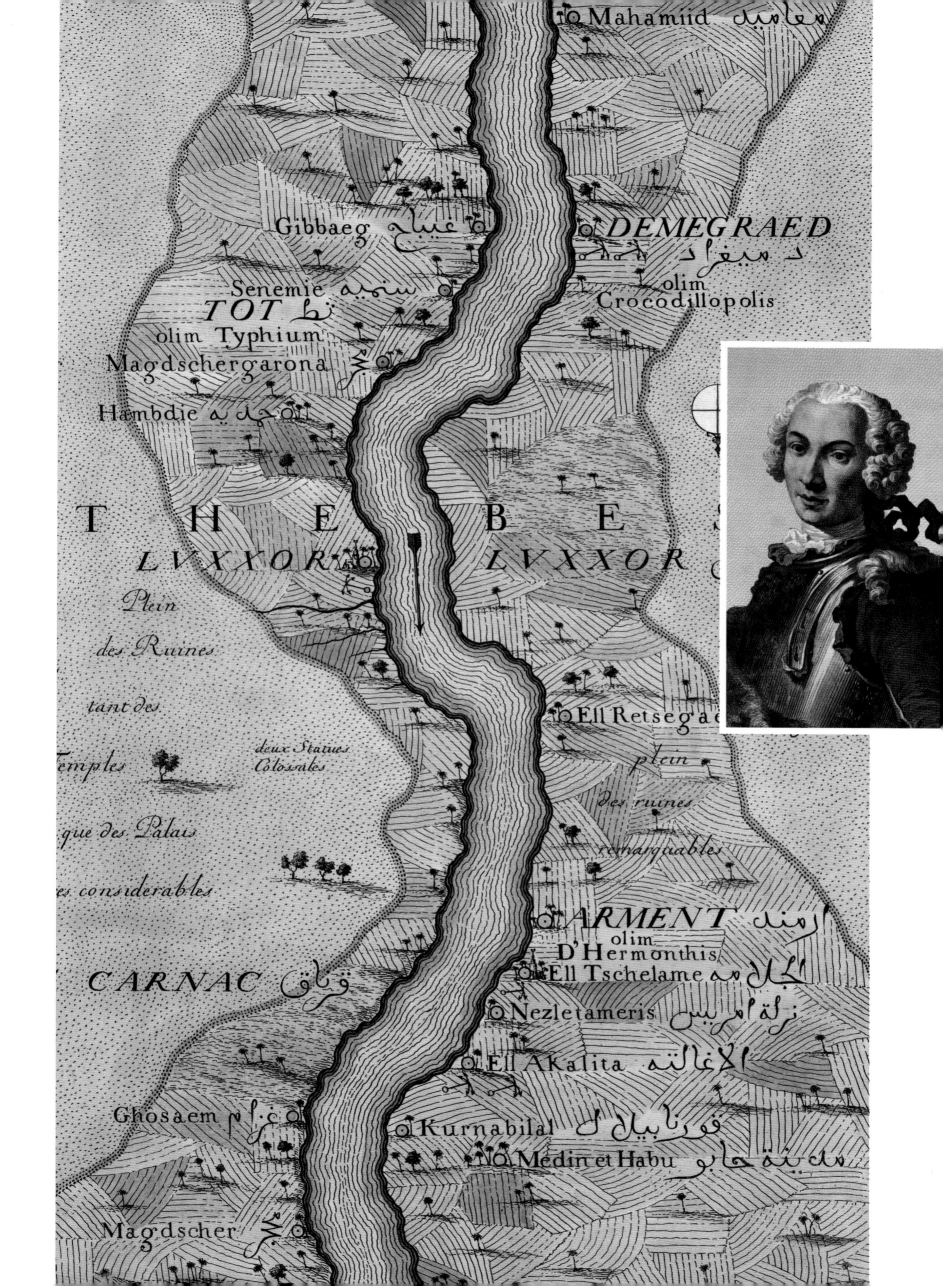

Mahamiid مهاميد

Gibbaeg جباع

DEMEGRAED
د ميغراد

Senemie سنمة

olim
Crocodillopolis

TOT ط
olim Typhium

Magdschergarona

Hambdie همبدية

T H E B E S

LVXXOR

LVXXOR

Plein

des Ruines

tant des

Temples

deux Statues
Colossales

que des Palais

es considerables

Ell Retsegad

plein

Des ruines

remarquables

ARMENT ارمنت
olim
D'Hermonthis
Ell Tschelame الجلام

Nezletameris نزلة امريس

CARNAC قرناق

Ell Akalita الاغالتة

Ghosaem غصام

Kurnabilal قرنابيلال

Médinet Habu مدينة حابو

Magdscher

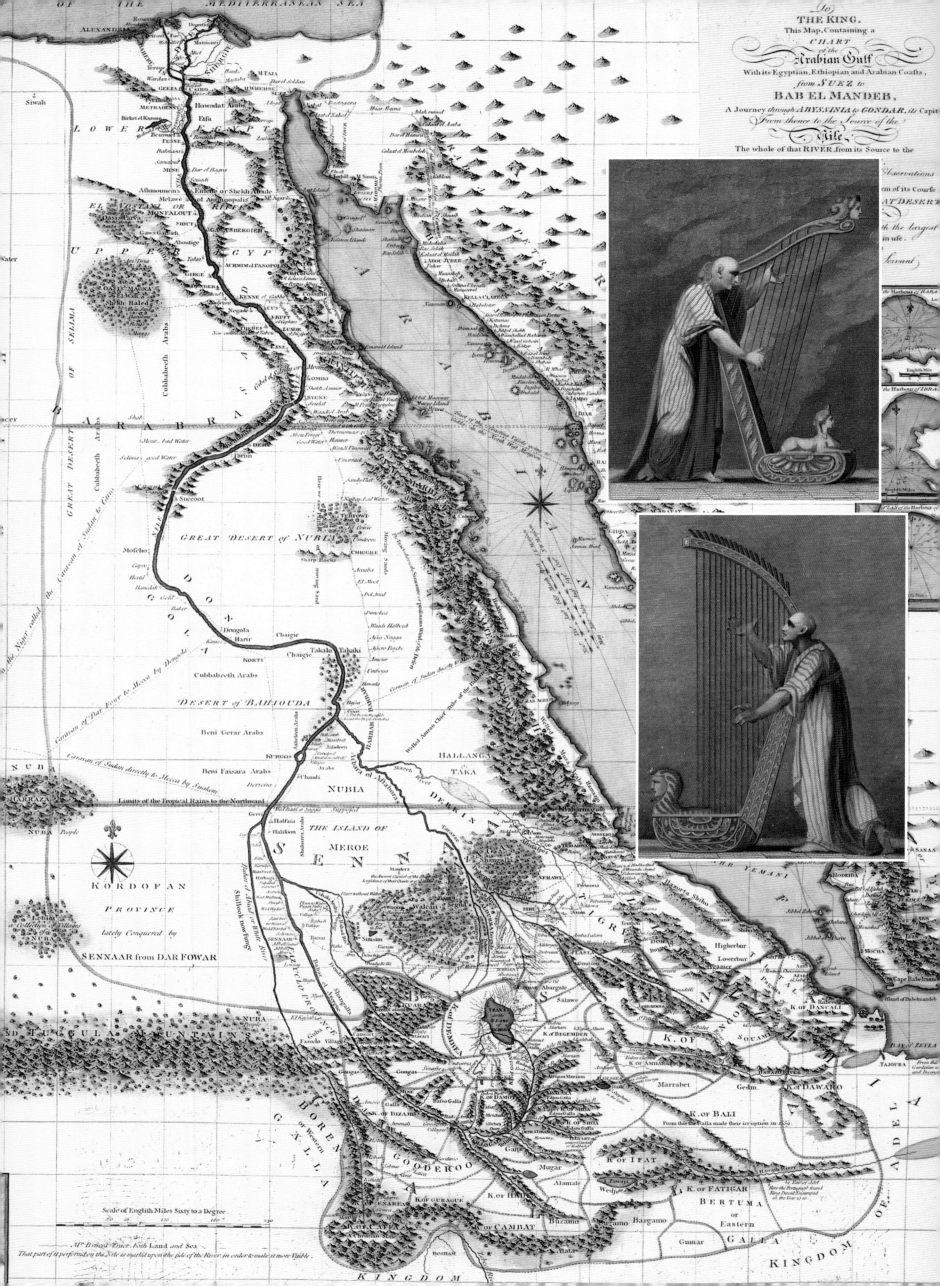

James Bruce

After serving as the British consul in Algiers from 1762-65, James Bruce (1730-94) traveled extensively in the eastern Mediterranean, reaching Egypt in July 1768. Bruce's aim was to discover the source of the Nile, but on his travels through Egypt, he stopped at Thebes and visited the royal tombs in the Valley of the Kings. Here, he became interested in the tomb of Ramesses III, which he partially cleared. Bruce was particularly taken with depictions of two blind harpers which he reproduced in a pair of fanciful etchings that bear little resemblance to the originals. The illustrations were first published in 1790 in Bruce's *Travels to discover the source of the Nile in the years 1768, 1769, 1770, 1771, 1772, and 1773.* These romanticized images of ancient Egyptians struck such a chord with all who saw them that the tomb became known as "Bruce's Tomb" or the "Harpers' Tomb"—designations that were used into the twentieth century, long after the name of the royal owner, Ramesses III, could be deciphered.

277 CENTER
James Bruce spent more than 10 years traveling in the eastern Mediterranean and northeastern Africa, where his travels took him to Ethiopia and the source of the Blue Nile.

277 BOTTOM
Like all visitors who traveled in Egypt before the middle of the twentieth century, Bruce sailed up the Nile by boat.

276 LEFT
At the end of 1768, James Bruce set out from Cairo with the intent of reaching the source of the Nile. After many difficulties, he eventually reached Ethiopia and the source of the Blue Nile in 1770, though he was not the first to do so.

276 RIGHT
These etchings, loosely based on paintings of two blind harp players in the tomb of Rameses III, are the best known illustrations from Bruce's Travels.

THE IMAGES REPRODUCED IN THIS SECTION ARE TAKEN FROM *TRAVELS TO DISCOVER THE SOURCE OF THE NILE,* BY JAMES BRUCE (EDINBURGH 1790).

Dominique Vivant Denon

Baron Dominique Vivant Denon (1747-1825) was a man of great learning and artistic talent. In spite of being a courtier and diplomat during the reigns of Louis XV and Louis XVI, he managed through his courage and personal charm to survive the French revolution. In 1897, at the age of 50, he embarked for Egypt with Napoleon's army and the *Commission des arts et des sciences*, becoming one of the 36 founding members of the *Institut d'Egypte*. At the end of August 1798, Denon accompanied General Desaix to Upper Egypt on his military campaign to defeat Murad Bey, commander of Egypt's Mameluke troops. The expedition caught its first site of the ruins of ancient Thebes on the morning of January 27, 1799. On this occasion, Denon was able to get only a glimpse of the monuments on the west bank, stopping briefly at one site, then racing on to the next as the armys progress left him behind. In his published account he writes that "at this time, I saw Thebes only at a gallop." In this fashion he visited the temple of Seti I, the Ramesseum, the colossi of Memnon, and Medinet Habu temple. Over the next six months, Denon was able to examine the monuments of Thebes several more times, making excellent plans and drawings. In early July, he finally saw the Valley of the Kings, where he entered eight tombs in a mere three hours. Like most of his visits to Thebes, this one had been too brief: "I found, as on all other occasions, that a visit to Thebes was like an attack of fever, it was a kind of crisis that left me with an impression of equal parts impatience, enthusiasm, irritation, and fatigue." Denon left Egypt with Napoleon in August 1799 and spent the next year preparing his notes and drawings for publication. Appearing in 1802, Denon's volumes remain valuable resources today.

278
At 50, Denon was among the oldest members of the Commission that accompanied Napoleon to Egypt. This sketch was made by one of his companions on the expedition, André Dutertre.

278-279
On their first visit to Thebes, Denon and General Desaix were attacked by local residents when they attempted to examine one of the Eleventh Dynasty saff tombs of western Thebes (foreground). These monuments are now almost completely obscured by the modern village of Tarif.

279 TOP
Denon was finally able to visit the Valley of the Kings in July 1899. Among others, he entered the tomb of Rameses IV, the entrance of which is seen here. The plans of this tomb (left) and the conjoined tombs of Rameses III and Amenmesse (right) seem to have been copied from Pococke, whose publication also reverses these last two.

279 BOTTOM
Denon's view of the gateway leading into the precinct of Medinet Habu temple captures the grandeur of this triumphal entrance that Rameses III patterned on a Near Eastern design. A Ptolemaic era pylon is visible at the right.

THE IMAGES REPRODUCED IN THIS SECTION ARE TAKEN FROM *VOYAGE DANS LA BASSE ET LA HAUTE EGYPTE*, BY DOMINIQUE VIVANT DENON (PARIS 1802).

Giovanni Battista Belzoni

Giovanni Battista Belzoni (1787-1823) was born in Padua. He arrived in England in 1803, having acquired some knowledge of hydraulic engineering. To support himself, the nearly 2 meters tall (six foot seven inch) Belzoni demonstrated ornamental fountains of his own design, and performed feats of strength for the public as the "Pategonian Samson." He eventually married an Irish woman and became a British citizen. In 1815, Belzoni travelled to Egypt hoping to interest the Khedive, Mohammed Ali, in a new method for raising water. After failing in this venture, Belzoni made the acquaintance of

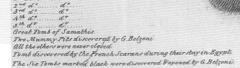

280 TOP
Giovanni Belzoni, though born in Italy, became a British citizen and married an Irish woman. He is most famous for discovering the tomb of Seti I, one of the largest and most completely decorated in the Valley of the Kings.

Henry Salt, the British Consul General, who wanted to acquire Egyptian antiquities. One piece in particular interested Salt—the head and shoulders of a colossal statue located in the Ramesseum, or Memnonium as it was then known. This had proven impossible for anyone to move, but Belzoni took on the task and left for Upper Egypt at the end of June 1816, arriving in late July. By August 12, using dozens of local workmen, he had succeeded in transporting the fragment to the edge of the Nile where it waited for some time until a large enough boat could be found to transport it to Cairo. The next day, Belzoni made his first visit to the tombs of western Thebes in order to see a sarcophagus that he also hoped to send to Cairo. In order to confuse Belzoni, his Egyptian guides took him in by a circuitous route which he describes as follows: "Previous to our entering the cave, we took off the greater part of our clothes, and, each having a candle, advanced through a cavity in the rock, which extended a considerable length in the mountain, sometimes pretty high,

280 BOTTOM
Belzoni's topographic map of the Valley of the Kings shows the tombs he discovered in black. The largest one, marked 6, belonged to Seti I. The one above this belonged to his father, Rameses I.

281 TOP
Belzoni's published illustrations of the decoration in Seti's tomb are not facsimile copies, however, they record many scenes that are only partially preserved today such as this pillar decoration showing the king embracing Osiris who is depicted as a djed-pillar.

281 CENTER
On his first visit to western Thebes, Belzoni succeeded in transporting a 7 ton statue fragment from the Ramesseum to the Nile.

281 BOTTOM
This pillar decoration is still largely preserved in Seti's tomb. Here the text is completely wrong and was perhaps substituted mistakenly from another area of the tomb.

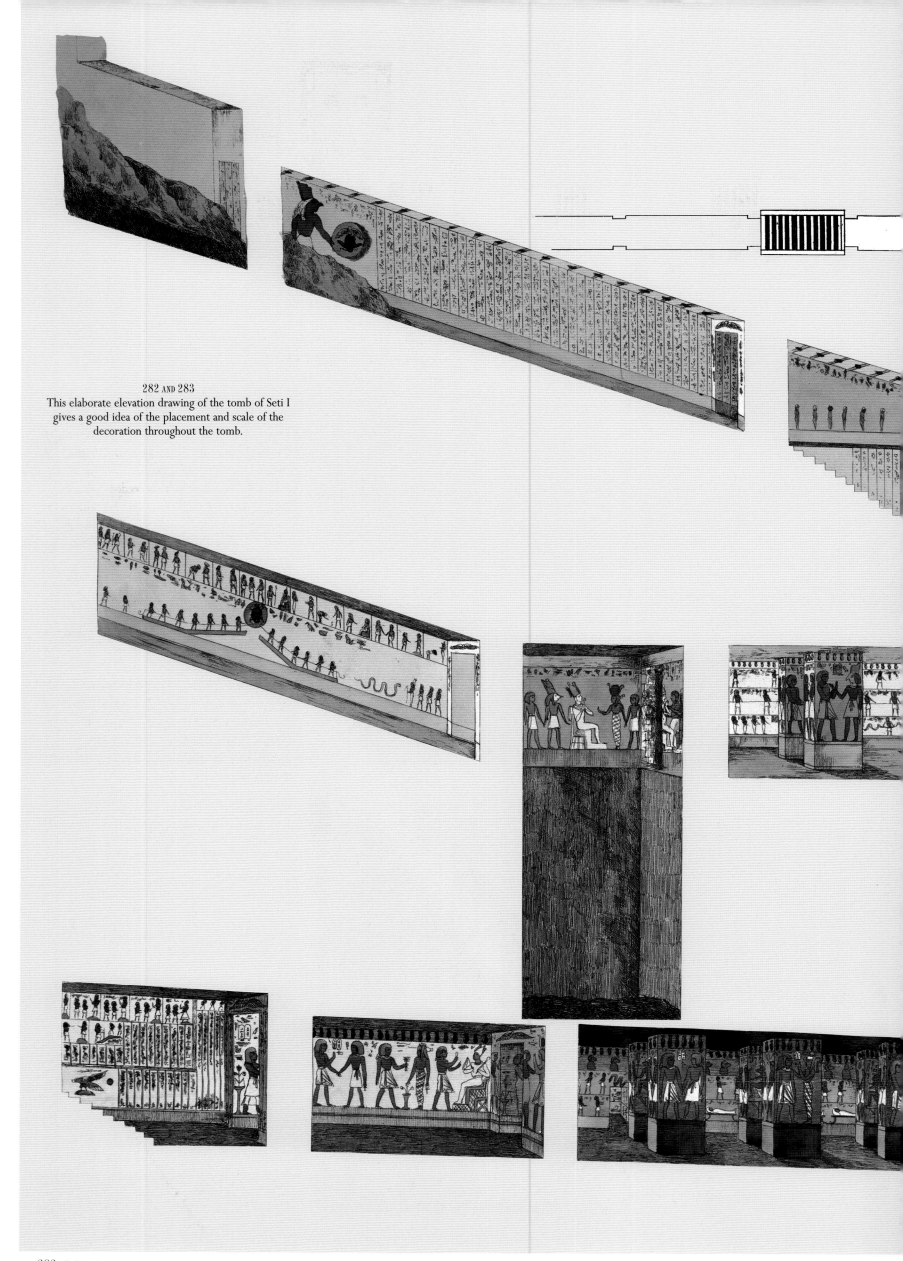

282 AND 283
This elaborate elevation drawing of the tomb of Seti I
gives a good idea of the placement and scale of the
decoration throughout the tomb.

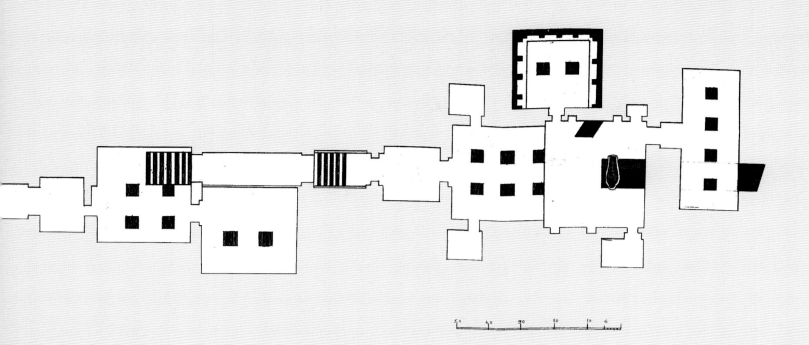

sometimes very narrow, and without any regularity. In some passages we were obliged to creep on the ground, like crocodiles." Eventually, the party reached a juncture beyond which the huge Belzoni was unable to pass, but one of the guides and an interpreter succeeded, going on ahead. A few minutes later, Belzoni heard a loud noise and a cry of "Oh, My God! My God! I'm Lost!" Managing to retrace his steps to the entrance of the "cave," Belzoni met the interpreter, who had found his own way out through a second entrance. The guide had fallen into a deep pit, and had to be rescued.

Toward the end of 1816, Belzoni visited the Valley of the Kings. While exploring the remote section of the royal cemetery known as the West Valley, where Napoleon's expedition had found the tomb of Amenhotep III, he located the tomb of Ay, the immediate successor of Tutankhamen. Nearby, in the summer of 1817 he found an unfinished tomb containing several undisturbed mummies.

However, his most significant discoveries were to come not long after this, when he began exploring the main Valley of the Kings. Belzoni was aware that the classical writers Strabo and Diodorus Siculus had set the number of tombs at between 40 and 47, 18 of which could still be viewed in ancient times. He was able to identify 16 tombs plus the two he himself had discovered in the West Valley, leaving a large number to be accounted for, and in October 1817 he accounted for four of them. First came the tomb of Montuherkhepshef, a son of Ramesses IX who ruled at the end of the New Kingdom. One of the last tombs carved in the valley, its painted decoration was still bright, but the royal burial had long since vanished. Belzoni's next discovery was an undecorated tomb containing two unwrapped mummies of women, but it provided little else of interest. A few days later, however, on October 10, he found the entrance to the

tomb of Ramesses I, founder of the Nineteenth Dynasty. The burial chamber of this relatively small tomb contained a sarcophagus of granite and a number of magical figures carved of wood. The room was decorated in expertly painted scenes and texts that retained their original brilliant colors. On October 16, about 30 feet from the tomb of Ramesses I, Belzoni made his greatest discovery when he uncovered the entrance to the tomb of Seti I, son of Ramesses I, and father of Rameses the Great (Ramesses II).

284 LEFT
This door jamb decoration from Seti's tomb depicts Maat, goddess of truth.

284-285
This scene depicts Seti being ushered into the presence of Osiris, god of the Afterworld. Seti's companion is the falcon headed god Horus, and behind Osiris is the goddess of the west who symbolizes the cemetery and the Afterlife. Even before the decipherment of hieroglyphs, the significance of this scene was partially understood, and the image of Osiris could be correctly identified.

285
Belzoni understood that the cartouches in this lintel decoration held the name of the tomb's owner, but he was unable to read them. They record the kings throne name, Men-maat-ra, at the left and his personal name, Seti-Merenptah at the right.

Known for many years thereafter as "Belzoni's tomb," the tomb of Seti I is considered the jewel of the Valley of the Kings to this day. By far the largest of the Kings' tombs (a crudely cut corridor extends at least 90 meters—100 yards—beyond the burial chamber), this is the first to have been decorated from the burial chamber all the way to the entrance. This decoration was carved in the finest low relief and then painted with exquisite detail. An account of Belzoni's travels and discoveries in Egypt and Nubia was published in 1820. This was accompanied by a folio volume of plates that included illustrations of the wall decoration in Seti's tomb. These copies, prepared with the assistance of Alessandro Ricci, are not facsimiles, but the scenes and texts are recognizable and they give an excellent idea of the colors, though the ancient hues may not have been duplicated exactly.

In 1821, Belzoni opened an exhibition in London which included a scale model of Seti's tomb measuring about 15 meters (50 feet) in length. The tomb itself is roughly 90 meters (300 feet) long, excluding the corridor that extends off the burial chamber. Belzoni also recreated two chambers of the tomb at full scale, using casts made from molds taken of the original decoration—a process that unfortunately removed much of the original paint. The alabaster sarcophagus that was found in the burial chamber was removed and eventually sold to Sir John Soane, who installed it in a "crypt" in his London town house, where it still may be seen.

In his search for antiquities, Belzoni excavated at Theban sites other than the Valley of the Kings. In 1818-19, he worked in the area behind the colossi of Memnon, the statues that actually represent the Eighteenth Dynasty pharaoh,

Amenhotep III, whose immense mortuary temple once stood behind them. Almost a century earlier, Richard Pococke had noted the remains of statues in this area. During his excavations, Belzoni unearthed a colossal head of Amenhotep III, which is now in the British Museum along with many of his other discoveries.

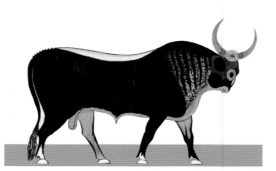

286 TOP AND BOTTOM
These two vignettes show a ritual sacrifice and a sacred bull.

286 CENTER
This brightly painted text records the kings full titulary and is located above the door inside what Belzoni called the "sideboard room." This room opens off of the burial chamber and contains two pillars and a bench around three sides.

287
This scene depicts Seti with the goddess Hathor (thought by Belzoni to be Isis). It was removed from the tomb by Champollion and is now in the Louvre.

THE IMAGES REPRODUCED IN THIS SECTION ARE TAKEN FROM
NARRATIVE OF THE OPERATIONS... IN EGYPT AND NUBIA...,
BY GIOVANNI BATTISTA BELZONI
(LONDON 1820).

Jean-Jacques Rifaud

Born in Marseilles, Jean Jacques Rifaud (1786-1852) was originally trained as a sculptor. After serving for a time in the French army, he travelled extensively in the eastern Mediterranean beginning in 1805. Arriving in Egypt in 1813, Rifaud became acquainted with Bernardino Drovetti, an Italian who served both Napoleon and later Louis XVIII as consul-general for France in Egypt. By far the most politically astute of the European consuls, Drovetti became a close friend of Mohammed Ali, who was appointed Khedive of Egypt in 1805 and ruled the country until 1848 with only tenuous ties to his Ottoman overlords. Drovetti provided the Khedive with valuable advice on reorganizing Egypt's military, updating agricultural and irrigation methods, and helping to develop industry. In return, Drovetti had

great personal influence and was given a free hand in the business of collecting Egyptian antiquities, which had become much sought after since Napoleon's expedition and the publication of the *Description de l'Egypte*.

Rifaud settled in Luxor and became one of Drovetti's chief agents, supervising many excavations in the Theban area. Although his methods were far from scientific, he sometimes did excavate with care. While working at Karnak temple on the east bank of the Nile, Rifaud came across the superb head of a king. Whereas many of his contemporaries would have been satisfied with the head alone, Rifaud carefully searched the area for the other fragments of this magnificent seated statue of Ramesses II. Thanks to his diligence, the statue could be reconstructed with minimal restoration and is now one of the

masterpieces of the Egyptian Museum in Turin. During his sojourn in Egypt, which lasted some fifteen years, Rifaud was instrumental in helping to bring together Drovetti's two great collections of Egyptian antiquities. The first, having been rejected by Louis XVIII of France, was acquired in 1824 for the newly created antiquities museum in Turin. The second group of antiquities was acquired in 1827 by Charles X of France for the newly created section for Egyptian antiquities at the Louvre. The French collection was under the care of its first curator, Jean-François Champollion, who in 1826 had been instrumental in acquiring for the Louvre a collection of Egyptian art belonging to Henry Salt, the British consul-general in Egypt, who was one of Drovetti's rivals in the collection of antiquities.

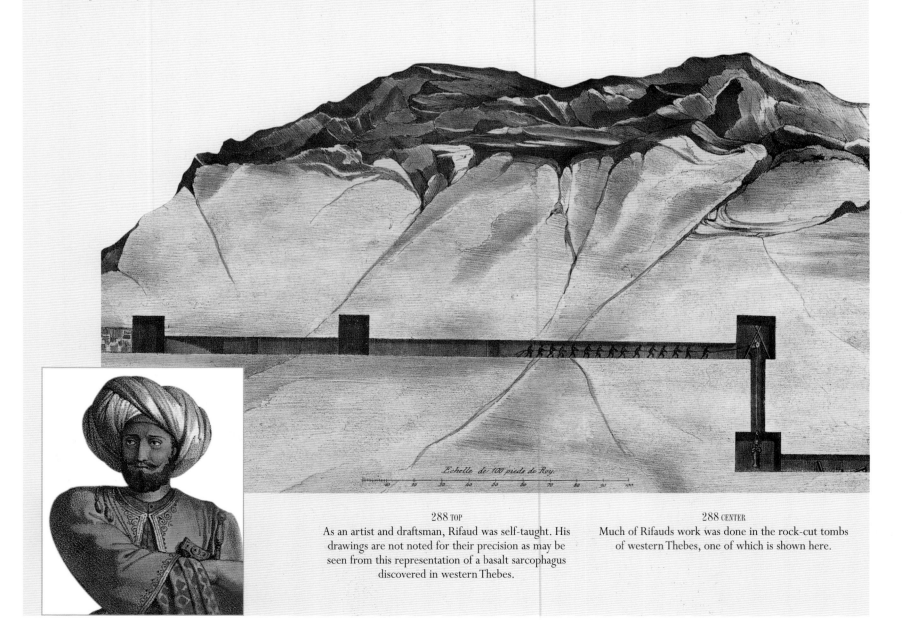

Echelle de 100 pieds de Roy.

288 TOP
As an artist and draftsman, Rifaud was self-taught. His drawings are not noted for their precision as may be seen from this representation of a basalt sarcophagus discovered in western Thebes.

288 CENTER
Much of Rifaud's work was done in the rock-cut tombs of western Thebes, one of which is shown here.

Jean Jacques Rifaud spent about fifteen years in Egypt during which he carried out numerous excavations on behalf of Bernardino Drovetti, who was consul-general for France.

In 1830, Rifaud published an account of his extensive travels in Egypt, Nubia, and the eastern Mediterranean. This contained long descriptions of the places he had visited and was illustrated by his drawings.

THE IMAGES REPRODUCED IN THIS SECTION ARE TAKEN FROM *VOYAGE EN EGYPTE, EN NUBIE, ET LIEUX CIRCONVOISINS*, BY JEAN JACQUES RIFAUD (PARIS 1830).

John Gardner Wilkinson

Sir John Gardner Wilkinson (1797-1875) is generally regarded as the founder of British Egyptology. Educated at Harrow and continuing his studies at Oxford, Wilkinson set off in 1819 to see something of Europe before beginning a career in the army. While in Italy, he met Sir William Gell, an antiquarian with a keen interest in ancient Egypt. Knowing that Wilkinson planned to travel in Egypt, Gell suggested that the young man learn something of the antiquities to be found there and offered the resources of his personal library and his own considerable knowledge of the subject. During the summer and fall of 1821, Wilkinson studied with Gell, reading accounts of earlier travelers and learning what was then known about ancient Egyptian hieroglyphs. He also studied Arabic and when he sailed for Egypt in late October, Wilkinson was better prepared than any of his predecessors. After spending some months in Egypt, he abandonned the idea of a military career. He remained in Egypt for twelve years, working on his own and living on a small independent income.

290 top
This detail was copied from the tomb of the vizier Rekhmire (TT 100) who oversaw gifts presented by foreigners from ancient Nubia and Kush (to the south of Egypt), and from western Asia.

290 center
When he reached Cairo in December of 1821, Wilkinson provided himself with Turkish dress, having been advised that this would make his journey both easier and safer.

291 bottom
These boats are from a funerary scene in the tomb of Neferhotep (TT 49). Although not facsimiles from the point of view of artistic style, the placement of the figures, their gestures and modes of dress are copied with great accuracy.

291 top
Wilkinson's map of the Theban area shows his intimate knowledge of the archaeological sites, many of which went unrecognized by the Napoleonic expedition.

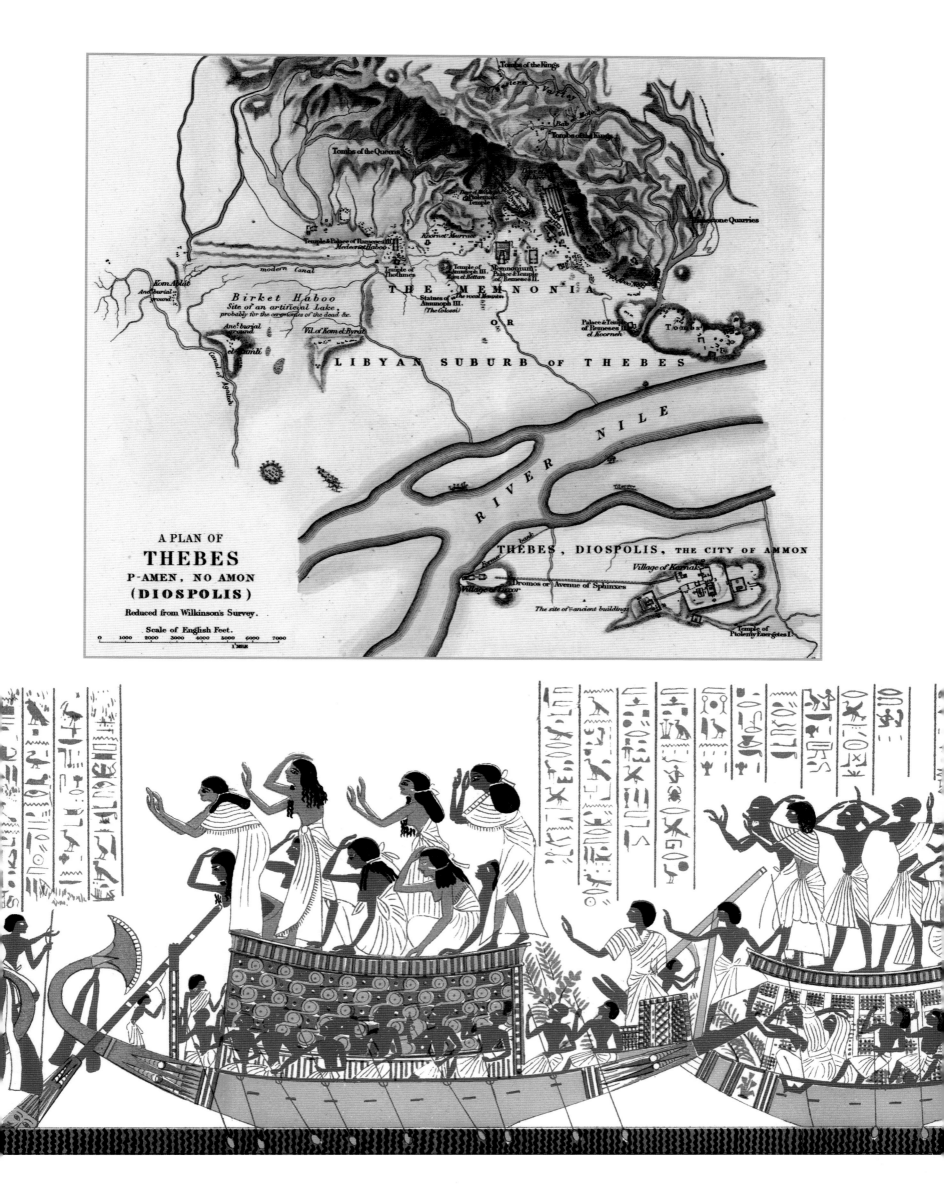

A PLAN OF
THEBES
P-AMEN, NO AMON
(DIOSPOLIS)

Reduced from Wilkinson's Survey.

Scale of English Feet.

THEBES, DIOSPOLIS, THE CITY OF AMMON

Thanks to his association with William Gell, Wilkinson was the first European scholar/traveler who was able to read Egyptian royal names with some accuracy and assign the ancient monuments to their proper owners, rather than following unquestioningly the often incorrect interpretations of the classical authors. While in Egypt, he added to his knowledge by incorporating the ground-breaking advances of Jean-François Champollion as these were published.

Beginning in 1824, a large part of Wilkinsons time was spent at Thebes, where he lived on Sheikh Abd el-Qurna hill in a house that included the courtyard and rock-cut chambers of an ancient tomb.

One of his early interests was to establish a chronology of the ancient rulers of Egypt. To determine the succession of the New Kingdom pharaohs he systematically studied the tombs in the Valley of the Kings, where he assigned numbers to the known tombs, twenty-one in

the main valley and four in the west valley. This numbering system has been used ever since, with each successive discovery receiving the next number. Thus, the tomb of Tutankhamen is no. 62. Wilkinson's chronology was published in 1828-30, and a topographical survey of Thebes and other sites appeared in 1830.

Although he recorded the scenes on temple walls and in kings tombs, some of Wilkinson's most important work was done in the tombs of officials on Sheikh Abd el-Qurna hill and other

non-royal cemeteries in western Thebes, which had been virtually ignored by earlier visitors. He was particularly interested in the evidence these provided for the day to day lives of the ancient Egyptians. Thus, he recorded dress and hairstyles, scenes of agricultural work and scenes showing the manufacturing of furniture, jewelry, sculpture, etc. The information he gathered during his long sojourn in Egypt led, in 1837, to the publication of his magnum opus, the title of which aptly explains its

comprehensive nature: *The Manners and Customs of the Ancient Egyptians, Including Their Private Life, Government, Laws, Arts, Manufactures, Religion, and Early History; Derived from a Comparison of the Paintings, Sculptures, and Monuments Still Existing, with the Accounts of Ancient Authors*. This monumental work, the only one of its kind ever produced, remains an important reference. Wilkinson's fifty-six volumes of notes and drawings, many of them unpublished, are now in the Bodleian Library at Oxford.

Emile Prisse D'Avennes

Educated as an engineer-architect, Achilles Constant Théodore Émile Prisse d'Avennes (1807-1879) went to Greece in 1826 to participate in the war for independence from Turkey. In 1827 he traveled to Egypt, where the Khedive, Mohammed Ali offered him a position as a lecturer at the military academy.

During the next decade, Prisse d'Avennes learned fluent Arabic and began studying Champollion's work on hieroglyphs, gaining a proficient knowledge of the ancient language. In 1836, he resigned his teaching position, and devoted the next eight years of his life to copying the ancient monuments, settling in

Thebes in 1838 and making it his home until 1843. Although much of his time in Upper Egypt was spent copying the reliefs of Karnak temple on the east bank of the Nile, he devoted himself to the monuments of western Thebes as well. An excellent draftsman, Prisse d'Avennes also possessed an artistic sense that is evident in his copies which reproduce ancient Egyptian relief and painting more accurately than those published by professional Egyptologists such as Champollion, Rosellini, and Lepsius.

Prisse left Egypt in 1844, but returned in June 1858 for a two year expedition sponsored by the French Ministry of Public Education.

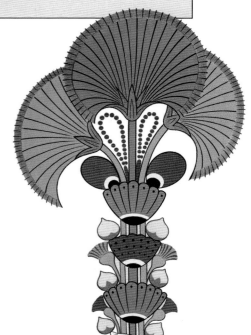

PLAN TOPOGRAPHIQUE
DES RUINES
DE
THÈBES

294
This battle scene from the second pylon of the
Ramesseum, depicts Ramesses II at the battle of Kadesh,
a city on the Orontes River. In this battle,
Ramesses claims a great victory over the Hittites,
some of whom are seen lying dead on the battlefield
beneath the king's horses.

295 TOP
Like many Europeans who lived and worked in Egypt
during the first half of the nineteenth century,
Prisse d'Avenne's wore Turkish dress.
He also adopted
the name Idriss Effendi.

295 CENTER
Prisse d'Avennes map is based on the one published
by Wilkinson in 1835. During his years working
at Thebes, Prisse corresponded with Wilkinson,
informing him of new discoveries, especially at
Karnak temple.

295 BOTTOM
Like Wilkinson before him, Prisse d'Avennes
was a keen observer of details, which he recorded
in his drawings.

On this trip, he was accompanied by Willem de Famars Testas, a young artist from the Netherlands. He also took along A. Jarrot, a young photographer from Paris. Nearly ten years earlier, the same ministry that was sponsoring Prisse d'Avennes had sent another photographer, Maxime du Camp to take photographs in Egypt and the Near East, and photography was now considered an essential part of any serious expedition. The resulting photographs, however, were usually employed as

preliminary studies for the final lithographs rather than as illustrations in their own right.

Prisse d'Avennes produced a number of publications based on his work in Egypt. The first of these was *Les Monuments égyptiennes* which appeared in 1847.

His most significant contribution to the study of Ancient Egypt was his two volume *Atlas de l'histoire de l'art égyptien, d'après les monuments, depuis les temps les plus reculés jusquà la domination romaine* (1868-78).

296
In this image of Ramesses III, from his tomb in the Valley of the Kings (KV 11), Prisse has attempted to reproduce the effect of the sunk relief decoration found at the entrance of the tomb.

296-297
Amenhotep Huy was a Viceroy of Kush, the Egyptian name for one of the lands to the south of Egypt. In his tomb (TT 40), Huy is shown accepting tribute from the southern lands. Although not quite a facsimile, this detail published by Prisse is more accurate than the copy published by Richard Lepsius.

297 TOP RIGHT
Nebet-tawy was a daughter of Ramesses II, who may have performed the ceremonial duties of queen during the last years of her fathers reign.
This image was copied from her tomb in the Valley of the Queens (QV 60).

Although he is best known for his copies of the ancient monuments, the name Prisse is also associated with two significant antiquities. One is the Papyrus Prisse, now in the Bibliothèque Nationale, Paris. Purchased in western Thebes, this nearly 4000 year old papyrus preserves the only complete copy of one of the great works of wisdom literature from ancient Egypt, "The Instructions of Ptah-hotep."

Prisse is also responsible for the removal from Karnak temple of the Table of Kings, a lengthy historical document carved on stone blocks that are now in the Louvre. Having recognized the importance of this inscription which dates to the reign of the Eighteenth Dynasty pharaoh, Tuthmosis III (ca. 1450 B.C.), Prisse spirited it away, practically under the nose of Richard Lepsius, who had received official permission to take it to Berlin.

298 TOP
His artistic sense allowed Prisse d'Avennes to copy with some accuracy the differences in artistic styles that are found in tombs of the Theban necropolis. This detail of relief in the tomb of Kha-em-hat (TT 57) is easily recognizable as dating to the reign of Amenhotep III.

298 BOTTOM
Some of Prisse d'Avennes finest copies were made in the tomb of Ramose (TT 55), who served as vizier during the reigns of Amenhotep III and his son Amenhotep IV, who later called himself Akhenaten. Here, foreigners make obeisance to Amenhotep IV.

299
The distinctive style of Amenhotep IV / Akhenaten is visible in this group of foreigners in the tomb of Ramose. Prisse d'Avennes was the first to recognize a similar artistic style on blocks found in one of the pylons at Karnak, which he mentioned in his letters to Wilkinson.

300

Although the position of this young womans left hand is slightly different than the original, other details of this figure from the tomb of Kenamen (TT 93), including the wisp of hair on her forehead, demonstrate Prisse d'Avennes keen sense of observation.

301 LEFT

This scene, depicting a native of Punt, a land believed to have been somewhere on the horn of Africa, was copied in 1859. It is from the temple of the female pharaoh, Hatshepsut, which was partially uncovered at this time.

301 RIGHT

Like a number of scenes that Prisse copied during his residence in Thebes, this one was missing when he returned in 1859.

302 top
Queen Tyti was probably a daughter of Ramesses III.
This image from her tomb in the Valley of the Queens
(QV 52) shows her wearing the vulture crown worn
by queens and goddesses.

302 bottom
These two offering bearers from an unknown Theban
tomb bring offerings of fruit and lotus flowers to the
deceased.

303
Even when Prisse copied this charming scene from the
tomb of Kenamen (TT 93), the head and front paws of
the dog were missing. This is indicated by the dotted
outline and the slightly different color. This unusual scene
shows the pharaoh, Amenhotep II, seated on the lap of
his nurse, Amenemopet, who was Kenamen's mother.

304 TOP AND 305 BOTTOM
These metalworkers from Rekhmire's tomb are making various types of vessels. Like Wilkinson, Prisse was careful to note differences in the dress and hairstyles of the figures.

304-305 TOP AND BOTTOM
These scenes of metal workers are from the tomb of Rekhmire (TT 100) who was vizier in the reign of Tuthmosis III. The men in the lower scene are casting a pair of doors from bronze imported from Retjenu, a land in western Asia.

305 CENTER RIGHT
As vizier, Rekhmire was in charge of goods produced in various parts of Egypt and imported from abroad. Here, wine, papyrus, and oil are brought to be stored.

THE IMAGES REPRODUCED IN THIS SECTION ARE TAKEN FROM *HISTOIRE DE L' ART EGYPTIEN*, BY ÉMILE PRISSE D'AVENNES (PARIS 1878).

Owen Jones

The son of a Welsh antiquarian, Owen Jones (1809-1874) was trained as an architect. At the age of 23, he set out on a journey through Greece, Turkey and Egypt, where he arrived in 1833. Jones traveled up the Nile as far as the second cataract, making sketches along the way. In 1843, he published *Views on the Nile from Cairo to the Second Cataract*, which included thirty lithographs made from his drawings.

Although Jones visited Egypt only once, his experience of the ancient monuments had a long lasting influence. In his most famous work, *The Grammar of Ornament*, published in 1856, he included nine plates showing multiple examples of ornamental patterns copied from wall paintings in tombs—many from Thebes. These included ceiling decoration, mat and textile patterns, border decorations, and floral patterns. Jones was also interested in the use of color and pattern in architecture: "The architecture of Egypt is thoroughly polychromatic—they painted everything; they dealt in flat tints and used neither shade nor shadow, yet found no difficulty in poetically conveying to the mind the identity of the object they desired to represent." To demonstrate this, he included two plates illustrating various types of column capitals, taking many of these from Theban temples."

306

In the mid-nineteenth century, the tomb of Ramesses IV, with its decorated walls and its huge, nearly complete granite sarcophagus, was one of the favorite stops for European travelers. The exotic figures smoking pipes are seated some distance from the tombs entrance. The brightness of the light on the successive door jambs and back wall of the burial chamber suggests early morning in the Valley of the Kings.

306-307

The pyramidal end of the Qurn, the highest point in western Thebes, dominates this view of the Valley of the Kings as seen in the early morning. The entrance of the tomb of Ramesses IV, the second on the right as one enters the Valley is probably indicated by the flag at the right.

307 BOTTOM

This unusual view of the Valley of the Kings in the mid-afternoon was drawn looking north from the branch of the wadi that contains the tombs of Seti II and Tausert/Setnakht, both of which were accessible in Jones's day.

308 TOP

Jones's sketch of the Ptolemaic addition to Medinet Habu shows the ruined entrance in the early morning sun.
As with most of his illustrations, Jones includes human figures for scale and local color.

308 BOTTOM

Like most European travelers, Jones visited the colossi of Memnon at dawn. In the distance at the right is the Ramesseum. Although he describes the faces of the statues as "perfect wrecks," Jones thought them beautifully executed, based on the areas that had been protected from erosion.

308-309

This view shows the Osiride pillars of the Ramesseum in the late afternoon sun. At the far right, beyond the fallen colossus, are the colossi of Memnon.
At the left, the spreading waters of the Nile flood approach the temple ruins.

309 BOTTOM

During his stay on the west bank, Jones visited Medinet Habu, which he ranked "among the magnificent remains of Thebes." In this interesting view, Jones includes some of the mud-brick ruins of the Coptic town of Djeme, which was constructed on and around the great enclosure wall of the earlier pharaonic temple.

THE IMAGES REPRODUCED IN THIS SECTION ARE TAKEN FROM *VIEWS OF THE NILE FROM CAIRO TO THE SECOND CATARACT*, BY OWEN JONES (LONDON 1843).

David Roberts

In his early career, David Roberts (1796-1864) worked as a scene painter at the Royal Theater in Glasgow, later moving to London where he eventually gave up theatrical work to concentrate on his skills as an artist. His great passion was for architectural painting and he travelled extensively in Europe and North Africa, in order to expand his subject matter. His introduction to the Moorish architecture of Spain and Morocco inspired Roberts to plan a voyage to Egypt, Nubia, and the Holy Land. Arriving in Alexandria in late September 1838,

310 TOP LEFT
Unlike his scholarly contemporaries, Roberts was interested in Egyptian monuments as works of art, not merely for the texts that they bore. This view of the colossi of Memnon is one of the few in which they are recognizable as ruined statues made in the time of Amenhotep III. For effect, Roberts has also made the statues far larger than they are in reality.

310 TOP RIGHT
The Scottish romantic painter David Roberts became justly famous for his lithographs of Egyptian and Near Eastern scenes. This portrait, by Robert Scott Laundler, was painted in 1840, shortly after Roberts returned from the east.

Roberts hired a boat for the journey up the Nile at the cost of thirteen Egyptian pounds. Roberts and his companions approached Thebes on October 21, but remained only three days before proceeding up the Nile as far as Abu Simbel. On the return trip, they stopped in Thebes for ten days, between November 26 and December 5.

Roberts was particularly impressed by the light in Egypt, commenting that the sunrises and sunsets were among the most glorious anywhere in the world. This is evident in his drawings, many of which were done in the rosy light of early morning and late afternoon. Among his greatest talents was his ability to

310 BOTTOM
Roberts adopted local dress during his travels in Egypt. Here, he shows himself sketching in the porch of the Ptolemaic temple near the village at Deir el-Medina.

311 TOP
In this view, the colossi of Memnon are set against the rising sun.

311 BOTTOM
On May 12, 1839, Roberts was given an audience with Mohammed Ali, the Khedive (Viceroy) of Egypt. Roberts is the gentleman in civilian dress, sitting with his compatriots at the right. This scene, drawn from memory, is the frontispiece of his volume on the Islamic architecture of Egypt.

choose the most striking vantage point for his subject—the back of the colossi of Memnon against sunrise; or the view of western Thebes from atop the colonnade of Luxor temple. Such choices make Roberts lithographs the most memorable to come from the Victorian Era. Unlike many European visitors, Roberts had not gone to Egypt to study and record the ancient monuments, or to collect antiquities. His purpose was to gather material for his own artistic endeavors. In his drawings of Egyptian scenes, he seeks to convey the contemporary atmosphere, rather than an exact documentation of the ancient structures, but his artists eye often captures more accurately the grandeur of a ruined temple, or the artistic style of a monumental statue than do the carefully measured drawings of his scholarly contemporaries.

After returning to London in 1839, Roberts prepared his drawings for publication in a series of six folio volumes. The majority of his Egyptian drawings appeared in three volumes containing 125 lithographs and entitled *Egypt and Nibia, from drawings made on the spot by David Roberts, R.A.* The first two volumes were dedicated to ancient Egyptian monuments and the third to Islamic monuments. These volumes, which appeared between 1846-1849, were a great success and published in two types. In the less expensive edition, the lithographs were printed in black, white and ocher, with one other color added in a few. The lithographs of the deluxe edition were hand painted with colors matching those in the original drawings. The colors used do not necessarily conform to reality, but were chosen for artistic effect.

THE IMAGES REPRODUCED IN THIS SECTION ARE TAKEN FROM *EGYPT AND NUBIA*, BY DAVID ROBERTS (LONDON 1846-1849).

312 top
One of Roberts most famous paintings shows the great fallen colossus of "Ozymandias" (Ramesses II) at the Ramesseum.

312 bottom
In his landscapes, Roberts made excellent use of unusual vantage points. In this early morning scene, he has climbed to the top of the colonnade at Luxor temple to get the full view of the west bank. I
n the distance one sees Medinet Habu at the left, the colossi of Memnon, the Ramesseum in the center, and the temple of Seti I at the far right.

312-313
This view of the Valley of the Kings, probably sketched from atop the hill overlooking the tomb of Ramesses VI (above the standing man) gives an excellent impression of the desolate landscape seen just after sunrise.
It is not particularly realistic, however, the tomb entrances having been placed for artistic effect rather than accuracy.

Karl Richard Lepsius

In 1842, King Friedrich Wilhelm IV of Prussia sponsored an expedition to Egypt for the purpose of documenting the ancient monuments and collecting antiquities for a new state museum to be built specially for the display of Egyptian art. The organizer of this great undertaking was Karl Richard Lepsius (1810-1884) who had just been appointed as temporary professor of Egyptology at the University of Berlin. Trained in Germany and later in France and Italy, where he studied with Ippolito Rosellini, Lepsius was a brilliant young scholar whose contributions to the

developing field of ancient Egyptian language studies earned him a reputation as the "German Champollion."

In preparation for the expedition, Lepsius gathered a group of scholars, artists, draftsmen, architects, and engravers. On a diplomatic level, the Prussian King contacted Mohammed Ali, the Khedive of Egypt, thus gaining almost *carte blanche* for the expedition's endeavors both in documentation and collection. Lepsius and his colleagues arrived in Egypt in September 1842. They worked for many months in the Old Kingdom cemeteries of Giza and Sakkara, and the Middle Kingdom sites not far south, none of which had been thoroughly explored or documented by previous expeditions.

Map text: General Karte von THEBEN.

314 TOP
This copy of a vignette in the tomb of the vizier Rekhmire (TT 100) contains a number of errors.

314 BOTTOM
Lepsius was a brilliant philologist who improved upon Champollions methods of translating ancient Egyptian and earned himself a reputation as the "German Champollion."

315 TOP
The map of Thebes printed in the Denkmäler improves on the one published by Wilkinson, adding new discoveries and more details. But it omits the limestone quarries at the northern end of western Thebes, and the avenue of sphinxes that connects the temples of Luxor and Karnak on the east bank, both of which were noted on Wilkinson's map.

314-315
This view of western Thebes was drawn from the area of Tarif looking toward the temple of Seti I, with the Qurn in the background. In the center distance is the Ramesseum, and to the left are the Colossi of Memnon surrounded by water from the Nile flood.

Lepsius finally moved his operations to Thebes in November 1844. After two years working in other parts of Egypt and in Nubia, Lepsius found Thebes inspirational, as he wrote in a letter dated Nov. 24: "Here, where the mighty pharaohs of the eighteenth and nineteenth dynasties meet me in all their splendor and magnificence, I feel once more as fresh as at the beginning of the journey." (trans. Underhill) Lepsius himself made a trip to Sinai early in 1845, but most of his colleagues remained at work in Thebes until he rejoined them in April.

Building on information gathered by previous scholars, particularly Champollion and Rosellini, but including John Gardner Wilkinson and others, the members of the Prussian team were able to accomplish a great deal of work in a relatively short amount of time. The expedition concentrated on architecture which Lepsius felt had been neglected by the Franco-Tuscan expedition. The precise plans and reconstructions of the ancient ruined temples that were made by Lepsius and his team are among the best ever produced, and their copies of texts are generally correct and easy to read, improving on those of their predecessors. This is partly because Lepsius perfected the technique of making paper molds (called squeezes) of the texts that were carved on stone. These exact copies could then be transferred to the appropriate drawings after the expedition returned to Berlin. However, with all their correctness, the texts, whether painted or carved, are reproduced in a standard hieroglyphic script that usually ignores differences in the writing styles among ancient scribes and artists. This is largely because Lepsius had gone to Egypt with a specific goal in mind, one that he states in a letter written from Thebes on February 25, 1845. "The great end which I have always had before my eyes, and for which I have principally made my selections, has been history.

316-317 TOP

These two illustrations show a panoramic view from the top of Sheikh Abd el-Qurna hill facing east towards the Nile valley and the plain of western Thebes. From north (left) to south (right) one sees the remains of the mud-brick superstructure of the tomb of Montuemhat (Dynasty 26) in the valley known as Assasif (far left). The Prussian headquarters is the building in the foreground of the second print (lower left), just below where the artist sat to do his drawings. Above this, at the edge of the desert is the Ramesseum, the Colossi of Memnon are visible in the cultivated fields, and Medinet Habu temple is at the far right. Karnak and Luxor temples are just visible in the distance on the east bank of the Nile.

This view of the Valley of the Kings seems to have been drawn from a point above the still unknown tomb of Tutankhamen. To the right is the entrance of the tomb of Ramesses VI (KV 9); to the left is probably the tomb of Amenmesse (KV 10), or perhaps the tomb of Ramesses III (KV 11); in the distance, beyond the people, is the tomb of Tausert/Setnakht (KV 14).

This drawing shows the view looking west, across the top of Sheikh Abd el-Qurna hill toward the Qurn, the highest point on the west bank.

When I thought I had collected the most essential information on this point, I remained satisfied." (trans. Mackenzie)

The Prussian team had spent many months copying Old Kingdom monuments at Giza, Saqqara and other northern sites before arriving at Thebes where the monuments they copied were primarily of New Kingdom date, and they noted a difference in the artistic style between the two periods. However, when they copied wall paintings in the tombs of Theban officials, they seem not to have recognized the subtle differences in style from one tomb to the next. Their primary interest was in the subject matter and what it could reveal about the ancient Egyptian culture. Thus the details of furniture, clothing, animals, plants, manufacturing and agricultural techniques, were usually copied with care.

318 AND 319
Some of the best copies made by the Prussian expedition were a group of drawings illustrating individual figures from tombs in the Valley of the Kings. The drawing on the left copies an outlined figure of the pharaoh Setnakht on a pillar in the burial chamber of Tausert in KV 14, which Setnakht extended for his own use.

The drawing at the center is a portrait of Ramesses III that was carved in sunk relief near the entrance of his tomb, KV 11. The figure on the right depicts Prince Montuherkhepshef. It is an excellent copy of one of the representations KV 19—one of the tombs discovered by Giovanni Belzoni more than 25 years before the Prussian expedition worked in the Valley.

On the other hand, the features of a human face, or the exact position of a hand or foot were often drawn incorrectly, either because these details didnt matter, or because they were unnoticed by the nineteenth century copyist. In a few exceptional cases, however, individual representations were treated as true works of art. There are a number of plates in which a specific figure, usually a king, has been copied with great care. These drawings were done on a 1:1 scale and are near facsimiles of the originals.

After three years in Egypt, the Prussian expedition returned with a wealth of information in drawings, watercolors, squeezes of inscriptions, and notes. They also arrived with some fifteen hundred antiquities that form a significant part of the collections of the Egyptian Museum in Berlin. In the report he made to the ministry after returning to Berlin in January of 1846, Lepsius compared his own efforts with the earlier Franco-Tuscan expedition: "The expedition most immediately comparable with ours was Champollions, but that was more a voyage of discovery, and necessarily suffered from the very deficiencies which we were easily able to supply. The advantages which he had as founder of the science and from his incomparable ability as a student of monuments, were for us more than counterbalanced by the firmer and broader foundations of the science... Added to this was our greater previous knowledge of the interesting localities which we had to investigate." (trans. Underhill)

The scholarly results of the expedition were published in the truly monumental *Denkmäler aus Ägypten und Äthiopien*. This eventually included twelve huge volumes of plates that appeared between 1849-1859. More than a decade after Lepsius died, five volumes of notes on the illustrations were finally published between 1897 and 1913.

320
Asian offering bearers from the tomb of Amenhotep Huy (TT 40).

321
This detail from the tomb of Amenhotep Huy (TT 40), in the cemetery of Gurnet Murai, demonstrates one of the weaknesses in some of the Denkmäler copies. Here, the four boats behind the standing figure are almost exact copies of one another. In reality, the cargo and crew of each is slightly different.

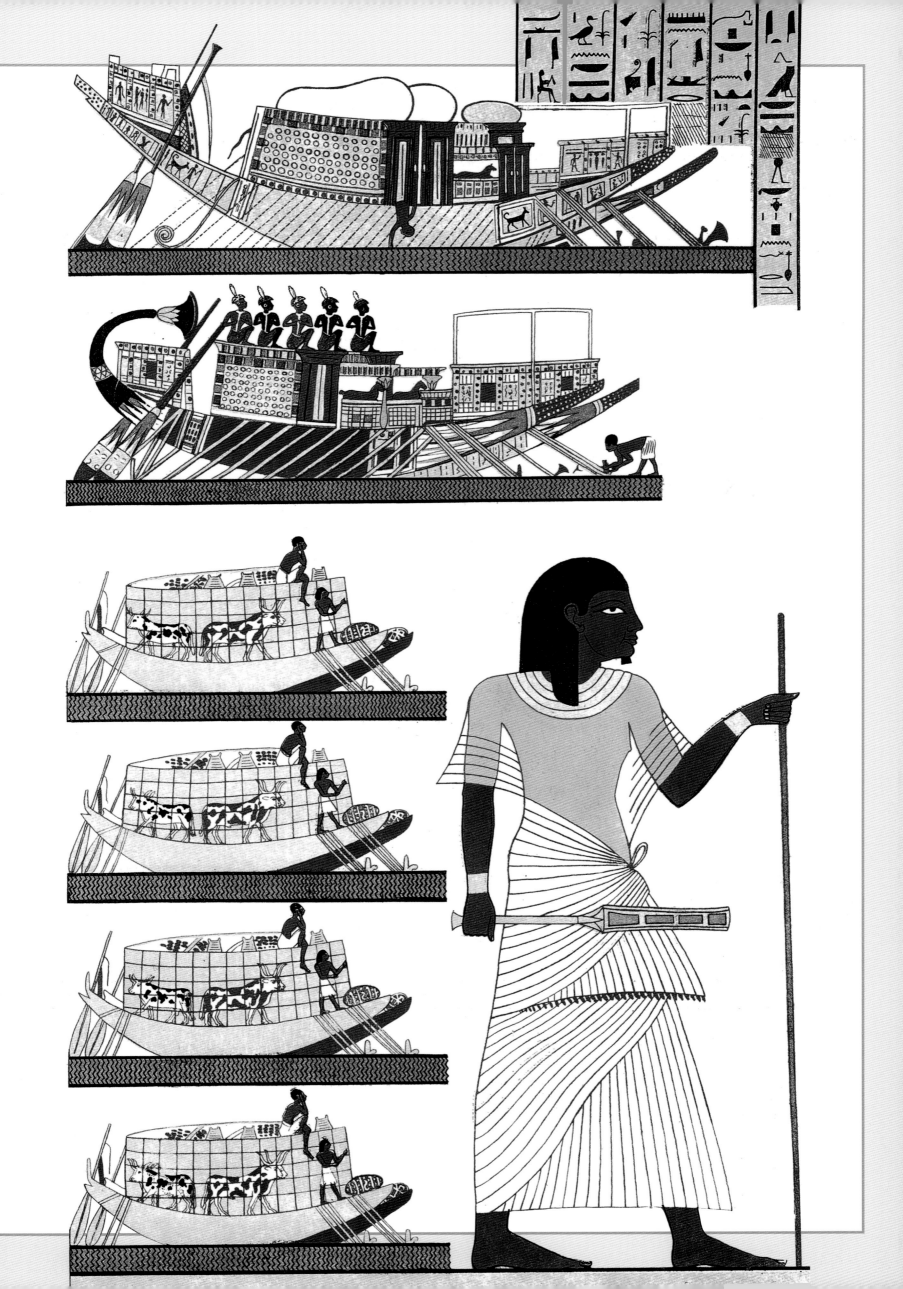

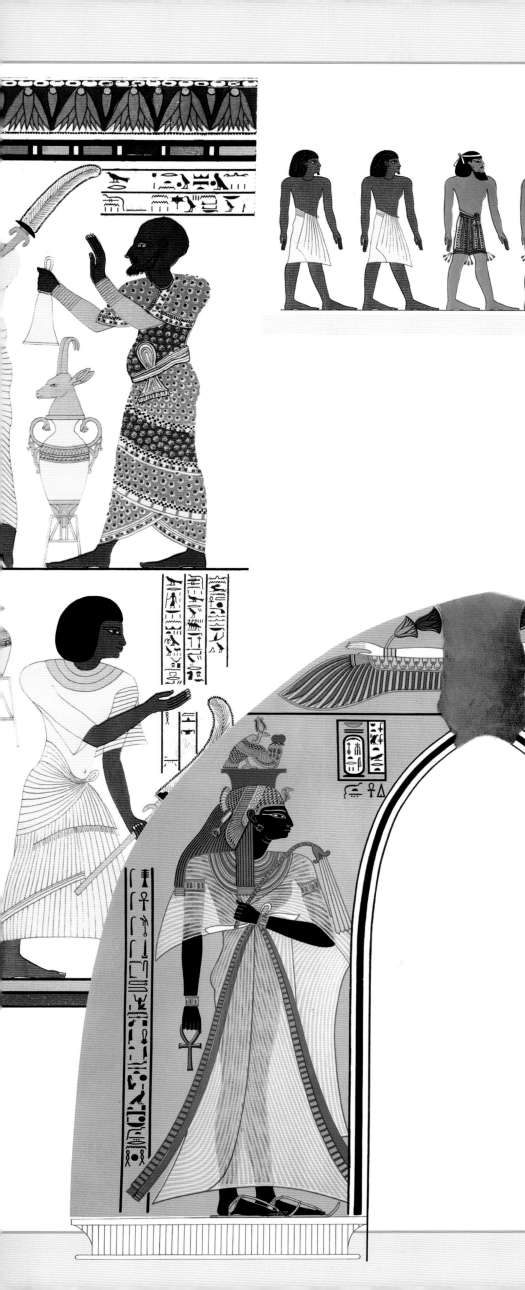

322·323

Amenhotep Huy was viceroy of Kush during the reign of Tutankhamen. His tomb in Qurnet Murai (TT 40) is full of scenes depicting foreign tribute being brought to the king. Here, the gifts are being brought by peoples from western Asia. Although the text and many details are accurate, the artistic style is nineteenth century European, academic, not late Eighteenth Dynasty Egyptian.

323 TOP

Two Asians and two Egyptians depicted in the tomb of Seti I.

323 BOTTOM

Originally on either side of a doorway in the tomb of Anherkhawy (TT 359) at the workmen's village of Deir el-Medina, these paintings are now in the Egyptian Museum, Berlin. The royal figures depicted here were considered the patrons of the royal tomb builders: queen Ahmose-Nefertari, principal wife of Ahmose, the first king of Dynasty 18; and Amenhotep I, their son, who is credited with establishing the workmen's village.

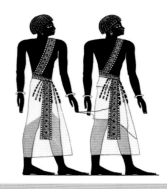

324 LEFT
Two Nubians from the tomb of Seti I.

324-325
Parts of this scene in the tomb of Amenhotep Huy (TT 40) were copied by both the Prussian expedition and by Prisse d'Avennes. A comparison shows that, while Lepsius and his colleagues copied the texts and many details with a standardized accuracy, Prisse was able capture the style of the ancient artists.

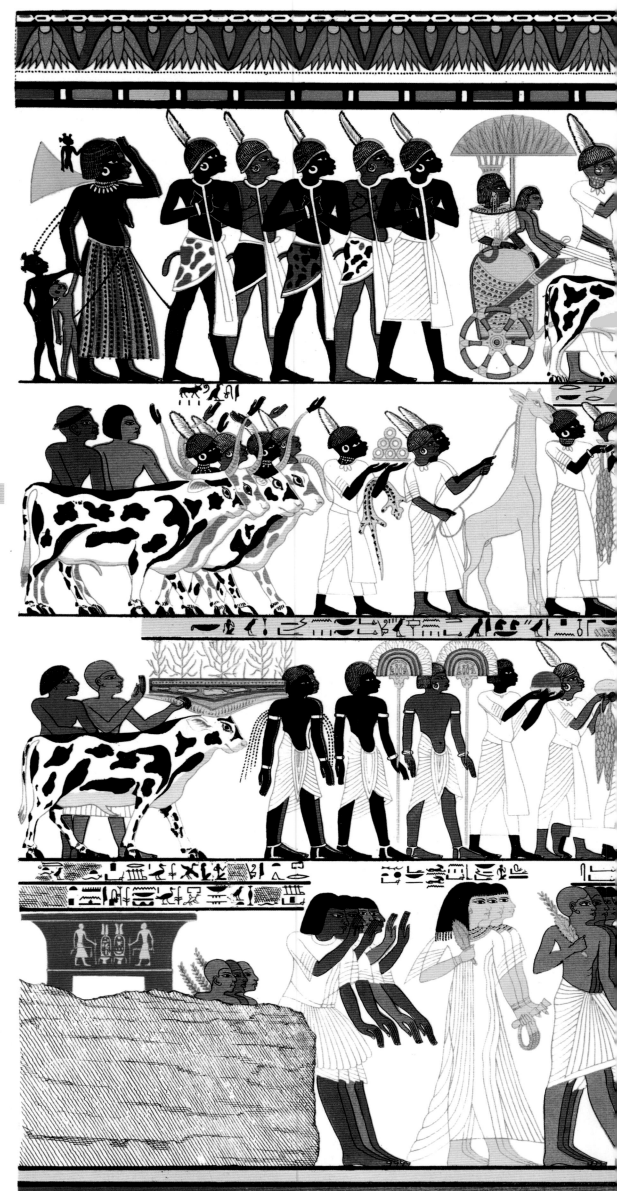

William Henry Bartlett

Apprenticed to an architect at age fourteen, William Henry Bartlett (1809-1854) worked as an architectural illustrator for a number of years before beginning his travels, which took him around Europe, America, Turkey and the Near East. In June of 1845, he arrived in Alexandria, just as Richard Lepsius and his expedition were finishing their three years of work in Egypt and Nubia. Bartlett had prepared himself well and was aware of Lepsius's work, but his principal references to the monuments of ancient Egypt were the works of John Gardner Wilkinson, especially *A Handbook for Egypt*, published in 1847.

Having visited Alexandria and sites around Cairo, Bartlett set off up the Nile. Arriving at Thebes at noon on a brilliant summer day, he was at first disappointed by the huge expanse of space separating the various ruins, and thus diminishing their impact in his view. "The only grand feature was the lofty barren mountain of yellow sandstone overhanging the western quarter of the city, with the dark orifices of its countless tombs, and which seemed to reverberate the ardent rays of the vertical sun." But, in the end, he was impressed by the antiquities, and the largest portion of his travel journal is taken up with descriptions of the sites in western Thebes.

326 TOP
Bartlett traveled from Cairo up the Nile in a boat he had rented for 9 Egyptian pounds per month. This included the wages of the captain and six crew members. It was loaded with supplies including a goat to provide milk for the journey.

326-327
In the Valley of the Kings, Bartlett visited the tomb of Seti I (KV 17), and was particularly struck by the decoration in the first pillared hall, Belzoni's "Hall of Beauty."

After his visit to the Valley of the Kings, Bartlett followed the path that leads out of the desert wadi and onto the cliffs that overlook the valley of the Nile. In *The Nile Boat*, an account of his travels which was published in 1849, he described this view of the site where the ancient city of Thebes once flourished: "It is, indeed, marked by nature for a great capital;—a grand valley many miles in width, divided by the Nile—defended on the west by the craggy range of mountains we stood upon, and on the east by the far distant hills on the Arabian side;—a mighty area, strewn for miles with the scattered remains of former magnificence..."

In the introduction to his book, Bartlett comments on the plethora of similar publications "To add another book on Egypt... may almost appear like a piece of presumption. But it should be remarked, that besides the army of erudite 'savans' who have enlisted themselves in the study of its antiquities, there has always been a flying corps of light-armed skirmishers, who...busy themselves chiefly with

the picturesque aspect; who aim at giving lively impressions of actual sights, and at thus creating an interest which may lead the reader to a further investigation of the subject...Of this slight texture is the composition of the present volume."

Bartlett's book contains about 50 marvelous etchings made from drawings he had done on the spot, many with the Camera Lucida. These evocative illustrations are usually described in great detail in the accompanying text, and it would have been a shame had he not added this volume to the other nineteenth century accounts of travel in Egypt.

326 BOTTOM
This view of Medinet Habu shows the Ramesseum in the center distance, and the Colossi of Memnon, reflected in the flood waters of the Nile at the far right.

327 TOP
This view of the Valley of the Kings was drawn from the same vantage point as that recorded by the Prussian expedition. At the right is the entrance of KV 9 (Ramesses VI). As with many of his illustrations, Bartlett includes contemporary Egyptians to give scale and set the scene.

327 BOTTOM
In this rather wide-angle view of the Nile valley from the western cliffs, Bartlett has included all of the principal Theban sites: Karnak and Luxor temples on the distant east bank, and the Ramesseum, Colossi of Memnon, and Medinet Habu on the western plain.

THE IMAGES REPRODUCED IN THIS SECTION ARE TAKEN FROM *THE NILE BOAT*, BY WILLIAM HENRY BARTLETT (LONDON 1850).

PHOTO CREDITS

328

TEMPLE OF RAMESSES II
DESCRIPTION, ANTIQUITÉS, VOLUME II, PLATE 12
THEBES, MEDINET HABU